I0015488

Mastering Data Mining with Python – Find patterns hidden in your data

Learn how to create more powerful data mining applications with this comprehensive Python guide to advance data analytics techniques

Megan Squire

[PACKT] PUBLISHING

open source*
community experience distilled

BIRMINGHAM - MUMBAI

Mastering Data Mining with Python – Find patterns hidden in your data

Copyright © 2016 Packt Publishing

All rights reserved. No part of this book may be reproduced, stored in a retrieval system, or transmitted in any form or by any means, without the prior written permission of the publisher, except in the case of brief quotations embedded in critical articles or reviews.

Every effort has been made in the preparation of this book to ensure the accuracy of the information presented. However, the information contained in this book is sold without warranty, either express or implied. Neither the author(s), nor Packt Publishing, and its dealers and distributors will be held liable for any damages caused or alleged to be caused directly or indirectly by this book.

Packt Publishing has endeavored to provide trademark information about all of the companies and products mentioned in this book by the appropriate use of capitals. However, Packt Publishing cannot guarantee the accuracy of this information.

First published: August 2016

Production reference: 1240816

Published by Packt Publishing Ltd.
Livery Place
35 Livery Street
Birmingham B3 2PB, UK.

ISBN 978-1-78588-995-0

www.packtpub.com

Credits

Author

Megan Squire

Reviewers

Sanjeev Jaiswal

Ron Mitsugo Zacharski

Commissioning Editor

Veena Pagare

Acquisition Editor

Lester Frias

Content Development Editor

Mamata Walkar

Technical Editor

Naveenkumar Jain

Copy Editors

Safis Editing

Sneha Singh

Project Coordinator

Shweta H Birwatkar

Proofreader

Safis Editing

Indexer

Pratik Shirodkar

Graphics

Kirk D'Penha

Production Coordinator

Shantanu N. Zagade

Cover Work

Shantanu N. Zagade

About the Author

Megan Squire is a professor of computing sciences at Elon University.

Her primary research interest is in collecting, cleaning, and analyzing data about how free and open source software is made. She is one of the leaders of the FLOSSmole.org, FLOSSdata.org, and FLOSSpapers.org projects.

About the Reviewers

Sanjeev Jaiswal is a computer graduate with 7 years of industrial experience. His works involves Perl, Python, and GNU/Linux. He is currently working on projects involving penetration testing, source code review, and security design and implementations.

He is very much interested in web and cloud security. He is also learning NodeJS and cloud security.

Sanjeev loves teaching engineering students and IT professionals. He has been teaching for the last 8 years in his free time. He founded Alien Coders (http://www.aliencoders.org), based on the learning through sharing principle for computer science students and IT professionals in 2010, which became a huge hit in India among engineering students.

You can follow him on Facebook at http://www.facebook.com/aliencoders, on Twitter at @aliencoders, and on GitHub at https://github.com/jassics.

Sanjeev wrote *Instant PageSpeed Optimization* and co-authored *Learning Django Web Development* for Packt Publishing. He has reviewed more than 5 books for Packt and looks forward to more such opportunities.

Ron Mitsugo Zacharski is a computational linguist working in the areas of information extraction and machine learning (zacharski.org). He has a BFA in music from the University of Wisconsin at Milwaukee and a PhD in computer science from the University of Minnesota, and he completed a post doctorate in linguistics at the University of Edinburgh. He authored the free online book *A Programmer's Guide to Data Mining: The Ancient Art of the Numerati* (www.guidetodatamining.com) and co-edited *The Grammar-Pragmatics Interface: Essays in Honor of Jeanette K. Gundel*, published by John Benjamins. For the majority of his academic life, he has focused on multilingual natural language processing, particularly with lesser-studied languages. Dr. Zacharski is a Zen monk in the Sōtō School lineage of Soyu Matsuoka. He lives in New Mexico.

www.PacktPub.com

eBooks, discount offers, and more

Did you know that Packt offers eBook versions of every book published, with PDF and ePub files available? You can upgrade to the eBook version at www.PacktPub.com and as a print book customer, you are entitled to a discount on the eBook copy. Get in touch with us at customercare@packtpub.com for more details.

At www.PacktPub.com, you can also read a collection of free technical articles, sign up for a range of free newsletters and receive exclusive discounts and offers on Packt books and eBooks.

https://www2.packtpub.com/books/subscription/packtlib

Do you need instant solutions to your IT questions? PacktLib is Packt's online digital book library. Here, you can search, access, and read Packt's entire library of books.

Why subscribe?

- Fully searchable across every book published by Packt
- Copy and paste, print, and bookmark content
- On demand and accessible via a web browser

Table of Contents

Preface

Over the past decade, cheaper data storage, faster hardware, and impressive advances in algorithms have combined to pave the way for a rapid ascendance of **data science** as one of the most important opportunities in computing. While the term data science can include everything from cleaning data and storing data to visualizing it in graphs and charts, the area that has made the most significant gain is the invention of intelligent and sophisticated algorithms for analyzing data. Using computers to find the interesting patterns buried within massive amounts of data is called **data mining**, an area that encompasses elements of database systems, statistics, and machine learning.

Right now there are dozens of great data mining and machine learning books available for software developers to get up to date on all these advances in the field. What most of these books have in common is that they all cover a small set of tried-and-true methods for finding patterns in data: classification, clustering, decision trees, and regression. Of course, all of these are critically important methods for any data miner to know and they are popular because they can be effective. But these same few techniques are not the whole story. Data mining is a rich field encompassing many dozens of techniques to uncover patterns and make predictions. A true master of data mining should have *many* tools in her toolbox, not just a few. Thus, the mission of this book, *Mastering Data Mining with Python*, is to introduce some of the lesser-known data mining concepts that are typically only covered in academic textbooks.

This book uses the Python programming language and a project-based approach to introduce diverse and often overlooked data mining concepts, such as association rules, entity matching, network analysis, text mining, and anomaly detection. Each chapter thoroughly illustrates the basics of one particular data mining technique, provides alternatives for evaluating its effectiveness, and then implements the technique using real-world data.

Our focus on real-world data is another feature of this book that sets it apart from many other data mining books. The true test of whether we have mastered a concept is whether we can apply a method to a new, unknown problem. In our case, this means applying each data mining method to a new problem area or a new data set. The emphasis on real data also means that our results may not always be as clean and tidy as results that come from a canned, example data set. For this reason, each chapter includes a discussion for how to critically evaluate the method. Do the results make sense? What do the results mean? How can the results be improved?

So, in many ways, this book picks up where some of the other data mining books leave off. If you want to round up your growing data mining toolbox with a set of interesting but often overlooked techniques, then read on to learn the specific topics we will cover and how they will be applied in each chapter.

What this book covers

Chapter 1, *Expanding Your Data Mining Toolbox*, gives an introduction to the field of data mining. In this chapter we pay special attention to how data mining relates to similar topics, such as machine learning and data science. We also review many different data mining methodologies, and talk about their various strengths and weaknesses. This foundational knowledge is important as we transition into the remaining chapters of the book, which are much more technique-oriented and focus on the application of specific data mining tools.

Chapter 2, *Association Rule Mining*, introduces our first data mining tool: mining for co-occurring sets of items, sometimes called frequent itemsets. We extend our understanding of frequent itemset mining to include mining for association rules, and we learn how to evaluate whether the rules we have found are helpful or not. To put our knowledge into practice, at the end of the chapter we implement a small project wherein we find association rules in the keywords chosen to describe a large set of software projects.

Chapter 3, *Entity Matching*, focuses on finding matching pairs of data elements that may look slightly different but are actually the same. We learn how to determine whether two items are actually the same thing by using the attributes of the data. At the end of the chapter, we implement an entity matching project where we learn to find the software projects that have moved from one hosting service to another, even after changing their names and other important attributes.

Chapter 4, Network Analysis, is a tour through the basics of network or graph analysis, as used to describe the relationships between various interconnected groups of entities. We investigate the various types of network and learn how to describe and measure them. Then we put our learning into practice to describe how a network of software developers has changed over time.

Chapter 5, Sentiment Analysis in Text, is the first of four text mining chapters in this book. This chapter serves as an introduction to the growing field of sentiment, or mood, analysis in text. After comparing various approaches to sentiment mining and learning how to evaluate the results, we practice using a machine learning classifier to determine the sentiment of a set of software developer chat logs and e-mail logs.

Chapter 6, Named Entity Recognition in Text, is about finding proper nouns and proper names in text. We spend some time learning why this task is useful, and why finding named entities can sometimes be more difficult than it sounds. At the end of the chapter we implement a named entity recognition system on several different types of real-world text data including e-mail, chat logs, and board meeting minutes. Along the way we apply different techniques for quantifying the success or failure of our results.

Chapter 7, Automatic Text Summarization, presents several strategies for automatically create condensed summaries of text. This chapter emphasizes extractive summarization tools, which are designed to find the most important sentences in a text sample. To this end, we experiment with three different tools for accomplishing this goal, testing the summarization methods, and learning how they differ. Following the introduction of each tool, we attempt to summarize a common set of text documents and compare the results.

Chapter 8, Topic Modeling in Text, shows how to use software tools to reveal what topics or concepts are present in a given text. Can we train a computer program to infer the themes that are present in large amounts of text? In a series of experiments, we learn how to use common topic modeling libraries to reveal the topics present in software developer e-mails, and how those topics change over time.

Chapter 9, Mining for Data Anomalies, is where we learn how to use data mining and statistical techniques to improve our own data mining process. While all of the other chapters in this book deal with finding different types of patterns in data, here we focus on finding data that is anomalous or that does not match a particular pattern. Whether it is because the data is empty, missing, or just plain weird, this chapter presents strategies for finding or fixing this type of data so that the rest of your data can be mined more effectively.

What you need for this book

To complete the projects in this book, you will need a version of Python 3.5 or higher. I recommend using Anaconda Python, but any Python distribution will do as long as it is updated and contains the following packages: Numpy, Matplotlib, NetworkX, PyMySQL, Gensim, and NLTK. In *Chapter 1, Expanding Your Data Mining Toolbox*, we will walk through an easy installation of Python and all these libraries, and each time a library is used later in the book, we will install it or upgrade it together.

Because data mining is obviously data-centric, and because the data sets we are working with are sometimes large or require some type of persistent data storage, I chose to implement some of the data mining algorithms alongside a relational database system. I chose MySQL for accomplishing this since it is an established, easy-to-download and install piece of infrastructure. The chapters where MySQL comes into play are in working with the memory-intensive algorithms in *Chapter 2, Association Rule Mining*, and *Chapter 3, Entity Matching*. I also use MySQL for some of the examples in *Chapter 9, Mining for Data Anomalies*, but it is possible to go through that chapter without MySQL.

Who this book is for

If you picked up a book on mastering data mining, you are probably familiar with the basics of data analysis and you have likely experimented with machine learning techniques such as regression, decision trees, classification, and cluster analysis. If you have intermediate experience with Python, understand basic relational database terminology, have some exposure to basic statistics, and can understand the rudiments of how supervised and unsupervised machine learning techniques work, then you are ready for this book. Let's build on what you already know to learn some more exotic, unusual strategies for mining your data!

Conventions

In this book, you will find a number of text styles that distinguish between different kinds of information. Here are some examples of these styles and an explanation of their meaning.

Code words in text, database table names, folder names, filenames, file extensions, pathnames, dummy URLs, user input, and Twitter handles are shown as follows: "We can include other contexts through the use of the `include` directive."

A block of code is set as follows:

```
MINSUPPORTPCT = 5
allSingletonTags = []
allDoubletonTags = set()
doubletonSet = set()
```

Any command-line input or output is written as follows:

```
conda install pymysql
```

New terms and **important words** are shown in bold. Words that you see on the screen, for example, in menus or dialog boxes, appear in the text like this: "Clicking the **Next** button moves you to the next screen."

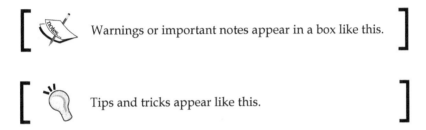

Warnings or important notes appear in a box like this.

Tips and tricks appear like this.

Reader feedback

Feedback from our readers is always welcome. Let us know what you think about this book—what you liked or disliked. Reader feedback is important for us as it helps us develop titles that you will really get the most out of.

To send us general feedback, simply e-mail feedback@packtpub.com, and mention the book's title in the subject of your message.

If there is a topic that you have expertise in and you are interested in either writing or contributing to a book, see our author guide at www.packtpub.com/authors.

Customer support

Now that you are the proud owner of a Packt book, we have a number of things to help you to get the most from your purchase.

Downloading the example code

You can download the example code files for this book from your account at
`http://www.packtpub.com`. If you purchased this book elsewhere, you can visit
`http://www.packtpub.com/support` and register to have the files e-mailed directly
to you.

You can download the code files by following these steps:

1. Log in or register to our website using your e-mail address and password.
2. Hover the mouse pointer on the **SUPPORT** tab at the top.
3. Click on **Code Downloads & Errata**.
4. Enter the name of the book in the **Search** box.
5. Select the book for which you're looking to download the code files.
6. Choose from the drop-down menu where you purchased this book from.
7. Click on **Code Download**.

You can also download the code files by clicking on the **Code Files** button on the
book's webpage at the Packt Publishing website. This page can be accessed by
entering the book's name in the **Search** box. Please note that you need to be
logged in to your Packt account.

Once the file is downloaded, please make sure that you unzip or extract the folder
using the latest version of:

- WinRAR / 7-Zip for Windows
- Zipeg / iZip / UnRarX for Mac
- 7-Zip / PeaZip for Linux

The code bundle for the book is also hosted on GitHub at `https://github.com/`
`megansquire/masteringDM`. We also have other code bundles from our rich catalog
of books and videos available at `https://github.com/PacktPublishing/`. Check
them out!

Errata

Although we have taken every care to ensure the accuracy of our content, mistakes do happen. If you find a mistake in one of our books—maybe a mistake in the text or the code—we would be grateful if you could report this to us. By doing so, you can save other readers from frustration and help us improve subsequent versions of this book. If you find any errata, please report them by visiting http://www.packtpub.com/submit-errata, selecting your book, clicking on the **Errata Submission Form** link, and entering the details of your errata. Once your errata are verified, your submission will be accepted and the errata will be uploaded to our website or added to any list of existing errata under the Errata section of that title.

To view the previously submitted errata, go to https://www.packtpub.com/books/content/support and enter the name of the book in the search field. The required information will appear under the **Errata** section.

Piracy

Piracy of copyrighted material on the Internet is an ongoing problem across all media. At Packt, we take the protection of our copyright and licenses very seriously. If you come across any illegal copies of our works in any form on the Internet, please provide us with the location address or website name immediately so that we can pursue a remedy.

Please contact us at copyright@packtpub.com with a link to the suspected pirated material.

We appreciate your help in protecting our authors and our ability to bring you valuable content.

Questions

If you have a problem with any aspect of this book, you can contact us at questions@packtpub.com, and we will do our best to address the problem.

1
Expanding Your Data Mining Toolbox

When faced with sensory information, human beings naturally want to find patterns to explain, differentiate, categorize, and predict. This process of looking for patterns all around us is a fundamental human activity, and the human brain is quite good at it. With this skill, our ancient ancestors became better at hunting, gathering, cooking, and organizing. It is no wonder that pattern recognition and pattern prediction were some of the first tasks humans set out to computerize, and this desire continues in earnest today. Depending on the goals of a given project, finding patterns in data using computers nowadays involves database systems, artificial intelligence, statistics, information retrieval, computer vision, and any number of other various subfields of computer science, information systems, mathematics, or business, just to name a few. No matter what we call this activity – knowledge discovery in databases, data mining, data science – its primary mission is always to find interesting patterns.

Despite this humble-sounding mission, data mining has existed for long enough and has built up enough variation in how it is implemented that it has now become a large and complicated field to master. We can think of a cooking school, where every beginner chef is first taught how to boil water and how to use a knife before moving to more advanced skills, such as making puff pastry or deboning a raw chicken. In data mining, we also have common techniques that even the newest data miners will learn: How to build a classifier and how to find clusters in data. The title of this book, however, is *Mastering Data Mining with Python*, and so, as a *mastering*-level book, the aim is to teach you some of the techniques you may not have seen in earlier data mining projects.

In this first chapter, we will cover the following topics:

- **What is data mining?** We will situate data mining in the growing field of other similar concepts, and we will learn a bit about the history of how this discipline has grown and changed.

- **How do we do data mining?** Here, we compare several processes or methodologies commonly used in data mining projects.

- **What are the techniques used in data mining?** In this section, we will summarize each of the data analysis techniques that are typically included in a definition of data mining, and we will highlight the more exotic or underappreciated techniques that we will be covering in this mastering-level book.

- **How do we set up a data mining work environment?** Finally, we will walk through setting up a Python-based development environment that we will use to complete the projects in the rest of this book.

What is data mining?

We explained earlier that the goal of data mining is to find patterns in data, but this oversimplification falls apart quickly under scrutiny. After all, could we not also say that finding patterns is the goal of classical statistics, or business analytics, or machine learning, or even the newer practices of **data science** or **big data**? What is the difference between data mining and all of these other fields, anyway? And while we are at it, why is it called **data mining** if what we are really doing is mining for patterns? Don't we already have the data?

It was apparent from the beginning that the term data mining is indeed fraught with many problems. The term was originally used as something of a pejorative by statisticians who cautioned against going on *fishing expeditions*, where a data analyst is casting about for patterns in data without forming proper hypotheses first. Nonetheless, the term rose to prominence in the 1990s, as the popular press caught wind of exciting research that was marrying the mature field of database management systems with the best algorithms from machine learning and artificial intelligence. The inclusion of the word *mining* inspires visions of a modern-day Gold Rush, in which the persistent and intrepid miner will discover (and perhaps profit from) previously hidden gems. The idea that data itself could be a rare and precious commodity was immediately appealing to the business and technology press, despite efforts by early pioneers to promote the holistic term **knowledge discovery in databases (KDD)**.

The term data mining persisted, however, and ultimately some definitions of the field attempted to re-imagine the term data mining to refer to just one of the steps in a longer, more comprehensive **knowledge discovery process**. Today, data mining and KDD are considered very similar, closely related terms.

What about other related terms, such as machine learning, predictive analytics, big data, and data science? Are these the same as data mining or KDD? Let's draw some comparisons between each of these terms:

- **Machine learning** is a very specific subfield of computer science that focuses on developing algorithms that can learn from data in order to make predictions. Many data mining solutions will use techniques from machine learning, but not all data mining is trying to make predictions or learn from data. Sometimes we just want to find a pattern in the data. In fact, in this book we will be exploring a few data mining solutions that do use machine learning techniques, and many more that do not.

- **Predictive analytics**, sometimes just called analytics, is a general term for computational solutions that attempt to make predictions from data in a variety of domains. We can think of the terms business analytics, media analytics, and so on. Some, but not all, predictive analytics solutions will use machine learning techniques to perform their predictions. But again, in data mining, we are not always interested in prediction.

- **Big data** is a term that refers to the problems and solutions of dealing with very large sets of data, irrespective of whether we are searching for patterns in that data, or simply storing it. In terms of comparing big data to data mining, many data mining problems are made more interesting when the data sets are large, so solutions discovered for dealing with big data might come in handy to solve a data mining problem. Nonetheless, these two terms are merely complementary, not interchangeable.

- **Data science** is the closest of these terms to being interchangeable with the KDD process, of which data mining is one step. Because data science is an extremely popular buzzword at this time, its meaning will continue to evolve and change as the field continues to mature.

To show the relative search interest for these various terms over time, we can look at Google Trends. This tool shows how frequently people are searching for various keywords over time. In the following figure, the newcomer term data science is currently the hot buzzword, with data mining pulling into second place, followed by machine learning, data science, and predictive analytics. (I tried to include the search term *knowledge discovery in databases* as well, but the results were so close to zero that the line was invisible.) The y-axis shows the popularity of that particular search term as a 0-100 indexed value. In addition, I combined the weekly index values that Google Trends gives into a monthly average for each month in the period 2004-2015.

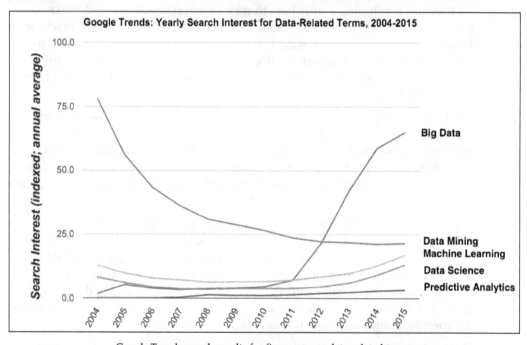

Google Trends search results for five common data-related terms

How do we do data mining?

Since data mining is traditionally seen as one of the steps in the overall KDD process, and increasingly in the data science process, in this section we get acquainted with the steps involved. There are several popular methodologies for doing the work of data mining. Here we highlight four methodologies: Two that are taken from textbook introductions to the theory of data mining, one taken from a very practical process used in industry, and one designed for teaching beginners.

The Fayyad et al. KDD process

One early version of the knowledge discovery and data mining process was defined by Usama Fayyad, Gregory Piatetsky-Shapiro, and Padhraic Smyth in a 1996 article (*The KDD Process for Extracting Useful Knowledge from Volumes of Data*). This article was important at the time for refining the rapidly changing KDD methodology into a concrete set of steps. The following steps lead from raw data at the beginning to knowledge at the end:

- **Data selection**: The input to this step is raw data, and the output of this selection step is a smaller subset of the data, called the **target data**.

- **Data pre-processing**: The target data is cleaned, oddities and outliers are removed, and missing data is accounted for. The output of this step is **pre-processed data**, or **cleaned data**.

- **Data transformation**: The cleaned data is organized into a format appropriate for the mining step, and the number of features or variables is reduced if need be. The output of this step is **transformed data**.

- **Data mining**: The transformed data is mined for patterns using one or more data mining algorithms appropriate to the problem at hand. The output of this step is the **discovered patterns**.

- **Data interpretation/evaluation**: The discovered patterns are evaluated for their ability to solve the problem at hand. The output of this step is **knowledge**.

Since this process leads from raw data to knowledge, it is appropriate that these authors were the ones who were really committed to the term *knowledge discovery in databases* rather than simply data mining.

The Han et al. KDD process

Another version of the knowledge discovery process is described in the popular data mining textbook *Data Mining: Concepts and Techniques* by Jiawei Han, Micheline Kamber, and Jian Pei as the following steps, which also lead from raw data to knowledge at the end:

- **Data cleaning**: The input to this step is raw data, and the output is **cleaned data**.

- **Data integration**: In this step, the cleaned data is integrated (if it came from multiple sources). The output of this step is **integrated data**.

- **Data selection**: The data set is reduced to only the data needed for the problem at hand. The output of this step is a **smaller data set**.

- **Data transformation**: The smaller data set is consolidated into a form that will work with the upcoming data mining step. This is called **transformed data**.

- **Data mining**: The transformed data is processed by intelligent algorithms that are designed to discover patterns in that data. The output of this step is one or more patterns.

- **Pattern evaluation**: The discovered patterns are evaluated for their interestingness and their ability to solve the problem at hand. The output of this step is an interestingness measure applied to each pattern, representing knowledge.

- **Knowledge representation**: In this step, the knowledge is communicated to users through various means, including visualization.

In both the Fayyad and Han methodologies, it is expected that the process will iterate multiple times over the steps, if such iteration is needed. For example, if, during the transformation step the person doing the analysis realized that another data cleaning or pre-processing step, is needed, both of these methodologies specify that the analyst should double back and complete a second iteration of the incomplete earlier step.

The CRISP-DM process

A third popular version of the KDD process that is used in many business and applied domains is called **CRISP-DM**, which stands for **CRoss-Industry Standard Process for Data Mining**. It consists of the following steps:

1. **Business understanding**: In this step, the analyst spends time understanding the **reasons** for the data mining project from a business perspective.

2. **Data understanding**: In this step, the analyst becomes familiar with the data and its potential promises and shortcomings, and begins to generate **hypotheses**. The analyst is tasked to reassess the business understanding (*step 1*) if needed.

3. **Data preparation**: This step includes all the data selection, integration, transformation, and **pre-processing** steps that are enumerated as separate steps in the other models. The CRISP-DM model has no expectation of what order these tasks will be done in.

4. **Modeling**: This is the step in which the algorithms are applied to the data to discover the **patterns**. This step is closest to the actual data mining steps in the other KDD models. The analyst is tasked to reassess the data preparation step (*step 3*) if the modeling and mining step requires it.

5. **Evaluation**: The model and discovered patterns are evaluated for their value in **answering the business problem** at hand. The analyst is tasked with revisiting the business understanding (*step 1*) if necessary.

6. **Deployment**: The discovered knowledge and models are **presented** and put into production to solve the original problem at hand.

One of the strengths of this methodology is that iteration is built in. Between specific steps, it is expected that the analyst will check that the current step is still in agreement with certain previous steps. Another strength of this method is that the analyst is explicitly reminded to keep the business problem front and center in the project, even down in the evaluation steps.

The Six Steps process

When I teach the introductory data science course at my university, I use a hybrid methodology of my own creation. This methodology is called the Six Steps, and I designed it to be especially friendly for teaching. My Six Steps methodology removes some of the ambiguity that inexperienced students may have with open-ended tasks from CRISP-DM, such as *Business Understanding*, or a corporate-focused task such as *Deployment*. In addition, the Six Steps method keeps the focus on developing students' critical thinking skills by requiring them to answer *Why are we doing this?* and *What does it mean?* at the beginning and end of the process. My Six Steps method looks like this:

1. **Problem statement**: In this step, the students identify what the problem is that they are trying to solve. Ideally, they motivate the case for why they are doing all this work.

2. **Data collection and storage**: In this step, students locate data and plan their storage for the data needed for this problem. They also provide information about where the data that is helping them answer their motivating question came from, as well as what format it is in and what all the fields mean.

3. **Data cleaning**: In this phase, students carefully select only the data they really need, and pre-process the data into the format required for the mining step.

4. **Data mining**: In this step, students formalize their chosen data mining methodology. They describe what algorithms they used and why. The output of this step is a **model** and **discovered patterns**.

5. **Representation and visualization**: In this step, the students show the results of their work visually. The outputs of this step can be **tables**, **drawings**, **graphs**, **charts**, **network diagrams**, **maps**, and so on.

6. **Problem resolution**: This is an important step for beginner data miners. This step explicitly encourages the student to evaluate whether the patterns they showed in *step 5* are really an answer to the question or problem they posed in *step 1*. Students are asked to state the limitations of their model or results, and to identify parts of the motivating question that they could not answer with this method.

Which data mining methodology is the best?

A 2014 survey of the subscribers of Gregory Piatetsky-Shapiro's very popular data mining email newsletter KDNuggets included the question *What main methodology are you using for your analytics, data mining, or data science projects?*

- 43% of the poll respondents indicated that they were using the CRISP-DM methodology
- 27% of the respondents were using their own methodology or a hybrid
- 7% were using the traditional KDD methodology
- The remaining respondents chose another KDD method

These results are generally similar to the 2007 results from the same newsletter asking the same question.

My best advice is that it does not matter too much which methodology you use for a data mining project, as long as you just pick one. If you do not have any methodology at all, then you run the risk of forgetting important steps. Choose one of the methods that seems like it might work for your project and your needs, and then just do your best to follow the steps.

For this book, we will vary our data mining methodology depending on which technique we are looking at in a given chapter. For example, even though the focus of the book as a whole is on the data mining step, we still need to motivate each chapter-length project with a healthy dose of *Business Understanding* (CRISP-DM) or *Problem Statement* (Six Steps) so that we understand why we are doing the tasks and what the results mean. In addition, in order to learn a particular data mining method, we may also have to do some pre-processing, whether we call that data cleaning, integration, or transformation. But in general, we will try to keep these tasks to a minimum so that our focus on data mining remains clear. One prominent exception will be in the final chapter, where we will show specific methods for dealing with missing data and anomalies. Finally, even though data visualization is typically very important for representing the results of your data mining process to your audience, we will also keep these tasks to a minimum so that we can remain focused on the primary job at hand: Data mining.

What are the techniques used in data mining?

Now that we have a sense of where data mining fits in our overall KDD or data science process, we can start to discuss the details of how to get it done.

Since the early days of attempting to define data mining, several broad classes of relevant problems consistently show up again and again. Fayyad et al. name six classes of problems in another important 1996 paper (*From Data Mining to Knowledge Discovery in Databases*), which we can summarize as follows:

- **Classification problems**: Here, we have data that needs to be divided into predefined classes, based on some features of the data. We need an algorithm that can use previously classified data to learn how to put unknown data into the correct class.

- **Clustering problems**: With these problems, we have data that needs to be divided into classes based on its features, but we do not know what the classes are in advance. We need an algorithm that can measure the similarity between data points and automatically divide the data up based on these similarities.

- **Regression problems**: We have data that needs to be mapped onto a predictor variable, so we need to learn a function that can do this mapping.

- **Summarization problems**: Suppose we have data that needs to be shortened or summarized in some way. This could be as simple as calculating basic statistics from data, or as complex as learning how to summarize text or finding a topic model for text.

- **Dependency modeling problems**: For these problems, we have data that might be connected in some way, and we need to develop an algorithm that can calculate the probability of connection or describe the structure of connected data.

- **Change and deviation detection problems**: In another case, we have data that has changed significantly or where some subset of the data deviates from normative values. To solve these problems, we need an algorithm that can detect these issues automatically.

In a different paper written that same year, those same authors also included a few additional categories:

- **Link analysis problems**: Here we have data points with relationships between them, and we need to discover and describe these relationships in terms of how much support they have in the data set and how confident we are in the relationship.

- **Sequence analysis problems**: Imagine that we have data points that follow a sequence, such as a time series or a genome, and we must discover trends or deviations in the sequence, or discover what is causing the sequence or how it will evolve.

Han, Kamber, and Pei, in the textbook we discussed earlier, describe four classes of problems that data mining can help solve, and further, they divide them into descriptive and predictive categories. Descriptive data mining means we are finding patterns that help us understand the data we have. Predictive data mining means we are finding patterns that can help us make predictions about data we do not yet have.

In the descriptive category, they list the following data mining problems:

- Data characterization and data discrimination problems, including data summarization or concept characterization or description.

- Frequency mining, including finding frequent patterns, association rules, and correlations in data.

In the predictive category, they list the following:

- Classification, regression
- Clustering
- Outlier detection and anomaly detection

It is easy to see that there are many similarities between the Fayyad *et al.* list and the Han *et al.* list, but that they have just grouped the items differently. Indeed, the items that show up on both lists are exactly the types of data mining problems you are probably already familiar with by now if you have completed earlier data mining projects. Classification, regression, and clustering are very popular, foundational data mining techniques, so they are covered in nearly every data mining book designed for practitioners.

What techniques are we going to use in this book?

Since this book is about *mastering* data mining, we are going to tackle a few of the techniques that are not covered quite as often in the standard books. Specifically, we will address link analysis via association rules in *Chapter 2, Association Rule Mining*, and anomaly detection in *Chapter 9, Mining for Data Anomalies*. We are also going to apply a few data mining techniques to actually assist in data cleaning and pre-processing efforts, namely, in taking care of missing values in *Chapter 9, Mining for Data Anomalies*, and some data integration via entity matching in *Chapter 3, Entity Matching*.

In addition to defining data mining in terms of the techniques, sometimes people divide up the various data mining problems based on what type of data they are mining. For example, you may hear people refer to text mining or social network analysis. These refer to the type of data being mined rather than the specific technique being used to mine it. For example, text mining refers to any kind of data mining technique as applied to text documents, and network mining refers to looking for patterns in network graph data. In this book, we will be doing some network mining in *Chapter 4, Network Analysis*, different types of text document summarization in *Chapter 6, Named Entity Recognition in Text*, *Chapter 7, Automatic Text Summarization*, and *Chapter 8, Topic Modeling in Text*, and some classification of text by its sentiment (the emotion in the text) in *Chapter 5, Sentiment Analysis in Text*.

If you are anything like me, right about now you might be thinking *enough of this background stuff, I want to write some code*. I am glad you are getting excited to work on some actual projects. We are almost ready to start coding, but first we need to get a good working environment set up.

How do we set up our data mining work environment?

The previous sections were included to give us a better sense of what we are going to build and why. Now it is time to begin setting up a development environment that will support us as we work through all of these projects. Since this book is designed to teach us how to build the software to mine data for patterns, we will be writing our programs from scratch using a general purpose programming language. The Python programming language has a very strong – and still growing – community dedicated to data mining. This community has contributed some very handy libraries that we can use for efficient processing, and numerous data types that we can rely on to make our work go faster.

At the time of writing, there are two versions of Python available for download: Python 2 (the latest version is 2.7), now considered legacy, and Python 3 (the latest version is 3.5). We will be using Python 3 in this book. Because we have so many related packages and libraries we need to use to make our data mining experience as painless as possible, and because some of them can be a bit difficult to install, I recommend using a Python distribution designed for scientific and mathematical computing. Specifically, I recommend the Anaconda distribution of Python 3.5 made by Continuum Analytics. Their basic distribution of Python is free, and all the pieces are guaranteed to work together without us having to do the frustrating work of ensuring compatibility.

To download the Anaconda Python distribution, point your browser to the Continuum Analytics web site at `https://www.continuum.io` and follow the prompts to download the free Anaconda version (currently numbered 3.5 or above) that will work with your operating system.

Upon launching the software, you will see a splash screen that looks like the following screenshot:

Continuum Anaconda Navigator

Depending on the version you are using and when you downloaded it, you may notice a few **Update** buttons in addition to the **Launch** button for each application within Anaconda. You can click each to update the package if your software version is indicating that you need to do this.

To get started writing Python code, click **Spyder** to launch the code editor and the integrated development environment. If you would rather use your own text editor, such as TextWrangler on MacOS or Sublime editor on Windows, that is perfectly fine. You can run the Python code from the command line.

Spend a few moments getting Spyder configured to your liking, setting its colors and general layout, or just keep the defaults. For my own workspace, I moved around a few of the console windows, set up a working directory, and made a few customization tweaks that made me feel at home in this new editor. You can do the same to make your development environment comfortable for you.

Now we are ready to test the editor and get our libraries installed. To test the Spyder editor and see how it works, click **File** and select **New File**. Then type a simple hello world statement, as follows:

```
print ('hello world')
```

Run the program, either by clicking the green arrow, by pressing *F5*, or by clicking **Run** from inside the **Run** menu. Either way, the program will execute and you will see your output in the console output window.

At this point, we know Spyder and Python are working, and we are ready to test and install some libraries.

First, open a new file and save it as `packageTest.py`. In this test program, we will determine whether Scikit-learn was installed properly with Anaconda. Scikit-learn is a very important package that includes many machine learning functions, as well as canned data sets to test those functions. Many, many books and tutorials use Scikit-learn examples for teaching data mining, so this is a good package to have in our toolkit. We will use this package in several chapters in this book.

Running the following small program from the Scikit-learn tutorial on its website (found at `http://scikit-learn.org/stable/tutorial/basic/tutorial.html #loading-an-example-dataset`) will tell us if our environment is set up properly:

```
from sklearn import datasets
iris = datasets.load_iris()
digits = datasets.load_digits()
print (digits.data)
```

If this program runs properly, it will produce output in the console window showing a series of numbers in a list-like data structure, like this:

```
[[  0.   0.   5. ...,    0.   0.    0.]
 [  0.   0.   0. ...,   10.   0.    0.]
 [  0.   0.   0. ...,   16.   9.    0.]
 ...,
 [  0.   0.   1. ...,    6.   0.    0.]
 [  0.   0.   2. ...,   12.   0.    0.]
 [  0.   0.  10. ...,   12.   1.    0.]
```

For our purposes, this output is sufficient to show that Scikit-learn is installed properly. Next, add a line that will help us learn about the data type of this `digits.data` structure, as follows:

```
print (type(digits.data))
```

The output is as follows:

```
<class 'numpy.ndarray'>
```

From this output, we can confirm that Scikit-learn relies on another important package called Numpy to handle some of its data structures. Anaconda has also installed Numpy properly for us, which is exactly what we wanted to confirm.

Next, we will test whether our network analysis libraries are included. We will use `Networkx` library later in the network mining we will do in *Chapter 4, Network Analysis* to build a graphical social network. The following code sample creates a tiny network with one node, and prints its type to the screen:

```
import networkx as nx
G=nx.Graph()
G.add_node(1)
print (type(G))
```

The output is as follows:

```
<class 'networkx.classes.graph.Graph'>
```

This is exactly the output we wanted to see, as it tells us that `Networkx` is installed and working properly.

Next we will test some of the text mining software we need in later chapters. Conveniently, the **Natural Language Toolkit** (**NLTK**), is also installed with Anaconda. However, it has its own graphical downloader tool for the various corpora and word lists that it uses. Anaconda does not come with these installed, so we will have to do it. To get word lists and dictionaries, we will create a new Python file, import the NLTK module, then prompt NLTK to start the graphical Downloader:

```
import nltk
nltk.download()
```

A new Downloader window will open in Anaconda that looks like this:

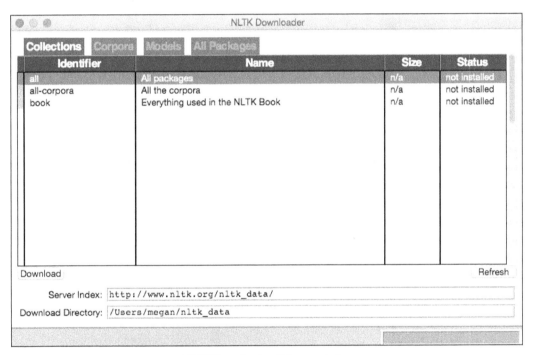

NLTK Downloader dialogue window

Inside this Downloader window, select **all** from the list of Identifiers, change the **Download Directory** location (**optional**), and press the **Download** button. The red progress bar in the bottom-left of the **Downloader** window will animate as each collection is installed. This may take several minutes if your connection is slow. This mid-download step is shown in the following screenshot:

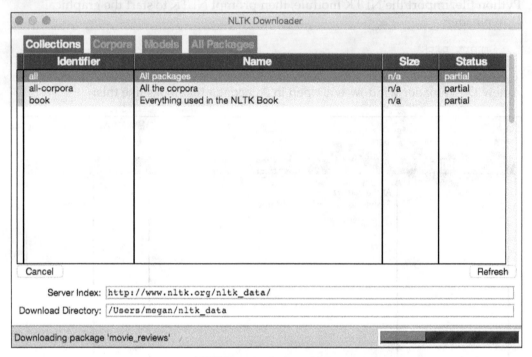

NLTK Downloader in progress

Once the **Downloader** has finished installing the NLTK corpora, we can test whether they work properly. Here is a short Python program where we ask NLTK to use the Brown University corpora and print the first 10 words:

```
from nltk.corpus import brown
print (brown.words()[0:10])
```

The output of this program is as follows, a list of the first 10 words in the NLTK Brown text corpus, which happens to be from a news story:

```
['The', 'Fulton', 'County', 'Grand', 'Jury', 'said', 'Friday', 'an',
'investigation', 'of']
```

With this output, we can be confident that NLTK is installed and all the necessary corpora have also been installed.

Next, we will install a text mining module called **Gensim** that we will need later for doing topic modeling. Gensim does not come pre-installed as part of Anaconda by default, but instead it is one of several hundred packages that are easily added by using Anaconda's built-in conda installer. From the **Anaconda Tools** menu, choose **Open a Terminal** and type `conda install gensim`. If you are prompted to update `numpy` and `scipy`, type *y* for yes, and the installation will proceed.

When the installation is finished, start up a new Python program and type this shortened version of the Gensim test program from its website:

```
from gensim import corpora, models, similarities
test = [[(0, 1.0), (1, 1.0), (2, 1.0)]]
print (test)
```

This program does not do much more than test if the module is imported properly and then print a list to the screen, but that is enough for now.

Finally, since this is a book about data mining, or knowledge discovery in databases, having some kind of database software to work with is definitely a good idea. Because it is free software, easy to install, and available for many operating systems, I chose MySQL to implement the projects in this book.

To get MySQL, head to the download page for the free Community Edition, available at `http://dev.mysql.com/downloads/mysql/` for whatever OS you are using.

To get Anaconda Python to talk to MySQL, we will need to install some MySQL Python drivers. I like the `pymysql` drivers since they are fairly robust and lack some of the bugs that come with the standard drivers. From within Anaconda, start up a terminal window and run the following command:

`conda install pymysql`

It looks like all of our modules are installed and ready to be used as we need them throughout the book. If we decide we need additional modules, or if one of them goes out of date, we now know how to install it or upgrade it as needed.

Summary

In this chapter, we learned what it would take to expand our data mining toolbox to the *master* level. First we took a long view of the field as a whole, starting with the history of data mining as a piece of the **knowledge discovery in databases (KDD)** process. We also compared the field of data mining to other similar fields such as data science, machine learning, and big data.

Next, we outlined the common tools and techniques that most experts consider to be most important to the KDD process, paying special attention to the techniques that are used most frequently in the mining and analysis steps. To really master data mining, it is important that we work on problems that are different than simple textbook examples. For this reason, we will be working on more exotic data mining techniques such as generating summaries and finding outliers, and focusing on more unusual data types, such as text and networks.

Finally, in this chapter we put together a robust data mining system for ourselves. Our workspace centers around the powerful, general-purpose programming language, Python, and its many useful data mining packages, such as NLTK, Gensim, Numpy, Networkx, and Scikit-learn, and it is complemented by an easy-to-use and free MySQL database.

Now, all this discussion of software packages has got me thinking: Have you ever wondered what packages are used most frequently together? Is the combination of NLTK and Networkx a common thing to see, or is this a rather unusual pairing of libraries? In the next chapter, we will work on solving exactly that type of problem. In *Chapter 2*, *Association Rule Mining*, we will learn how to generate a list of frequently-found pairs, triples, quadruples, and more, and then we will attempt to make predictions based on the patterns we found.

2

Association Rule Mining

In our data mining toolbox, measuring the frequency of a pattern is a critical task. In some cases, more frequently occurring patterns may end up being more important patterns. If we can find frequently occurring pairs of items, or triples of items, those may be even more interesting.

In this chapter, we begin our exploration of frequent itemsets, and then we extend those to a type of pattern called association rules. We will cover the following topics:

- What is a frequent itemset? What are the techniques for finding frequent itemsets? Where are the bottlenecks and how can we speed up the process?

- How can we extend a frequent itemset to become an association rule?

- What makes a good association rule? We will learn to describe the value of a particular association rule, given its level of support in the database, our confidence in the rule itself, and the value added by the rule we found.

To do this, we will write a program to find frequent itemsets in an open dataset of metadata (facts) about a group of software projects. Then we will learn to find frequent itemsets among the tags used to describe those projects. Next, we will learn how to extend a frequent itemset into an association rule by calculating its support in the database and then adding a probabilistic direction (X implies Y) confidence interval. Finally, we will learn how to interpret an association rule. Specifically, we want to understand what an association rule shows, and what it does not show.

What are frequent itemsets?

Finding frequent itemsets is a type of counting activity. But unlike producing a simple tally of items we observe in a dataset (*today we sold 80 carrots and 100 tomatoes*), finding frequent itemsets is slightly different. Specifically, to find frequent itemsets we look for co-occurring sets of items within some larger group. These larger groups are sometimes imagined as supermarket transactions or shopping baskets, and the entire exercise is sometimes called **market basket analysis**. Staying with the supermarket analogy, the items co-occurring within those baskets are sometimes imagined to be combinations of products purchased at the supermarket. For example, given a set of supermarket transactions or baskets, we might be interested in whether the itemset of {carrots, tomatoes} occurs more frequently in baskets than does the {cucumbers, lemons} itemset.

The purpose of frequent itemset mining is to make interesting discoveries of co-occurring items within a set of transactions. In other words, it may be useful if we found out that there are some combinations of items that occur together frequently across multiple baskets. It will be especially interesting if the frequent itemsets we found are slightly unusual or unexpected in some way. The canonical example of an interesting, highly desirable rule in frequent itemset mining is usually described by retelling an urban legend called the *diapers and beer* story.

The diapers and beer urban legend

I remember first hearing this story in a data mining graduate course I took in 1998. My professor was trying to explain the usefulness of frequent itemsets and association rules, and he told our class the following story:

"A midwestern grocery store chain mined for frequent itemsets in order to discover what interesting combinations of groceries were purchased together. Their plan was to optimize the sales by co-locating these products in the store. To their delight, the grocery store data mining team learned that on Thursday nights between 5 and 7pm, men would frequently purchase a combination of diapers and beer. The grocery store placed these items together by moving a small display of diapers into the beer aisle, and sales of both products soared."

Being a skeptic, I had many questions about this story right away. How did the store know it was men who were doing the buying? After all, this was well before the advent of electronic loyalty cards or rewards cards in grocery stores. How could a store possibly fit a proper selection of diapers in a small display case in the middle of the beer aisle? After all, diapers come in five different sizes and there are usually at least three brands, and - as I quickly learned as a new parent - it is not a good idea to substitute one size or brand for another on a whim, or you may have disastrous results.

It turns out that several other folks were suspicious as well, and some went as far as to attempt to track down the history of this urban legend. The best-researched examples include Dan Powers' *DSS Resources* newsletter, with its November 10, 2002 issue (Volume 3, Number 23) dedicated to finding out the true origin of this story. This fascinating piece of work is available at `http://www.dssresources.com/newsletters/66.php`. Later, in 2006, The Register in the UK also ran a story about this urban legend. This article is available at `http://www.theregister.co.uk/2006/08/15/beer_diapers`.

If you believe the details relayed in both these pieces, the diapers and beer story started as a working example of what was possible with early attempts at data mining: *Use our database product and you can query for unusual patterns like diapers and beer!* Somehow, that working example extended to a *this really happened to me* story, which then morphed into an urban legend as the facts were stretched to accommodate various details and motives of the storytellers. As told in recent years, the common variants of this story include:

- It was Walmart that did the data mining
- The retailer used its discovered knowledge to raise the price of beer on Thursdays
- The motivation for buying the beer was as a reward for taking care of the children (presumably the children were the reason for buying the diapers)
- The retailer was particularly excited about these patterns because diapers are a profitable item

The truth of this story is indeed more mundane than the legend, but its popularity as a motivating case endures. It is very likely that if you do any research into frequent itemsets or association rule mining, the diapers and beer story, showing how market basket analysis is used in the real world, will come up as a case-in-point. It is used in nearly every book, article, and presentation ever given about association rules.

Frequent itemset mining basics

For our purposes, we will use the diapers and beer story as a useful metaphor. Specifically, we can use the terminology in this story to help define the three salient pieces in so-called market basket analysis, or frequent itemset mining:

- First, to do market basket analysis, we need a **market**. In the metaphor, the market is an actual supermarket.
- Next, we need a **basket**. In the example, the basket is a single shopping transaction. Sometimes we will use the word "basket," sometimes you will hear "transaction" used.

- We need **items**. In the metaphor, the grocery items are placed into the basket, or transaction, for purchase.

As long as we have the concepts of a market, a basket, and items, and as long as these things work the way we describe here, we are well on our way to having a dataset that we can mine for frequent itemsets.

There are a few more assumptions buried in the market basket story though, and these will affect whether or not we have a minable dataset. So let's be explicit about those now:

- There should be a many-to-many relationship between items and baskets. Baskets are made up of many items, and an item can appear in many baskets.

- The quantity of items is not considered. If the person bought six pack of diapers or one pack of diapers, the relevant fact is that the basket contains *diapers*.

- An item may not appear in any basket (I am sure we can all think of an unpopular grocery item), but every basket will contain at least one item. Empty baskets are not interesting!

- The order of the items in a basket does not matter. In terms of the metaphor, it does not matter whether your beer or your package of diapers was placed in the shopping basket first, nor does it matter which one was placed on the conveyer belt first, nor does it matter which one was entered into the cash register first. Instead, we will metaphorically group items together that were purchased as a single transaction or basket, regardless of their position in that basket.

At this stage in the analysis of our market baskets, we are most interested in finding **frequent itemsets**. These are groups of items that are found frequently together in baskets. In a grocery store, some combinations of items that people purchase together can be guessed easily using common sense, but some combinations are rare. Cake mix and frosting is a predictable set of items that will be purchased together, but beer and diapers would be a more unusual pair.

Sometimes certain combinations are more expected than others due to the weather, holidays, or regional preferences. As with any data mining exercise, it is important to understand the **domain** you are studying. In the case of shopping baskets, there are probably wide regional variations due to different food preferences. For example:

- I live in the southern part of the United States, and there are many interesting combinations that we have in our stores that might seem unusual elsewhere. For example, vanilla wafer cookies and bananas are often purchased together in order to make banana pudding, a popular dessert.

- A common meal to serve on New Year's Day in my state contains black-eyed peas (a legume) and collard greens (a leafy vegetable), so baskets containing these items may increase around the end of the year.

- I also live in a place where snow events are fairly rare. Each time the weather forecast calls for snow for our area, everyone panics and buys up all the milk and bread in the store. Even though milk and bread are both very common items to purchase on any day, regardless of the weather, on these snow event days, we may find that the combination of milk and bread is a more common frequent itemset.

We can express these itemsets using a **set notation** like this:

```
itemset1 = {vanilla wafers, bananas, whipped cream}
itemset2 = {black eyed peas, collard greens}
itemset3 = {milk, bread}
```

Itemsets with two items in them are called **2-itemsets**, or pairs, and itemsets with three items in them are called **3-itemsets**, or triples, and so on. Sometimes pairs and triples are called **doubletons** and **tripletons**, respectively.

Towards association rules

All of this frequent itemset stuff is fine, but we are ultimately on the hunt for association rules, which are much more exciting. Association rules are formed from frequent itemsets, with a few small twists. We are interested in making a statement about the frequent itemsets like this: *people who buy vanilla wafers also buy bananas 60% of the time*. In order to do so, we need to learn how to calculate a few additional metrics, starting with two we call support and confidence.

Support

If we are looking for **frequent** itemsets, then we also need a way to express how often we see these sets occurring in baskets, and whether that number qualifies as frequent. If I see {vanilla wafers, bananas} in 90% of baskets, is that considered frequent? What about 50% of baskets? What about 5%? We call this number the support of the itemset. The support is just the number of times we saw that itemset over all the baskets.

To make support more meaningful, and to begin talking about "interestingness," we need to set a **minimum support threshold**. The minimum support threshold is any percentage between 0-100 that makes sense to our problem domain. If we set the minimum support threshold to 5%, this means that itemsets will only be considered frequent if they are found in at least 5% of all our baskets.

Support for a 2-itemset is typically written using a probability notation, like this:

```
support(X->Y) = P(XuY)
```

In other words, we can read this equation as *The support of X->Y equals the percentage of baskets that contain both X and Y*. Item X could be vanilla wafers and item Y could be bananas in this example. To calculate support of an itemset, we count how many baskets contain both these items, and divide by the total number of baskets. If the support of an itemset exceeds the minimum support threshold, then we can consider the itemset to be potentially interesting.

Confidence

Once we have discovered the frequent itemsets, we can start to consider whether one or more items in the set are directing the purchase of other items. For example, it would be interesting to know that 75% of customers who have vanilla wafers in their basket will also have bananas in that same basket. But, on the other hand, maybe only 1% of customers with bananas in their basket will also buy vanilla wafers. Why? This is because many, many more people buy bananas than buy vanilla wafers. Bananas are common and vanilla wafers are rare. So the direction of the purchasing relationship here is not necessarily symmetrical.

This brings us to a critical concept called **confidence**. The confidence of a directional relationship is written like this:

```
confidence(X->Y) = P(Y|X)
```

We can read this as *the confidence of X leading to Y is the probability of Y given X*. Or written differently:

```
confidence(X->Y) = support(XuY) / support(X)
```

The confidence of X->Y is just the percentage of baskets that contain both X and Y divided by the percentage of baskets that contain just X.

Once we have both support and confidence, we can begin to extend frequent itemsets into association rules.

Association rules

Now that we know how to determine if an itemset is frequent, and how to set up support and confidence levels, we can make a possible association rule from that frequent itemset.

An example of an association rule might look like this:

```
vanilla wafers -> bananas, whipped cream
[support=1%, confidence=40%]
```

We read this rule as follows, *1% of all baskets have the combination of vanilla wafers, bananas, and whipped cream; 40% of customers who purchased vanilla wafers also purchased bananas and whipped cream.*

The left-hand side of that rule is the determining item, called the **antecedent**. The right-hand side is the resulting item(s), called the **consequent**. If we switch around the items on the left-hand and right-hand sides, we need to calculate a different association rule, which, due to the high popularity of bananas, might look something like this:

```
bananas -> vanilla wafers, whipped cream
[support = .001%, confidence=10%]
```

An example with data

Imagine we have a store, and we have 10 baskets of goods, as shown in the following table. Right away you can see that this is clearly a contrived case, as all the baskets in this store have exactly three items in them and that is highly unlikely in a real store:

Basket	Item1	Item2	Item3
1	vanilla wafers	bananas	dog food
2	bananas	bread	yogurt
3	bananas	apples	yogurt
4	vanilla wafers	bananas	whipped cream
5	bread	vanilla wafers	yogurt
6	milk	bread	bananas
7	vanilla wafers	apples	bananas
8	yogurt	apples	vanilla wafers
9	vanilla wafers	bananas	milk
10	bananas	bread	peanut butter

First, we need to calculate the support of all the individual items in this store. We have nine items across those 10 baskets:

Item	Support
apples	3
bananas	8
bread	4
dog food	1
milk	2
peanut butter	1
vanilla wafers	6
yogurt	4
whipped cream	1

To make the example easy, let's consider only one frequent itemset, {vanilla wafers, bananas}, at this point. The support of the itemset, {vanilla wafers, bananas}, is the percentage of baskets that contain both vanilla wafers and bananas. There are four baskets (numbers 1, 4, 7, and 9) that contain both of these items. Thus the support for either rule vanilla wafers -> bananas or bananas -> vanilla wafers is 40%, because 4/10 baskets contain both of these items.

Now we can use these support values to calculate the confidence for two proposed association rules:

```
vanilla wafers -> bananas

bananas -> vanilla wafers

confidence(vanilla wafers -> bananas) =  support(vanilla wafers U
bananas) / support(vanilla wafers) = 4/6 = 67%

confidence(bananas -> vanilla wafers) = support (vanilla wafers U
bananas) / support(bananas) = 4/8 = 50%
```

Written as association rules, we have:

```
vanilla wafers -> bananas [support=40%, confidence=67%]
bananas -> vanilla wafers [support=40%, confidence=50%]
```

The rule, vanilla wafers -> bananas, is stronger (same support, higher confidence) than the rule, bananas -> vanilla wafers.

Added value – fixing a flaw in the plan

It is very appealing to look at a rule like `vanilla wafers->bananas[s=40%,c=67%]` and feel satisfied. However, this is a very small dataset and was contrived just for this example. In some cases, association rules can be very misleading, and we should proceed with caution. Consider the following example.

Imagine in a different store, where the support numbers for vanilla wafers and bananas look more like this:

Item	Support
{vanilla wafers}	50%
{bananas}	80%
{vanilla wafers, bananas}	30%

In this case, the support for the items individually is quite high, but the support for the items together is lower.

The confidence of `vanilla wafers -> bananas` in this scenario is .3/.8 = 37.5%

So what is the problem? Well, it turns out that *some items might do better on their own than as the consequence of an association rule*. Even if the rule meets some minimum support threshold of support, we need to consider how the items behaved outside of the rule. To do this, we calculate a measure called added value of a given association rule. The added value of the rule `vanilla wafers -> bananas` is calculated by subtracting the support of bananas from the confidence of the rule. If the added value number is large and positive, then the rule is good and interesting. If the added value number is close to zero, then the rule may be true, but boring. If the added value number is large and negative, then the items in the rule are actually negatively associated and would do better on their own.

We calculate added value like this:

```
added value = confidence of rule - support of right-hand side
```

Using the preceding table, here are some calculations:

```
confidence of rule = .375
support of right-hand side (bananas) = .8

added value = .375 - .8 = -0.425
```

This number tells us that bananas actually would have done better by themselves. Furthermore, our proposed move of the display case of bananas next to the vanilla wafers in this store might be a mistake since there is nothing gained from attempting to exploit a relationship between bananas and wafers.

We can change the data slightly to contrive a positive, interesting rule:

Item	Support
{vanilla wafers}	50%
{bananas}	30%
{vanilla wafers, bananas}	30%

The confidence of `vanilla wafers -> bananas` in this scenario is .3/.3 = 100%

```
confidence of rule = 1.0
support of bananas = .3
added value = 1 - .3 = .7
```

In this case, bananas really should be placed with the vanilla wafers in the store, because apparently no one is buying bananas as their only product!

There are many more ways to measure the interestingness of association rules, but these are beyond the scope of this book. I would encourage interested readers to search Google Scholar for current academic papers covering this topic. Multiple good sources can be found by using a search phrase such as **interestingness measures for association rules**. In these papers, there are many good "interestingness" measures for different types of data and problems.

Methods for finding frequent itemsets

So far we have learned that finding association rules is based on first finding frequent itemsets. After that, we are simply calculating based on previously found counts. An important principle that will help us find frequent itemsets faster is called the **upward closure property**. Upward closure states that an itemset can only be frequent if all the items in it are also frequent. In other words, there is no sense in calculating the support for any itemset if all the itemsets contained in it are not also frequent.

Why is it important to know about closure? Because knowing this rule will save us a lot of time in calculating the possible itemsets. Calculating the support for every possible itemset in a store that has hundreds of thousands of items is clearly not practical! It is definitely to our advantage to reduce the number of itemsets as much as possible. One strategy to reduce the number of itemsets is to take advantage of upward closure to construct an algorithm that works as follows:

1. First, we will set a support threshold.

2. Construct a list of 1-itemsets, or singletons:
    - To do this, start with a list of every possible item. This list is called `CandidateSingletonList`.
    - Calculate the support for every individual item in `CandidateSingletonList`.
    - Keep only the singletons that meet the support threshold, and add them to a list called `SingletonList`.

3. Construct a list of 2-itemsets, or doubletons:
    - To do this, start with `SingletonList`.
    - Make a list of every possible pairing of the items from `SingletonList`. This is called `CandidateDoubletonList`.
    - Keep only the candidate doubletons that meet the support threshold, and add them to a list called `DoubletonList`.

4. Construct a list of 3-itemsets, or `tripletons`:
    - To do this, start with `DoubletonList`.
    - Make a list of every possible single item that appears in `DoubletonList`, and match them to each item in `DoubletonList`, making triples. This is called `CandidateTripletonList`.
    - Keep only the candidate `tripletons` that meet the support threshold, and add them to a list called `TripletonList`.

5. Repeat step 4, growing the n-itemsets by one, using the single items from the previously constructed list, until you run out of frequent itemsets.

This algorithm is called Apriori, and it was first outlined in a 1994 paper written by Agarwal and Srikant called *Fast algorithms for mining association rules in large databases*. Since that time, numerous other algorithms have been proposed that attempt to optimize Apriori, including those that exploit parallelism and more interesting data structures, such as trees. There are also separate algorithms for some special types of basket data; for example, if we had baskets with sequential items, or baskets with categorical or hierarchical data. Still, for doing basic frequent itemset generation, Apriori is a classic choice.

Before we implement Apriori, we will draw special attention to a few important guidelines for generating candidate itemsets. While it is definitely time consuming to count the 2-itemsets, this is by far the most intensive work of the entire process. Due to closure property mentioned earlier, each successive pass over the data will construct fewer potential itemsets. As such, it is definitely to our advantage to reduce the number of items that have to be compared at the doubleton phase. To do this, we will set a minimum support threshold, but this threshold can be adjusted depending on the needs of the project you are working on.

In the next section, we will implement the Apriori algorithm in Python and use it to find association rules in a real-world database.

A project – discovering association rules in software project tags

In 1997, the website, Freshmeat, was created as a directory that tracked free, libre, and open source software (FLOSS) projects. In 2011, the site was renamed Freecode. After sales and acquisitions and several site redesigns, in 2014 all updates to the Freecode site were discontinued. The site remains online, but it is no longer being updated and no new projects are being added to the directory. Freecode now serves as a snapshot of facts about FLOSS projects during the late 1990s and 2000s. These facts about each software project include its name, its description, the URL to download the software, tags that describe its features, a numeric representation of its popularity, and so on.

As part of my FLOSSmole project, I have catalogued data from Freshmeat/Freecode since 2005. Freshmeat/Freecode provided periodic RDF downloads describing each project on the site. I downloaded these, parsed out the project data, organized it into database tables, and provided basic visualizations of the data. For our purposes here, we can use this data to answer a question about which project tags are most frequently found together on FLOSS projects. To do this, we will find frequent itemsets from the project tags and generate subsequent association rules. A sample frequent itemset will take the form {GPL, Linux, C}. A sample association rule might be GPL, Linux -> C [s=.60, c=.90, av=.15].

To get started, log in to your MySQL server, and select a database to use for this project (mine is called test) and create a database table to hold the master list of projects and their tags:

```
CREATE TABLE IF NOT EXISTS fc_project_tags (
  project_id int(11) NOT NULL DEFAULT '0',
  tag_name varchar(50) NOT NULL DEFAULT '0',
  PRIMARY KEY (`project_id`,`tag_name`)
) ENGINE=MyISAM DEFAULT CHARSET=latin1;
```

In this dataset, each project will be identified a number, given by the Freecode site itself, and a list of tags, given by the person who added the project to the directory. For example, project number 8 has been given the tags GPL, multimedia, and Sound/Audio.

To populate this table, use the data file available on the GitHub site for this book, which is https://github.com/megansquire/masteringDM. This specific file is located in the chapter 2 directory at https://github.com/megansquire/masteringDM/blob/master/ch2/fc_project_tags.sql.gz.

To load this into your MySQL database from the command line, unzip the file into your working directory, then login to your MySQL server, use the correct database, and then issue a source command to run all the INSERT statements into that file. The process is as follows:

```
mysql> use test;
Database changed
mysql> source fc_project_tags.sql;
```

Each project is only identified by its number in this chapter project. However, if you want to find out more detail about the individual projects, or use this data for another project, all the Freshmeat/Freecode data is freely available on the FLOSSmole website in the following directory: `http://flossdata.syr.edu/data/fc/`. The data dump that we are using for this chapter is from March 2014, and in the FLOSSmole system that dataset has been given the number 8079. To keep things simple, you will not see that number in the examples for this chapter.

To get started in answering our question (*Which tags are most frequently found together?*), we first need to explore the data a little bit. First, we can discover the total number of project-tag combinations, keeping in mind that a project can have multiple tags:

```
SELECT COUNT(*)
FROM fc_project_tags;
```

```
353400
```

Next, we can calculate the total number of projects. In terms of association rule terminology, we can think of a Freecode project as a shopping basket or a transaction, and each project tag is equivalent to an item in a shopping basket:

```
SELECT count(DISTINCT project_id)
FROM fc_project_tags;
46510
```

How many unique items are in our dataset?

```
SELECT count(DISTINCT tag_name)
FROM fc_project_tags;
11006
```

So there are 46,510 baskets, and 11,006 items. To reduce the number of possible association rules, we can count how many projects have each tag (how many baskets include each product), and prune the tags that are very rare. The following table shows the required number of projects required to reach each possible support threshold:

Support rate for tag	Number of projects needed
50%	23,255
40%	18,604
30%	13,953
10%	4,651
5%	2,325

For example, by using a 5% threshold, we are able to reduce the possible set of items to 29, down from 11,006. This reduced set of tags will become our singletons. All the frequent doubletons will be based on these singletons, and the tripletons will in turn be built from those doubletons. Here is the SQL to generate the list of singletons, keeping a 5% minimum support threshold:

```
SELECT tag_name, COUNT(project_id)
FROM fc_project_tags
GROUP BY 1
HAVING COUNT(project_id) >= 2325
ORDER BY 2 DESC;
```

The first few results are shown in the following table:

Tag name	Number of projects
GPL	21,182
POSIX	16,875
Linux	16,288
C	10,292
OS Independent	10,180

Our program, the code for which can be found in the GitHub repository for this book at https://github.com/megansquire/masteringDM/tree/master/ch2, calculates the number of baskets and then uses the minimum support threshold percentage to find the singletons, as shown in the following code. MINSUPPORTPCT is a constant that you can set to whatever you like. It is set to 5 at the beginning:

```
import itertools
import pymysql

# set threshold as a percent
# (for example, 5% of Freecode baskets is about 2325)
MINSUPPORTPCT = 5
```

```
    allSingletonTags = []
    allDoubletonTags = set()
    doubletonSet = set()

    # Open local database connection
    db = pymysql.connect(host='localhost',
                         db='test',
                         user='megan',
                         passwd='',
                         port=3306,
                         charset='utf8mb4')
    cursor = db.cursor()
```

Next we calculate the number of baskets as the number of projects in the database table:

```
    queryBaskets = "SELECT count(DISTINCT project_id) FROM fc_project_
    tags;"
    cursor.execute(queryBaskets)
    baskets = cursor.fetchone()[0]
```

Using that number of baskets and our minimum support threshold set earlier, we can calculate the minimum number of baskets:

```
    minsupport = baskets*(MINSUPPORTPCT/100)
    print("Minimum support count:",minsupport,"(",MINSUPPORTPCT,"%
    of",baskets,")")
```

Now we can get a set of tags that meets our minimum support threshold:

```
    cursor.execute("SELECT DISTINCT tag_name \
            FROM fc_project_tags \
            GROUP BY 1 \
            HAVING COUNT(project_id) >= %s ORDER BY tag_
    name",(minsupport))
    singletons = cursor.fetchall()

    for(singleton) in singletons:
        allSingletonTags.append(singleton[0])
```

Next we use these frequent singletons to create our candidate doubletons. We encapsulate this task into a function called `findDoubletons()`. We will discuss the `findDoubletons()`, `findTripletons()`, and `generateRules()` functions later. The final line of our program closes the database connection when we are done with it:

```
findDoubletons()
findTripletons()
generateRules()
db.close()
```

As we discussed, when outlining the Apriori strategy earlier, it is not practical to pre-populate the database with all possible candidate doubletons and then count them there, since there are so many possible pairs. Instead, we will generate candidate doubletons in memory, count their support threshold, and only keep the ones that pass our support threshold. Just as with the preceding singleton counting, the support threshold remains at 5% (2,325 projects) for both doubletons and tripletons. We use a constant, called `MINSUPPORT`, to hold this support value. Additionally, we rely on the `itertools.combinations()` function to generate all possible combinations of `size=2` from our `allSingletonTags` list. Finally, we add these frequent tags to a new list called `allDoubletonTags`, which we will use in our `findTripletons()` function, shown here:

```
def findDoubletons():
    print("======")
    print("Frequent doubletons found:")
    print("======")
    # use the list of allSingletonTags to make the doubleton
candidates
    doubletonCandidates = list(itertools.
combinations(allSingletonTags, 2))
    for (index, candidate) in enumerate(doubletonCandidates):
        # figure out if this doubleton candidate is frequent
        tag1 = candidate[0]
        tag2 = candidate[1]
        cursor.execute("SELECT count(fpt1.project_id)
                    FROM fc_project_tags fpt1
                    INNER JOIN fc_project_tags fpt2
                    ON fpt1.project_id = fpt2.project_id
                    WHERE fpt1.tag_name = %s
                    AND fpt2.tag_name = %s", (tag1, tag2))
        count = cursor.fetchone()[0]
```

```
                  # add frequent doubleton to database
              if count > minsupport:
                  print (tag1,tag2,"[",count,"]")

                  cursor.execute("INSERT INTO fc_project_tag_pairs
                                  (tag1, tag2, num_projs)
                                  VALUES (%s,%s,%s)",(tag1, tag2, count))

                  # save the frequent doubleton to our final list
                  doubletonSet.add(candidate)
                  # add terms to a set of all doubleton terms (no
        duplicates)
                  allDoubletonTags.add(tag1)
                  allDoubletonTags.add(tag2)
```

Our program writes the doubletons (and later, the tripletons) to two new database
tables, but if you do not want to do this, you can remove the INSERT statements. The
CREATE statements for these two tables are shown in the following code. These SQL
statements can be found in the additionalQueries.sql file, downloadable from the
GitHub site for this book, as referenced earlier:

```
CREATE TABLE IF NOT EXISTS fc_project_tag_pairs (
  tag1 varchar(255) NOT NULL,
  tag2 varchar(255) NOT NULL,
  num_projs int(11) NOT NULL
) ENGINE=MyISAM DEFAULT CHARSET=latin1;

CREATE TABLE IF NOT EXISTS fc_project_tag_triples (
  tag1 varchar(255) NOT NULL,
  tag2 varchar(255) NOT NULL,
  tag3 varchar(255) NOT NULL,
  num_projs int(11) NOT NULL
) ENGINE=MyISAM DEFAULT CHARSET=latin1;
```

Once we have the list of doubletons, the program uses those to find the candidate
tripletons. The findTripletons() function is similar to findDoubletons(), except
that we must take into account the closure property. By this I mean that we cannot
generate any candidate tripletons that have doubletons inside that are not frequent.
Just before we ended the findDoubletons() function, we created a list of all the
doubletons (called doubletonList). Now we use the enumerate() function to
get a list of all possible doubletons inside the candidate tripleton, and if all those
doubletons were not already on our list of frequent doubletons, we can reject
the tripleton.

This may seem a little bit confusing, so an example is in order. Suppose we have generated frequent doubletons as follows:

```
foo, bar
bar, baz
```

If we simply used all the items inside and created a candidate tripleton of foo, bar, baz, that tripleton would be invalid, since it contains a doubleton of {foo, baz}, which is not a frequent doubleton. Therefore, we need to only generate tripletons for which every possible doubleton inside is also frequent. The code to find tripletons is shown here:

```
def findTripletons():
    print("======")
    print("Frequent tripletons found:")
    print("======")
    # use the list of allDoubletonTags to make the tripleton
candidates
    tripletonCandidates = list(itertools.combinations(allDoubletonTa
gs,3))

    # sort each candidate tuple and add these to a new sorted
candidate list
    tripletonCandidatesSorted = []
    for tc in tripletonCandidates:
        tripletonCandidatesSorted.append(sorted(tc))

    # figure out if this tripleton candidate is frequent
    for (index, candidate) in enumerate(tripletonCandidatesSorted):
        # all doubletons inside this
        # tripleton candidate MUST also be frequent
        doubletonsInsideTripleton = list(itertools.
combinations(candidate,2))
        tripletonCandidateRejected = 0
        for (index, doubleton) in enumerate(doubletonsInsideTriplet
on):
            if doubleton not in doubletonSet:
                tripletonCandidateRejected = 1
                break
        # add frequent tripleton to database
        if tripletonCandidateRejected == 0:
            cursor.execute("SELECT count(fpt1.project_id)
                FROM fc_project_tags fpt1
                INNER JOIN fc_project_tags fpt2
                ON fpt1.project_id = fpt2.project_id
```

```
                    INNER JOIN fc_project_tags fpt3
                    ON fpt2.project_id = fpt3.project_id
                    WHERE (fpt1.tag_name = %s
                    AND fpt2.tag_name = %s
                    AND fpt3.tag_name = %s)", (candidate[0],
                                               candidate[1],
                                               candidate[2]))
        count = cursor.fetchone()[0]
        if count > minsupport:
            print (candidate[0],",",
                    candidate[1],",",
                    candidate[2],
                    "[",count,"]")
            cursor.execute("INSERT INTO fc_project_tag_triples
                            (tag1, tag2, tag3, num_projs)
                            VALUES (%s,%s,%s,%s)",
                            (candidate[0],
                             candidate[1],
                             candidate[2],
                             count))
```

When run against the Freecode dataset, our program produces 37 doubletons, which are shown in the following table in order from the highest support to the lowest support:

tag1	tag2	num_projs
C	GPL	5543
C	Linux	5653
C	POSIX	6956
C++	GPL	2914
C++	Linux	3428
C++	POSIX	3502
Communications	GPL	2578
Dynamic Content	Internet	3173
Dynamic Content	Web	3171
English	Linux	2662
GPL	Internet	4038
GPL	Linux	8038
GPL	Multimedia	2883
GPL	OS independent	4405

tag1	tag2	num_projs
GPL	PHP	2376
GPL	POSIX	10069
GPL	Software development	3319
GPL	Web	2901
GPL	Windows	2605
Internet	OS	3007
Internet	POSIX	2832
Internet	Web	5978
Java	OS independent	3436
Java	Software development	2360
Libraries	Software development	5638
Linux	Mac OS X	2974
Linux	POSIX	11903
Linux	Software development	2336
Linux	Unix	2494
Linux	Windows	5281
Mac OS X	Windows	3131
Multimedia	POSIX	2539
OS independent	Software development	3566
OS independent	Web	2605
POSIX	Software development	3503
POSIX	Unix	2326
POSIX	Windows	4467

The program also produces four tripletons, as shown in the following table, in highest-to-lowest support order:

Tag1	Tag2	Tag3	Num_projs
Internet	OS independent	Web	2519
GPL	Linux	POSIX	7384
C	GPL	Linux	3299
C	GPL	POSIX	4364
GPL	Internet	Web	2878
Dynamic Content	Internet	Web	3166
Linux	POSIX	Windows	3315

Tag1	Tag2	Tag3	Num_projs
C++	Linux	POSIX	2622
C	Linux	POSIX	4629

Once we have the frequent itemsets, we can begin to design association rules from these, assigning support and confidence to each. Here is code for a rule generation routine that generates rules from tripletons. We start with generating rules with a single item on the right-hand side, due to the same closure properties as with generating frequent itemsets. In other words, if a rule like this {vanilla wafers, bananas -> marshmallows} is not interesting, then there is no sense in measuring the other options that have marshmallows on the right side such as {vanilla wafers -> bananas, marshmallows}.

Finally, this code also prints the added value score for each rule, calculated by subtracting the support of the right-hand side from the confidence of the whole rule:

```python
def generateRules():
    print("======")
    print("Association Rules:")
    print("======")

    # pull final list of tripletons to make the rules
    cursor.execute("SELECT tag1, tag2, tag3, num_projs \
        FROM fc_project_tag_triples")
    triples = cursor.fetchall()
    for(triple) in triples:
        tag1 = triple[0]
        tag2 = triple[1]
        tag3 = triple[2]
        ruleSupport = triple[3]

        calcSCAV(tag1, tag2, tag3, ruleSupport)
        calcSCAV(tag1, tag3, tag2, ruleSupport)
        calcSCAV(tag2, tag3, tag1, ruleSupport)
        print("*")

def calcSCAV(tagA, tagB, tagC, ruleSupport):
    # Support
    ruleSupportPct = round((ruleSupport/baskets),2)

    # Confidence
    query1 = "SELECT num_projs \
        FROM fc_project_tag_pairs \
        WHERE (tag1 = %s AND tag2 = %s) \
```

```
            or (tag2 = %s AND tag1 = %s)"
    cursor.execute(query1, (tagA, tagB, tagB, tagA))
    pairSupport = cursor.fetchone()[0]
    confidence = round((ruleSupport / pairSupport),2)

    # Added Value
    query2 = "SELECT count(*) \
            FROM fc_project_tags \
            WHERE tag_name= %s"
    cursor.execute(query2, tagC)
    supportTagC = cursor.fetchone()[0]
    supportTagCPct = supportTagC/baskets
    addedValue = round((confidence - supportTagCPct),2)

    # Result
    print(tagA,",",tagB,"->",tagC,
            "[S=",ruleSupportPct,
            ", C=",confidence,
            ", AV=",addedValue,
            "]")
```

The Freecode rules that are generated from this code are shown next. Since each tripleton can generate three rules, each having a single item on the right-hand side, we have divided these into groups of three lines each for display purposes:

```
C++ , Linux -> POSIX [S= 0.06 , C= 0.76 , AV= 0.4 ]
C++ , POSIX -> Linux [S= 0.06 , C= 0.75 , AV= 0.4 ]
Linux , POSIX -> C++ [S= 0.06 , C= 0.22 , AV= 0.09 ]

C , Linux -> POSIX [S= 0.1 , C= 0.82 , AV= 0.46 ]
C , POSIX -> Linux [S= 0.1 , C= 0.67 , AV= 0.32 ]
Linux , POSIX -> C [S= 0.1 , C= 0.39 , AV= 0.17 ]

GPL , Linux -> POSIX [S= 0.16 , C= 0.92 , AV= 0.56 ]
GPL , POSIX -> Linux [S= 0.16 , C= 0.73 , AV= 0.38 ]
Linux , POSIX -> GPL [S= 0.16 , C= 0.62 , AV= 0.16 ]

Linux , POSIX -> Windows [S= 0.07 , C= 0.28 , AV= 0.12 ]
Linux , Windows -> POSIX [S= 0.07 , C= 0.63 , AV= 0.27 ]
POSIX , Windows -> Linux [S= 0.07 , C= 0.74 , AV= 0.39 ]

C , GPL -> POSIX [S= 0.09 , C= 0.79 , AV= 0.43 ]
C , POSIX -> GPL [S= 0.09 , C= 0.63 , AV= 0.17 ]
GPL , POSIX -> C [S= 0.09 , C= 0.43 , AV= 0.21 ]
```

```
Dynamic Content , Internet -> Web [S= 0.07 , C= 1.0 , AV= 0.87 ]
Dynamic Content , Web -> Internet [S= 0.07 , C= 1.0 , AV= 0.83 ]
Internet , Web -> Dynamic Content [S= 0.07 , C= 0.53 , AV= 0.46 ]


Internet , OS Independent -> Web [S= 0.05 , C= 0.84 , AV= 0.71 ]
Internet , Web -> OS Independent [S= 0.05 , C= 0.42 , AV= 0.2 ]
OS Independent , Web -> Internet [S= 0.05 , C= 0.97 , AV= 0.8 ]


GPL , Internet -> Web [S= 0.06 , C= 0.71 , AV= 0.58 ]
GPL , Web -> Internet [S= 0.06 , C= 0.99 , AV= 0.82 ]
Internet , Web -> GPL [S= 0.06 , C= 0.48 , AV= 0.02 ]


C , GPL -> Linux [S= 0.07 , C= 0.6 , AV= 0.25 ]
C , Linux -> GPL [S= 0.07 , C= 0.58 , AV= 0.12 ]
GPL , Linux -> C [S= 0.07 , C= 0.41 , AV= 0.19 ]
```

Based on these results, how do we know which rules are interesting? Just looking at the support does not yield particularly interesting clues, since we specified that every rule had to have a 5% support in order to even be considered.

Confidence, combined with support, could be an interesting measure. For example, the rule {GPL , Linux -> POSIX} has the highest support (16%) and a confidence over 90%. On the other side, the rule {Linux , POSIX -> C++} has a support barely above the threshold (6%) and the lowest confidence in the list (22%).

Added value tells us how much better the association rule predicts the right-hand side of the equation as opposed to simply looking at the right-hand side by itself. This collection of rules does not have any outright negatively-correlated items, but it does have several rules that are extremely close to zero, indicating that the right-hand side might do just as well on its own as part of the shown rules. Examples of very low added value scores are, {Internet , Web -> GPL}, indicating that GPL would probably do just as well on its own, as it is a very high-scoring item even as a singleton. The rule {Linux , POSIX -> C++} also falls into this category of having a very low added value score, the second lowest in the list. This, along with the very low support and confidence scores, makes it one of the least valuable rules on the list.

Rules with high added value scores include {Dynamic Content , Internet -> Web} and {Dynamic Content , Web -> Internet}. These two rules are especially interesting because the third rule in the group, {Internet, Web -> Dynamic Content}, has an unremarkable added value score (.53). Next we notice that all of the highest scoring added value rules in this list have either *Web* or *Internet* on the right-hand side, with the other term appearing somewhere on the left. This shows that *Web* and *Internet* are very tightly coupled as terms in this dataset, but are not themselves as predictive of other terms as they are predictive of each other.

Finding this relationship means that we can probe more deeply into the relationship between *Web* and *Internet*. Specifically, we should look at the rules `Web -> Internet` and `Internet -> Web`. Since we helpfully stored the support counts in the database, we can use a query in SQL to figure out the support, confidence, and added value for these two rules as well:

```
SELECT

round(num_projs / (SELECT count(DISTINCT project_id) FROM fc_project_
tags),2) as 'support',

round((num_projs / (SELECT count(DISTINCT project_id) FROM fc_
project_tags)) / ((SELECT count(*) FROM fc_project_tags WHERE tag_
name='Internet') / (SELECT count(DISTINCT project_id) FROM fc_project_
tags)),2) as 'conf I-> W',

round((num_projs / (SELECT count(DISTINCT project_id) FROM fc_project_
tags)) / ((SELECT count(*) FROM fc_project_tags WHERE tag_name='Web')
/ (SELECT count(DISTINCT project_id) FROM fc_project_tags)),2) as
'conf W-> I',

round(((num_projs/(SELECT count(DISTINCT project_id) FROM fc_
project_tags)) / ((SELECT count(*) FROM fc_project_tags WHERE
tag_name='Internet')/(SELECT count(DISTINCT project_id) FROM fc_
project_tags))) - ((SELECT count(*) from fc_project_tags where
tag_name='Web')/(SELECT count(DISTINCT project_id) FROM fc_project_
tags)),2) as 'AV I->W',

round(((num_projs / (SELECT count(DISTINCT project_id) FROM fc_
project_tags)) / ((SELECT count(*) FROM fc_project_tags where
tag_name='Web') / (SELECT count(DISTINCT project_id) FROM fc_
project_tags))) - ((SELECT count(*) from fc_project_tags where tag_
name='Internet') / (SELECT count(DISTINCT project_id) FROM fc_project_
tags)),2) as 'AV W->I'

FROM fc_project_tag_pairs where tag1='Internet' and tag2='Web'
```

This yields the following result from SQL:

```
support  conf I-> W  conf W-> I  AV I->W  AV W->I
0.13   0.74      0.95      0.77     0.60
```

That SQL code is pretty hairy, so here is a little Python script to run each individual query against the database, and use those numbers to calculate support, confidence, and added value. As before, fill in your database connection details, and fill in the constants X and Y with the two terms you are interested in comparing:

```python
import pymysql

X = 'Internet'
Y = 'Web'

# Open local database connection
db = pymysql.connect(host='',
    db='',
    user='',
    passwd='',
    port=3306,
    charset='utf8mb4')
cursor = db.cursor()

# grab basic counts from the database that we need
numBasketsQuery = "SELECT count(DISTINCT project_id) \
    FROM fc_project_tags"
cursor.execute(numBasketsQuery)
numBaskets = cursor.fetchone()[0]

supportForXQuery = "SELECT count(*) \
    FROM fc_project_tags \
    WHERE tag_name=%s"
cursor.execute(supportForXQuery, (X))
supportForX = cursor.fetchone()[0]

supportForYQuery = "SELECT count(*) \
    FROM fc_project_tags \
    WHERE tag_name=%s"
cursor.execute(supportForYQuery, (Y))
supportForY = cursor.fetchone()[0]

pairSupportQuery = "SELECT num_projs \
    FROM fc_project_tag_pairs \
    WHERE tag1=%s AND tag2=%s"
cursor.execute(pairSupportQuery, (X,Y))
pairSupport = cursor.fetchone()[0]
```

```
# calculate support : support of pair, divided by num baskets
pairSupportAsPct = pairSupport / numBaskets

# calculate confidence of X->Y
supportForXAsPct = supportForX / numBaskets
confidenceXY = pairSupportAsPct / supportForXAsPct

# calculate confidence of Y->X
supportForYAsPct = supportForY / numBaskets
confidenceYX = pairSupportAsPct/ supportForYAsPct

# calculate added value X->Y
AVXY = confidenceXY - supportForYAsPct
AVYX = confidenceYX - supportForXAsPct

print("Support for ",X,"U",Y,":", round(pairSupportAsPct, 2))
print("Conf.",X,"->",Y,":", round(confidenceXY, 2))
print("Conf.",Y,"->",X,":", round(confidenceYX, 2))
print("AV",X,"->",Y,":", round(AVXY, 2))
print("AV",Y,"->",X,":", round(AVYX, 2))

db.close()
```

The results are the same for the pair of terms *Internet* and *Web* as they were for the longer SQL query, as shown here:

```
Support for Internet U Web : 0.13
Conf. Internet -> Web : 0.74
Conf. Web -> Internet : 0.95
AV Internet -> Web : 0.6
AV Web -> Internet : 0.78
```

Even if these results seem somewhat underwhelming - after all, it is not particularly shocking that *Internet* and *Web* are such closely related terms - there are a few important lessons we can learn from this process. First, the results can be used to make suggestions. If a person tags their project *Web*, maybe we would also like to suggest *Internet* as a related tag. Alternatively, perhaps we want to cross-promote *Web* projects to people looking at *Internet* projects, and vice versa. Unlike in a store where we have to physically co-locate items next to each other, the costs of making recommendations or suggestions in a digital environment is not as high. In any case, finding frequent itemsets and generating association rules are useful tasks that can either confirm what we already suspect about our data, or that can help us understand underlying patterns in the data that we would not necessarily know about otherwise.

Summary

In this chapter, we learned how to generate frequent itemsets from a dataset using the Apriori algorithm. We then proposed association rules from these itemsets by describing their support and confidence. We used one additional check, an added value measure, to ensure that the proposed rules were interesting. We implemented all these concepts using a freely available dataset of Freecode open source projects and their tags. We calculated support for single tags, then generated doubletons and tripletons that met a minimum support threshold. For rules with one item on the right-hand side, we calculated confidence and added value for each. Finally, we looked closely at the rules that were generated and tried to figure out which ones were interesting, using the metrics we had calculated.

In the next chapter, we will continue our quest to make connections between items in a data set. However, unlike in this chapter where we were trying to find groups of two or three items that are already connected in some way, in the next chapter we will be trying to connect items that we are not sure are connected at all!

3
Entity Matching

In my set of outdoor tools, I have a large hand axe that I have always called a mattock. But my friend from the western United States calls it a *Pulaski*. When he asks me to hand him the Pulaski, it always gives me a moment of pause. Sometimes, we might know a thing by more than one name, or two things might share the same name, which can lead to confusion. This happens with people all the time. Have you ever been mistaken for someone else who shares your same first and last name? Have you ever used a nickname or an alias? In a children's playground, 10 women might turn around when they hear a child call out *Mom!* A man who always goes by the name *Bob* would be immediately suspicious when an unfamiliar telephone caller asks to speak with *Robert*. A pharmacy technician gives *John T. Smith* the medicine intended for *John M. Smith*, leading to disastrous results.

In this chapter, we are concerned with the accurate identification of entities, or things, and the correct assignment of matching entities. Are these two things really the same, or are they different? Can we determine that two similar-looking things really are the same, based on their other characteristics? To extend the market basket example from *Chapter 2, Association Rule Mining*, suppose we are a grocery store, and we have our own database full of information about our shoppers and items they have purchased from our store. Now, imagine our store merges with another grocery store chain, and we are now the caretakers of all of their shopping data as well. We would like to see if any of our shoppers also shopped at this other store. But how do we connect the first dataset to the second? Typically, we will look for some unique identifier that is in common between the two datasets. But what if that identifier does not exist? Or what if there is an attribute that both datasets have in common, but its values are not unique?

How can we solve this challenge of entity matching where there is no clear, unambiguous connection between two datasets? In this chapter we will learn:

- Common strategies for entity matching, including attribute matching, disjoint sets, contextual matching, and profiling a typical match

- How to evaluate efficacy of the chosen methods, including calculating the precision, recall, and F-measure for a result set

- How to apply entity matching methods to a real-world problem using data from two separate collections of data about free, libre, and open source software (FLOSS) projects

Before we get started, you may be wondering where in the data mining workflow entity matching fits. Is it data cleaning, or data integration, or data analysis, or what? Typically, entity matching would be considered primarily a data cleaning and data integration step, since its main purpose is to produce a dataset that is as accurate as possible, and one that is ready to be mined for other patterns. However, because we will use pattern-finding techniques in order to accomplish the matching, you will probably notice that it does have some of the flavor of a data analysis step as well.

What is entity matching?

Finding matching items is one of the oldest tasks in database processing, and as databases get larger and more distributed, this task becomes more and more important. Each time two datasets are merged, questions arise about how to identify duplicates, how to connect items from the first dataset to the similar items in the second data set. When we find ourselves asking *Are these two things different even though they have the same name?* or *Are these other two things the same, even though they have different names?* we can apply entity matching techniques to find out the answer.

In light of all this concern with the names for an item, it is perhaps appropriate that this task itself has many names: entity matching, entity disambiguation, object consolidation, duplicate identification, merge/purge, and record linkage, to name a few. We will use the term **entity matching** in this chapter to generically describe this class of activities.

Consider the following examples where entity matching might be helpful. How many different people are likely to be represented in this dataset? Which of these are the same person?

Name
John Smith
John R. Smith

Name
John R. Smith, Jr.
Jon Smith
JON R SMITH, JR

It is very difficult to tell whether these are five different individuals or all variations of the same person, or some number in between. There could be missing middle initials, missing suffixes, spelling problems, and mistakes. We have no idea of the data quality, and no strong clues about how to match these individuals. Suppose we add an `Address` attribute to the data. Now which of these are the same person?

Name	Address
John Smith	123 Main St.
John R. Smith	46 Pine Way
John R. Smith, Jr.	46 Pine Way
Jon Smith	12587 34th St.
JON R SMITH, JR	46 Pine Way

With the addition of the `Address` field, it now appears that there might be three distinct individuals in this dataset: one that lives on Main St, one that lives on Pine Way, and one that lives on 34th St. Of course, we also still have the possibility of an error; for example, John Smith at 123 Main St. might be showing an old address, or the `Name` value may be spelled wrong.

What if we add an `Age` attribute? Now which of these are the same person?

Name	Address	Age
John Smith	123 Main St.	55
John R. Smith	46 Pine Way	48
John R. Smith, Jr.	46 Pine Way	16
Jon Smith	12587 34th St.	34
JON R SMITH, JR	46 Pine Way	16

By adding additional details, such as `Address` and `Age`, we gain information that helps us determine that it is likely that there are actually four distinct people represented here. Two of the 46 Pine Way rows are much younger than the other row. Both of those younger individuals have a *Jr.* suffix, perhaps indicating that a father and son both live at that address.

To keep the rows separate, we can now add unique identifiers, as shown with the Id attribute:

Name	Address	Age	Id
John Smith	123 Main St.	55	1
John R. Smith	46 Pine Way	48	2
John R. Smith, Jr.	46 Pine Way	16	3
Jon Smith	12587 34th St.	34	4
JON R SMITH, JR	46 Pine Way	16	3

In an ideal world, we would start with a unique identifier for every entity in our database. But unfortunately, this is not the reality of many data projects. Not only will the unique identifiers be missing or non-existent, but these clear-cut attributes like Age and Address will also be missing, dirty, or non-existent. We might have attribute A for half the data and attribute B for the other half. Consider this dataset:

Name	Address	Age	State issuing driver's license
John Smith	123 Main St.	55	NC
John R. Smith	46 Pine Way	48	VA
John R. Smith, Jr.	46 Pine Way	16	
Jon Smith	12587 34th St.	34	
JON R SMITH, JR	46 Pine Way		FL

In this example, one of the ages is missing, and two of the driver's license issuing states are missing. Are these two *Jr.* people really the same in this dataset? Why do they have the same street address as the father but a different driver's license state? Did the son just get his Florida driver's license when he turned 16 but the father forgot to renew his license when they moved from Virginia to Florida? There is a lot of **domain knowledge** required here to make sense of the potential matches. We must make many complicated assumptions in order to properly assign a match, and yet this is just a simple example with five rows and four columns! Imagine the logic we would have to employ if we really were merging the grocery store shopping data, or data from two banks, or data from two different university record-keeping systems.

Merging data

In the previous examples, we were looking at five records stored in the same simple dataset. Unfortunately, with many data mining projects, we do not begin with entities that are already stored in the same dataset. In such a case, we must **merge** the data from multiple datasets together into one. Merging data means that we will need to combine multiple datasets, either physically or logically. Physically moving data from one dataset into another may mean moving it into the same tables or files, for example. Creating logical connections between two or more datasets may mean creating views or queries that join multiple disparate tables using a column in common. Either way, we must keep a few **data quality** principles in mind before merging data:

- Generally, we want to **keep as much data as possible**. Throwing away data is anathema and we want to avoid it if at all possible. Create a new column, create a new table, or otherwise move the data rather than deleting it. You never know when you will need that column again.

- **Clean** data is better. Merged data should be as uniform as possible, with standardized character sets, formatting, and so forth. I admit I am a bit fussy about having clean data (I did write a book on it, after all), but as you can see from the previous example with John Smith, our job of matching entities will be hard enough without introducing additional cleaning issues on top of everything else!

- Data should be **atomic**. This means it needs to be broken down into the smallest parts possible, without losing meaning. Separate address, city, state, and postal code fields will probably be more useful than one giant field with all parts of the address in it.

Merging datasets vertically

Merging two data sets vertically is sometimes called a **data append**. Usually when a vertical merge works best is when we have two datasets with the same columns, in the same order, and we just stack one dataset on top of the other. The resulting dataset may require duplication identification and purging of the duplicate data. Traditionally, for example in a relational database environment, vertical merging requires that both datasets have the same columns, or else there will be null values. Here is an example of a vertical merge between Dataset 1 and Dataset 2.

Dataset 1:

Name	Address	Age	State issuing driver's license
Frank Edwards	123 Main St.	55	NY
Kathryn White	460 Pine Cr.	54	NC
Laura Hartley	460 Pine Cr.	20	NC

Dataset 2:

Name	Address	Age	State issuing driver's license
Kathleen Richard	990 Michigan Ave.	23	FL
Susie Murphy	22 Butterfield Cir.	60	MO
Laura Hartley	460 Pine Cr.	18	NC

The vertically merged dataset is shown here:

Name	Address	Age	State issuing driver's license
Frank Edwards	123 Main St.	55	NY
Kathryn White	460 Pine Cr.	54	NC
Laura Hartley	460 Pine Cr.	20	NC
Kathleen Richard	990 Michigan Ave.	23	FL
Susie Murphy	22 Butterfield Cir.	60	MO
Laura Hartley	460 Pine Cr.	18	NC

The task following a vertical merge is to identify whether Laura Hartley on row 3 is the same Laura Hartley on row 6. If these two people are the same, we may wish to remove one of the rows so that we do not have a **duplicate**. However, it may not be obvious at first which row is the correct one to keep, since these two entities show different ages, but the same street address. Is Laura 18 or is she 20? Depending on our goals, we may want to merge the data first and remove duplicates second, or we may want to identify duplicates before creating the merged dataset. Or, we may wish to leave both records in, and somehow identify or tag them as being possible duplicates. Different strategies will work for different datasets and different problem domains.

Merging datasets horizontally

A horizontal merge is used when we have datasets that represent the same type of entity, but we have different attributes that describe each one. In this case, a vertical merge will not work because there are too many attributes in one dataset that are not in the other one. Here is an example. Notice that there are some attributes in Dataset 1 that do not appear in Dataset 2.

Dataset 1:

Name	Address	Age	State issuing driver's license
Kathleen Richard	990 Michigan Ave.	23	FL
Susie Murphy	22 Butterfield Cir.	60	MO
Laura Hartley	460 Pine Cr.	18	NC

Dataset 2:

Name	Year of first subscription	Favorite color	Home state
Kathleen Richard	1999	blue	FL
Susie Murphy	1998	purple	MO
Laura Hartley	2012	green	NC

This problem definitely requires entity matching and consolidation. Ideally, we will end up with a dataset that has the attributes from both datasets, and one row for each entity, like the following horizontally merged dataset:

Name	Year of first subscription	Favorite color	Home state	Address	Age	State issuing driver's license
Kathleen Richard	1999	blue	FL	990 Michigan Ave.	23	FL
Susie Murphy	1998	purple	MO	22 Butterfield Cir.	60	MO
Laura Hartley	2012	green	NC	460 Pine Cr.	18	NC

Horizontal merging does not require that both datasets have all the same columns, but there should be something to match on, in order to ensure that we have only one row per entity. In this example case, the Name column is unique and serves as the column in common between the two sets. However, in a real entity matching scenario, we may not be so lucky. Columns may have to be split, transformed, combined, adjusted, or otherwise tweaked in order to find a match.

Techniques for matching

No matter whether we are working with horizontally or vertically merged data, we will need some way of matching entities. If we are vertically merging, we will use entity matching to find duplicates, and if we are horizontally merging, we will use entity matching to identify a minimum set of rows. What are the common techniques for finding entity matches? What kind of technique works best in various situations, and what are the pros and cons of each?

It turns out that there is no one single best entity matching algorithm, just as there is no one *best* string similarity algorithm. But we will outline a few of the options in the following sections so that we can choose from among them later in this chapter when we are working on a real project.

Attribute-based similarity matching

Similarity matching on attributes is one of the oldest techniques for matching entities. To do this, we set up a similarity function on the different attributes of each entity, and score each pairwise combination between 0 and 1 as to how similar they are on that attribute. For example, given the datasets of people that we presented earlier, we could use the name and street address columns, along with a string matching function. Each pair of records would be scored 0 to 1 on their similarity to each other. This method is not limited to string values, but categorical and numeric values can also be mapped to an agree/disagree result on a scale of 0 to 1.

Be careful of pairwise comparisons

This method has some strengths in that it is quite flexible and can be used on many different types of data. However, as we learned in *Chapter 2*, *Association Rule Mining*, any time we need to perform pairwise comparisons, we are looking at a very large number of possible combinations. This means we need to take pains to reduce the set of possible matches, and we may need to use persistent storage (as we did in *Chapter 2*, *Association Rule Mining*) to *remember* the comparisons we have already made in the past.

Leverage rare values

Another interesting feature of attribute-based similarity matching is that very rare values can be leveraged to increase accuracy of the match. In other words, it is easier to find a match between two entities with very rare values, than it is to match entities with common values. We can use this knowledge to adjust the probability of matching entities based on the rarity or commonness of the attribute values. A common illustration of this idea given by geneticist Howard Newcombe in a 1959 *Science* paper (*Automatic Linkage of Vital Records*), and expanded in later highly-cited papers (such as Winkler's *The State of Record Linkage and Current Research Problems*) is to compare the ease of matching entities where there is a rare first and last name with the difficulty of matching a common name. For example, it will be easier to match two entities with the name Finklestein McGlockenspiel, which is a very rare name in English-speaking countries. It will be relatively difficult to match people who have a common name, for example John Smith.

Methods for matching attributes

Attribute matching strategies requires that the analyst define what qualifies as a match. Equality of values seems like an obvious matching goal: Smith equals Smith, 43 equals 43. However, in the absence of *precisely* equal values, we may need to be a little more creative about performing a match. What values are close enough to count as a match?

Range-based or distance from target

When working with numeric values or dates, *close enough* could be indicated by setting a range or a distance from the target. For example, in some domain dealing with age, we may declare *any value in the low 40s* is good enough to match the age 43. In another domain, we may decide that the eye colors green and hazel are close enough to be counted as matching. The rules governing this type of rule-based proximity matching will often depend on the domain and the goals of the problem.

String edit distance

Measuring the approximate equality of two strings is a very interesting exercise. How close are the names *Jones* and *James*?

There are a number of basic string metrics that can quantify the amount of **edit distance** between two strings. The edit distance is the number of edits that would transform one string into another. Two commonly-used methods for measuring the edit distance between two strings are the Hamming distance and the Levenshtein distance.

Hamming distance

For strings of equal length, the **Hamming distance** is a measure of the number of character substitutions needed to turn one string into the other. The Hamming distance between *blue* and *glue* is 1, since there is only a single edit needed to change the *b* character to a *g*. The Hamming distance is not designed for strings of different lengths, so we can pad the shorter word with dummy characters to account for this problem. To get the Hamming distance between *cat* and *catch*, we can turn cat into *cat***, which has a Hamming distance of 2 from *catch*.

Levenshtein distance

For any two strings, the **Levenshtein distance** is a measure of the minimum number of substitutions, deletions, or insertions required to change one string into another. The Levenshtein distance between *blue* and *glue* is also 1. And the Levenshtein distance between *cat* and *catch* is 2, since there are two additions, zero deletions, and zero changes. The Levenshtein distance between *catch* and *cap* is 3, since there are two deletions and one substitution. The Hamming distance between *catch* and *cap* is also 3, using the padding method described previously.

Do Hamming and Levenshtein always return the same value? No. Since the Hamming distance does not allow for insertions or deletions, sometimes it requires more actions than Levenshtein. Consider the strings *scat* and *cats*. The Hamming distance is 4 since this transformation requires the following substitutions: *s* changes to *c*, *c* changes to *a*, *a* changes to *t*, and *t* changes to *s*. The Levenshtein distance between *scat* and *cats* is only 2: delete *s* from the first position, insert *s* at the final position. So while the Hamming distance has the potential to be greater than the Levenshtein distance, the Hamming distance is less complicated, and easier to estimate than Levenshtein.

There are many other variations on edit distance calculation, and different techniques will work in different scenarios. Does your data only have strings of the same length? Do you need to handle fuzzy (approximate) string matches, or are you more interested in exact string matches? No matter what technique we choose, we must remember that for this chapter, our overarching goal is matching entities, and the purpose of the string metrics is to determine how similar the string attributes are between some pair of entities. Knowing how similar these string attributes are is just one additional clue as to how similar the entities are. Are there other ways of measuring the similarity of strings?

Soundex

Invented in 1918, **Soundex** is another rudimentary technique for measuring how similar two strings are to each other. But, just as its name suggests, Soundex is a measure of how phonetically similar the strings are. Soundex only works with English pronunciations. With Soundex, each word can be encoded into a character sequence, for example a traditional four-character Soundex algorithm encodes the name *Peters* as *P362*. The encoding rules are fairly simple. The first letter of a word is retained as the first letter of the new code. Subsequent vowels are ignored, along with the letters *W*, *Y*, and *H*. Consonants are assigned numbers in groups, chosen from a list as follows:

Letter	Becomes
B, F, P, V	1
C, G, J, K, Q, S, X, Z	2
D, T	3
L	4
M, N	5
R	6

Smith thus becomes *S530*. The first letter *S* is retained, the *M* becomes a 5, the *I* is dropped, the *T* becomes a 3, and the *H* is dropped. A *0* character is added to pad the code to four characters. *Smythe* also becomes *S530*. The first letter *S* is retained, the *M* becomes a 5, the *Y* is dropped, the *T* becomes a 3, the *H* is dropped, and the *E* is dropped.

James becomes *J520*. The first letter *J* is retained, the *M* becomes a 5, the *S* becomes a 2, and the vowels *A* and *E* are dropped. Since *M* and *N* are both in the same group, the code for *James* and *Jones* are exactly the same.

Consider a longer word, such as *Ellington*. Its code will be *E452*. Here we retain the *E* as the starting letter, substitute 4 for the letter *L*, drop the second 4 representing the second letter *L*, drop the *I*, substitute 5 for *N*, substitute 2 for *G*, substitute 3 for *T*, drop the *O*, and substitute 5 for the final *N*. Drop any digits that follow the first four characters. The result for *Ellington* is *E452*.

For our purposes, calculating the Soundex of strings is just another way to prepare data so that we can compare values. We are seeking entity matches, and, depending on the data we have, a Soundex comparison between two strings may be a very useful determinant of similarity. Another good application for Soundex is to use it to narrow down which strings should be compared. Rather than performing pairwise comparisons on every pair of strings in a database, we may find efficiency gains by only comparing pairs of strings that have similar Soundex codes.

Both edit distances and Soundex can be used in an entity matching scenario where we are trying to use the attributes of each entity as the matching criteria. But what happens when we do not have enough attributes, or where the attributes are different across our different sets of entities?

Leveraging disjoint sets

An alternate formulation of the attribute matching similarity solution can be used when we have disjoint attribute sets. **Disjoint sets** are those where the attributes in one dataset overlap with, but are not identical to, the attributes in another set. Consider the example earlier in this chapter where we attempted to horizontally merge two sets {name, address, age, drivers_license_state} and {name, year_of_first_subscription, favorite_color, home_state}. These two sets overlap on the *name* attribute, but nothing else.

We could proceed with attribute-based similarity matching using the common attribute, *name* in this case, but to ensure accuracy in those matched entities, we could also add a sanity check by way of a profile. We do this by setting up a concept of a typical **profile** that a matched record will have. Each profile is set up based on the disjoint attributes of the resulting record. For example, we can mandate that a typical user will have a *drivers_license_state* attribute that matches the *home_state* attribute. Additionally, we may mandate that if *drivers_license_state* is not null, then the age will be greater than 16 (or whatever age is considered a typical driving age in this domain). By doing this, we ensure that even though we only have a single matching attribute, which is *name*, we are still able to use the values present in the disjoint attributes to assist the overall matching process.

Disjoint set attribute matching is useful, but still requires that we have entities with some attributes in common, and that the attributes we have are trustworthy enough to serve as the match criteria. What happens if we do not have good attributes, or if the values are unreliable in some way?

Context-based similarity matching

An alternative to attribute-based matching is to take into account the way each entity relates to others within some sort of contextual space. To do this, imagine setting up a hierarchy or a graph structure for each dataset, and match entities based on their similar positions in the graph. For example, suppose we have one dataset that includes a roster of family members listed by name and connected by relationships:

- Richard is the father of Margaret
- Margaret is the mother of Steven

Next, we have a separate list of nicknames and relationships, such as:

- Grandpa is the father of Mom
- Mom is the mother of Bob
- Peg is the mother of Bob

Our task is to match the nicknames to the real names and find the matching identities. Because we have the same hierarchy between the entities in both datasets, we can more easily match the nicknames to real names, learning that Richard is known as Grandpa, Margaret is known as Mom and Peg, and Steven is known as Bob. Making the inference that Peg and Margaret are the same person assumes that in this particular family context, we have decided that each entity can have only one mother.

Context-based similarity matching works especially well with entities that have hierarchical or membership relationships to one another. Depending on how many entities and relationships there are in the sets, and how complicated the relationships are, it is also possible to put a likelihood score on a pairwise match. For example, if there are entities that appear in one list but not in the other list, we may have to assign a score of zero, whereas if the relationships are not exactly equivalent between two entities, we can assign a score to the match that is positive, but closer to zero. This kind of matching can work well when there are limited attributes, or unreliable or sparse attribute values.

Machine learning-based entity matching

If you have read any of the current literature on machine learning and data mining, you may be thinking that it would be clever to use something like a Bayesian classifier, support vector machine, or a decision tree to perform entity matching. After all, entity matching could be considered a binary classification problem (match/no match), so a trained classifier might work here. In such a case, the analyst would design training sets of accurate and inaccurate pairwise matches. Then the machine learning algorithm can use these training sets to learn which attributes contribute to true and false matches. Many of these systems have been developed in academic literature, using both theoretical and real-world data.

At this early stage, the researchers are finding that the effectiveness of the training-based entity matchers is good, but that their efficiency scales negatively with the size of the dataset. A large dataset simply takes too long to train on, especially with a wide set of attributes. So the construction of the training set takes time above and beyond the actual discovery of the matches, which takes even more time. If we attempt to reduce the dataset size by way of additional training activity, we find that this also is difficult and time-consuming.

A number of solutions have been proposed for these issues, including using parallel processing. Building machine learning-based matchers is an open research area with a lot of exciting developments and experimentation going on. Interested readers should look into the current academic comparisons of training-based, non-training-based, and hybrid entity matching solutions, for example the Köpcke et. al. 2010 article (*Evaluation of entity resolution approaches on real-world match problems*) or the 2011 Kolb et al. paper (*Learning-based Entity Resolution with MapReduce*).

There are many more variations on entity matching presented in the academic literature, but in this chapter we have focused on gaining a broad understanding of the most common matching strategies in use today. Improvements to the basic techniques will include greater concern for two things: speed and accuracy. In the next section, we will learn how to evaluate the speed and accuracy of whatever entity matching strategy we choose.

Evaluation of entity matching techniques

No matter what strategy we choose for entity matching, we will likely be concerned with how efficiently we can generate the matches, and how accurate those matches are. We mentioned previously that any time we can reduce the number of pairwise matches, we can improve the speed of the matching activity. Also, we mentioned that we can improve the accuracy of the matches by taking into account different types of data, and by leveraging other aspects of domain-specific knowledge such as hierarchies, relationships between attributes, and profiles of a *typical* result. In this section we will learn how to communicate in more detail about the different measures of success for any entity matching strategy we choose.

Efficiency – how long does it take to do the matching?

How long it takes to execute the entity matching exercise, called its execution time or runtime, is a critically important factor in choosing and evaluating an entity matching strategy. Without taking specific precautions to reduce the size of the sets being compared, the bulk of the execution time will likely be spent doing pairwise comparisons. This is a similar situation to where we found ourselves in *Chapter 2, Association Rule Mining* when finding frequent itemsets. Just like with the frequent itemset generation, we need to put some concerted effort into finding ways to limit the number of comparisons we have to make. Herman Wells is not likely the same person as Edward White, so we should not waste time comparing them, but Herman Wells and Harmon Walls might be the same person after all.

The good news is that we have many strategies for reducing the size of the lists of pairs that have to be compared. Numeric ranges, date ranges, string edit distances, and Soundex were mentioned earlier as very simple ways of reducing the number of comparisons. In the research literature, these techniques - and many, many more - are called **blocking** methods. A good blocking method will reduce the number of possible comparisons just enough to impact efficiency in a positive way, but will not reduce the comparisons to the point that it is impossible to find a match.

Aside from blocking to reduce the number of entities to be compared, we also want to reduce the number of attributes that need to be compared, as well as the number and complexity of the comparisons in the procedure overall. A matching task that relies on a single, simple numeric test will be more efficient than a matcher that relies on a half-dozen blockers and complicated string matches.

Effectiveness – how accurate are the matches that we generate?

Assuming that our procedure manages to propose some candidate matches, how do we know they are correct? We would like entities that are the same to be correctly matched (**true positives**), entities that are not the same to remain unmatched (**true negatives**), and we would like to minimize both types of incorrectly matched entities (**false positives** and **false negatives**).

We can measure the effectiveness of our procedure with classical information retrieval terms: accuracy, precision, recall, and specificity. **Precision** is the number of correct guesses (true positives) divided by the number of guesses that we proposed. Our proposals are comprised of both true positives and false positives.

Recall is the number of correct guesses (true positives) divided by the total number of actual matches. The total number of actual matches is comprised of both true positives and false negatives.

Accuracy is simply the number of correct guesses divided by the total number of all guesses. **Specificity** is the actual negatives divided by the sum of the guessed negatives and the actual negatives.

To clarify these important concepts, an example is probably in order. Consider the following table showing various proposed entity matches and the result given by our (fictitious) matching procedure. The right-most column shows whether the proposed match was a true positive, true negative, false positive, or false negative:

Proposed entity match	Our Guess	Correct Answer	Verdict
Richard Lewis matches Rick Lewis	YES	YES	TP
Richard Lewis matches Rich L. Lewis	NO	YES	FN
Ricky Lewis matches Rich Lewis	NO	YES	FN
lupin84 matches rlupin84	YES	YES	TP
R. J. Louis matches R. J. Lewis	YES	YES	TP
RLU matches RLIU	YES	NO	FP
Richard Liu matches Richard Lu	NO	NO	TN
Richard Lou matches Richard Lu	YES	YES	TP
R. J. Lupin matches R. J. Lewpin	NO	NO	TN

In this example, we got six guesses correct out of 10 possible, for an overall accuracy of 6/10 or .60. The specificity of our method is calculated as two true negatives divided by four total negatives, which yields 2/4 or .50.

We can calculate precision as follows:

```
precision = tp/(tp+fp)
precision = 4/(4+1)
precision = 4/5 = .80
```

A perfect precision score of 1.0 means that there were no false positives, which is good, but precision does not take into account false negatives.

Recall, on the other hand, does take into account false negatives. We can calculate recall as follows:

```
recall = tp/(tp+fn)
recall = 4/(4+2)
recall = 4/6 = 2/3 = .66
```

A perfect recall score of 1.0 means that there were no false negatives, which is also good, although it does not take into account false positives like precision did.

The F-measure, abbreviated as F1, takes both precision and recall into account, producing the harmonic mean of the two:

```
f1 = 2((precision * recall) / (precision + recall))
f1 = 2((.8*.66) / (.8 + .66))
f1 = .72
```

These measures, accuracy, precision, recall, specificity, and F-measure, can be used to compare two classification procedures, such as entity match procedures, to each other. With these, we are able to determine which procedure produces results with the highest values.

It is worth remembering at this point that in order to calculate these values, we have to know whether the class we chose (is a match, is not a match) is actually correct. This means one of two things will need to happen: if we have a small enough set of matched entities, we will need to be able to check them by hand to see whether they are correct, or if we have a large set of matches, we will need to practice by using a test set in which we have pre-coded the correct results.

Usefulness – how practical is the matching procedure to use?

Ideally, a matching procedure will be efficient, effective, and practical. What do we mean by practical? A practical procedure will be both generalizable and composed of minimal manual steps. **Generalizable** means that the entity matching procedure is broadly applicable to many situations. These various situations could include different domains, different times, or different systems. For example, if we design a procedure that matches person entities based on names, but we use a dataset comprised of book characters from Victorian fiction, it might work well for a particular academic project, but probably will not be of much use to a global social media platform in 2016. Similarly, a procedure designed for a niche test scenario may not be easily applied to real-world data. It is not always required that a procedure be generalizable to every possible situation, but we need to at least acknowledge in advance the likely boundaries of the thing we are designing.

Additionally, if the procedure we design has a lot of manual steps, it may not be practical to expect that using the procedure is **sustainable** into the future, as it will be very time-consuming and tedious. While manual procedures may promise higher accuracy, the time it takes to do the manual work does threaten overall the efficiency of a matching procedure. Even in a machine learning scenario, we should take into account whether or not the training sets are being constructed manually, and how long this takes. To increase efficiency, it is tempting to try to automate manual procedures. However, automation of a manual process can result in higher errors, which will defeat any gains made in accuracy. Correcting those errors then leads to less efficiency. As with many things in life, it seems like there is always a tradeoff!

At this point, we have considered different strategies for finding matching entities, and we have learned how to evaluate the matches we found. It is time to put our learning into practice with a real-world application.

Entity matching project

As with the application example in *Chapter 2*, *Association Rule Mining*, where we found frequently occurring sets of tags from Freecode projects, this project will also use data from the free, libre, and open source software (FLOSS) realm. Our task here is to find software projects that are being hosted on different code repositories, but actually represent the same entity. Specifically, we are interested in finding projects that were formerly hosted on the now defunct RubyForge.org site, but have subsequently migrated to its successor, the `https://rubygems.org/` site. RubyForge and RubyGems are both code repositories for software written in the Ruby language, but are slightly different in what they offer. RubyForge was a hosting site for software projects, and it included file downloads, source code control, mailing lists, discussion forums, and so on. On RubyForge, each project could be comprised of many files, including libraries, documentation, and the like. RubyGems.org does away with many of those project hosting features and simply hosts the gems, or library files, individually.

However, there is some thread of continuity between the two sites. RubyGems was created as a successor to RubyForge and many of the projects migrated to it. If we can connect projects as they move between these two sites, we will be able to create a longer history for each project. For those of us who study software evolution, having a longer record of project activity is a worthy goal. We can easily imagine the same goal being applied to other domains. For example, it may be important to match customers after an acquisition of one company by another, or matching graduates of a university as they move from the academic world into the working world.

Difficulties with matching software projects

Matching projects as they move around between hosting facilities is complicated by problems such as:

- Different projects on different sites using the same project name

- The same project using different names on different sites

- The same projects using slightly different variations for their URLs on different sites

- Projects gaining or losing team members across sites

- Different metadata attributes on one site versus the other

- No guarantee of whether a project on one site ever was actually hosted on the other site

Two examples

First, consider the project called *Rmagick* on RubyForge. Is this the same thing as the project called *Rmagick* on RubyGems? Let's compare the values for similar attributes for each project:

RubyForge Attribute	Value
System name	rmagick
URL	`http://rmagick.rubyforge.org`
Topic	Editors
Topic	Graphic Conversion
Topic	Viewers
Description	RMagick is moving to GitHub! See our new repository at: `http://github.com/rmagick/rmagick`. RMagick is an interface to the ImageMagick and GraphicsMagick image processing libraries. See `http://rmagick.rubyforge.org/ for prereqs`, install FAQ, and more.
Developer username	mmaiza
Developer real name	Moncef Maiza

RubyGems Attribute	Value
System name	rmagick
URL	`https://github.com/rmagick/rmagick`
Description	RMagick is an interface between Ruby and ImageMagick.

RubyGems Attribute	Value
Owner username	baror
Owner username	bentomas
Owner username	bf4
Owner username	vasilesky
Owner username	mmaiza
Author name	Tim Hunter, Omer Bar-or, Benjamin Thomas, Moncef Maiza (this is listed as one long string)

Next, consider the project called *Vapor* on both RubyForge and RubyGems.

RubyForge Attribute	Value
System name	Vapor
URL	`http://vapor.rubyforge.org`
Topic	Database
Description	A persistent Object-Repository for Ruby, providing transparent persistence of interrelated Ruby application objects to a PostgreSQL database.
Developer username	oliver
Developer real name	Oliver M. Bolzer

RubyGems Attribute	Value
System name	Vapor
URL	`http://helabs.com.br/opensource`
Description	Retrieve user information from Steam.
Owner username	guilleiguaran
Owner username	lunks
Owner username	maurogeorge
Author name	Pedro Nascimento

Are these *Rmagick* projects the same? Are the *Vapor* projects the same? Which attributes are most helpful in making this determination? Let's investigate the different possibilities.

Matching on project names

Matching on the name of project is problematic, especially for projects that have dictionary words (such as *vapor*) as the name. Just as we discussed earlier, it is easier to confirm a match between people who have unusual names than it is to confirm or reject a match between people with common names. The same holds true for software projects. *Rmagick* is a much less common word than is *vapor*. In fact, it turns out that currently there are four projects on RubyGems with the word *vapor* somewhere in their names.

Matching on people names

Matching on developer or owner names is also problematic, but not so much because of the risk of false positives with overly common names. After all, with such a small developer pool, the risk of having the same name as another developer or project owner is small, especially when similar project names are taken into account. However, there are real risks of false negatives with matching people names, due to variations in name spelling, including nicknames and usernames. In the *RMagick* example, the developer username *mmaiza* does appear in both lists, which is a strong indication that these projects are the same.

Matching on URLs

Matching projects using their home page or URL is easy in some ways and problematic in others. First, the risk of false positives is low. Since URLs are unique, we can be fairly confident that if a RubyForge project and a RubyGems project both state that they are using the same URL, that they are the same project. There are two exceptions to this rule that will help us find false positives. First, a rare exception might be if one project was using the expired or lapsed domain of another project, but this is so unlikely as to be impractical to plan around. Second, a more common exception would be if two projects listed the same generic URL, such as `http://rubyforge.org`, perhaps as a placeholder. This might unintentionally connect projects.

There are also small differences in URLs that might yield false negatives if we are not careful. Common differences include a trailing / at the end of a URL, the presence or absence of *www* at the front of a domain, *http* versus *https* in the protocol, and so on. String manipulation and edit distance metrics may be able to help with some of these differences. As with unusual names, a homepage URL is useful for confirming a positive match, but less useful for ruling out a match.

Matching on topics and description keywords

Matching on the topic and keywords found in the textual description of a project is an interesting option. In the *Vapor* example, it is obvious that these projects are quite different when we read their descriptions: one is a database storage software package, the other is related to gaming. However, in the *Rmagick* example, even though the RubyGems description of the software package is very generic, and the RubyForge topic seems to be serving as a notification that the project has moved to GitHhub, we do find words in common between the two. The keyword *ImageMagick* appears in both, as does the word *interface*.

So given these attributes and what we know about minimizing risks of both false positives and false negatives, how do we move forward with a matching strategy?

1. Consider matching by URLs. We will start by identifying matches using the technique for which the risk of false positives is lowest. We stated that it would be highly unlikely for two unrelated projects to use the same URL, therefore a very low (ideally, zero) Levenshtein edit distance between URLs is a good indicator that these projects are a match. In addition, as a blocking strategy, any 100% matches we find at this stage can be removed from the candidate sets, thus reducing the number of comparisons in later rounds.

2. Consider matching by project names. Matching project names is the next-easiest step, but it has a low risk of false positives for rare names, and a moderate risk of false positives for projects with common names or dictionary word names. As a blocking step, we will only consider RF projects at this stage if they have not already been found in Step 1.

Recall, however, the case of the two *Vapor* projects that turned out to be completely different, despite sharing the same name. Are there additional clues we can look for that will indicate whether the matching pair we have found is actually a match? Here are some things we can look for.

Is the RubyForge project name found anywhere in the RubyGems URL? If so, this match candidate might really be a match. An example of this is the `Abstractstack` project:

```
RF_project_name: abstractstack
RF_url: http://github.com/kachick/abstractstack

RG_project_name: abstractstack
RG_url: http://kachick.github.com/abstractstack
```

Are any of the RubyForge project developer names found in the RubyGems project list of owners or authors? If so, this might indicate that these projects really do match. An example of this is the *aerial* project:

```
RF_project_name: aerial
RF_url: http://aerial.rubyforge.org
RF_dev_username: mattsears
RF_dev_realname: Matt Sears

RG_project_name: aerial
RG_url: http://github.com/mattsears/aerial
RG_person_name: mattsears
RG_person_name: Matt Sears
```

The dataset

To get started on finding these matches, first we will need a database of projects from both RubyForge and RubyGems. The FLOSSmole project (`http://flossmole.org`) has been collecting data from both of these sites for several years. For this book, we have excerpted the relevant attributes from the FLOSSmole data and created the following five database tables (primary key columns are shown with (PK)):

- `Rf_entities`: The attributes are `project_name` (PK), `long_name`, `url`, description
- `Rf_entity_people`: The attributes are `project_name` (PK), `dev_username` (PK), `dev_realname`
- `Rf_entity_topics`: The attributes are `project_name` (PK), `topic` (PK)
- `Rg_entities`: The attributes are `project_name` (PK), `url`, description
- `Rg_entity_people`: The attributes are `project_name` (PK), `person_name` (PK)

These tables are available for loading into a MySQL database by downloading the `gzipped` file containing the `CREATE` and `INSERT` statements from the GitHub site for this book: `https://github.com/megansquire/masteringDM/blob/master/ch3/RFRGdata.sql.gz`.

Once the file has been downloaded, `gunzip` it and load the data into your MySQL environment. A fast way to do this is by using the command line MySQL client and the command line `gunzip` program. Note that in this example we have already created a database called *rfrg* to hold this data:

```
$ gunzip RFRGdata.sql.gz
$ mysql -h localhost -u username -p password
mysql> use rfrg;
mysql> source RFRGdata.sql;
```

The source command will load the CREATEs and INSERTs needed to populate the five data tables. When you are done, you can use show tables to see five tables loaded, as follows:

```
mysql> show tables;
+-------------------------+
| Tables_in_test          |
+-------------------------+
| book_rf_entities        |
| book_rf_entity_people   |
| book_rf_entity_topics   |
| book_rg_entities        |
| book_rg_entity_people   |
+-------------------------+
```

Now we need to create a table to hold the candidate matches. I have called this table book_entity_matches and we can CREATE it as follows:

```
CREATE TABLE IF NOT EXISTS book_entity_matches (
  rf_project_name varchar(100) NOT NULL,
  rg_project_name varchar(100) NOT NULL,
  url_levenshtein int(11) DEFAULT NULL,
  rf_name_soundex varchar(5) DEFAULT NULL,
  rg_name_soundex varchar(5) DEFAULT NULL,
  name_levenshtein int(11) DEFAULT NULL,
  rf_name_in_rg_name tinyint(1) DEFAULT NULL,
  rf_name_in_rg_url tinyint(1) DEFAULT NULL,
  rf_dev_in_rg_dev tinyint(1) DEFAULT NULL,
  PRIMARY KEY (rf_project_name,rg_project_name)
) ENGINE=MyISAM;
```

The table is created and empty, and is ready to hold our candidate entity matches. The next section will show the code needed to find candidates and populate this book_entity_matches table.

The code

To implement our proposed strategy for finding candidate matched pairs, we are going to write a short procedure that does the following:

1. Run a simple SQL select to find project pairs with matching URLs. Add these to the candidate list.

2. Run a simple SQL select to find project pairs with matching names. Add these to the candidate list.

3. For each candidate pair:

  ° Calculate the Levenshtein distance on URLs

  ° Calculate the Levenshtein distance on names

  ° Set Boolean: is the RubyForge name found in the RubyGems name?

  ° Set Boolean: is the RubyForge name found in the RubyGems URL?

  ° Set Boolean: is any RubyForge developer found on the list of RubyGems developers?

Once we have done these things, we can evaluate how good our matches are and decide how to refine the procedure or how to change it. The following code for this procedure is divided into chunks for easier understanding. As with previous chapters, the entire code base can be found on the GitHub repository for this book at https://github.com/megansquire/masteringDM.

Let's start off with some import statements for the three libraries we will need. These should already be in your Anaconda installation if you followed along in the previous chapters:

```
import pymysql
import sys
from nltk.metrics import *
```

Next we will set up our database connection. You should fill in the connection details with your own. We also need two database cursors. Our first two SQL statements will simply find projects with matching URLs and populate those as candidates, and then find projects with matching names, and populate those as candidates:

```
db = pymysql.connect(host='localhost',
                     db='rfrg',
                     user='',
                     passwd='',
                     port=3306,
                     charset='utf8mb4')
cursor = db.cursor()

# get all projects with matching URLs
cursor.execute("INSERT INTO book_entity_matches ( \
            rf_project_name, \
            rg_project_name) \
            SELECT rf.project_name, rg.project_name \
            FROM book_rf_entities rf \
            INNER JOIN book_rg_entities rg \
```

```
                    ON rf.url = rg.url")

    # get projects that have matching project names
    cursor.execute("INSERT INTO book_entity_matches(rf_project_name, \
                                                    rg_project_name) \
              SELECT rf.project_name, rg.project_name \
              FROM book_rf_entities rf \
              INNER JOIN book_rg_entities rg \
              ON rf.project_name = rg.project_name \
              WHERE rf.project_name NOT IN ( \
                  SELECT bem.rf_project_name \
                  FROM book_entity_matches bem)")
```

Our next step is to calculate the string metrics for each pair. First we will select out these pairs, then we will set up a loop to process each pair individually:

```
    cursor.execute("SELECT bem.rf_project_name, \
                          bem.rg_project_name, \
                          rfe.url, \
                          rge.url \
              FROM book_entity_matches bem \
              INNER JOIN book_rg_entities rge \
                ON bem.rg_project_name = rge.project_name \
              INNER JOIN book_rf_entities rfe \
                ON bem.rf_project_name = rfe.project_name \
              ORDER BY bem.rf_project_name")
    projectPairs = cursor.fetchall()
```

The `for` loop operates on lowercase versions of the names and URLs because the two systems, RubyForge and RubyGems, are not consistent in their requirement for casing of names and URLs. RubyGems allows case-sensitive project names, but RubyForge does not, and both sites allow capital letters in their URLs:

```
    for(projectPair) in projectPairs:
        RFname = projectPair[0]
        RGname = projectPair[1]
        RFurl  = projectPair[2]
        RGurl  = projectPair[3]

        # lowercase everything
        RFnameLC = RFname.lower()
        RGnameLC = RGname.lower()
        RFurlLC  = RFurl.lower()
        RGurlLC  = RGurl.lower()
```

The next section relies on two string metric functions, one of which, `edit_distance()`, is loaded with the `nltk` package, and one of which is a public domain function called `soundex()` written by Gregory Jorgensen and reproduced here. The code and explanation for `soundex()` is shown at the end of this section:

```
levNames = edit_distance(RFnameLC, RGnameLC)
levURLs  = edit_distance(RFurlLC, RGurlLC)
soundexRFname = soundex(RFnameLC)
soundexRGname = soundex(RGnameLC)
```

In the next few lines, we test whether the RubyForge name is found inside the RubyGems project name, and whether the RubyForge name is found inside the RubyGems URL string. If so, this is a good indication that the projects are a match, even if their names or URLs do not match exactly. We use Boolean variables `rf_in_rg` and `rf_in_rgurl` to hold the answers:

```
# is the RF project name inside the RG project name?
if RFnameLC in RGnameLC:
    rf_in_rg = 1
else:
    rf_in_rg = 0

# is the RF project name inside the RG project URL?
if RFnameLC in RGurl:
    rf_in_rgurl = 1
else:
    rf_in_rgurl = 0
```

Next we test whether the developers listed on the RubyForge list are found anywhere in the RubyGems list. We only need one developer match in common, so we let the SQL do the heavy lifting here for creating the matches. We `fetchone()` and set our Boolean `rfdev_in_rgdev`:

```
# do RF devs match the RG devs?
cursor.execute("SELECT rf.dev_username, rf.dev_realname \
                FROM book_rf_entity_people rf \
                WHERE rf.project_name =  %s \
                AND (rf.dev_username IN ( \
                    SELECT rg.person_name \
                    FROM book_rg_entity_people rg \
                    WHERE rg.project_name =  %s) \
                    OR \
                    rf.dev_realname IN ( \
                    SELECT rg.person_name \
                    FROM book_rg_entity_people rg \
```

```
                              WHERE rg.project_name = %s))",
                             (RFname, RGname, RGname))
        result = cursor.fetchone()
        if result is not None:
            rfdev_in_rgdev = 1
        else:
            rfdev_in_rgdev = 0
```

Now we have a bunch of string metrics and Booleans and we are ready to write all these to the database table. For each match candidate pair, we will UPDATE the row indicating what these values are:

```
        cursor.execute("UPDATE book_entity_matches \
                        SET rf_name_soundex    = %s, \
                            rg_name_soundex    = %s, \
                            url_levenshtein    = %s, \
                            name_levenshtein   = %s, \
                            rf_name_in_rg_name = %s, \
                            rf_name_in_rg_url  = %s, \
                            rf_dev_in_rg_dev   = %s \
                        WHERE rf_project_name = %s \
                        AND rg_project_name = %s",
                        (soundexRFname,
                         soundexRGname,
                         levURLs,
                         levNames,
                         rf_in_rg,
                         rf_in_rgurl,
                         rfdev_in_rgdev,
                         RFname,
                         RGname))
    db.close()
```

We close the database connection and we are all set. Before we discuss evaluating the results, here is the soundex() function written by Gregory Jorgenson and described earlier. This function takes two parameters. The first is the word for which you are generating the Soundex code. The second parameter is the length of the Soundex code you want to generate. The initial Soundex algorithm called for a 4-character code, which is also the default in this program. However, this length is configurable. If you find that you are dealing in a domain with very long and consonant-heavy words, you should increase the length. Remember that Soundex is designed for English pronunciations, so proceed with caution in non-English settings:

```
        def soundex(name, len=4):
            """
            soundex module conforming to Knuth's algorithm
```

```
        implementation 2000-12-24 by Gregory Jorgensen
        public domain
        available at: http://code.activestate.com/recipes/52213-soundex-
algorithm/
        """
        # digits holds the soundex values for the alphabet
        digits = '01230120022455012623010202'
        sndx = ''
        fc = ''

        # translate alpha chars in name to soundex digits
        for c in name.upper():
            if c.isalpha():
                if not fc: fc = c   # remember first letter
                d = digits[ord(c)-ord('A')]
                # duplicate consecutive soundex digits are skipped
                if not sndx or (d != sndx[-1]):
                    sndx += d

        # replace first digit with first alpha character
        sndx = fc + sndx[1:]

        # remove all 0s from the soundex code
        sndx = sndx.replace('0','')

        # return soundex code padded to len characters
        return (sndx + (len * '0'))[:len]
```

At this point we have a fully populated match table, and it is time to look at our results.

The results

A typical result in our result set now looks like the following:

```
rf_project_name: aafc
rg_project_name: acts_as_flux_capacitor
url_levenshtein: 0
rf_name_soundex: A120
rg_name_soundex: A232
name_levenshtein: 18
rf_name_in_rg_name: 0
rf_name_in_rg_url: 1
rf_dev_in_rg_dev: 1
```

What this means is that the RubyForge project *aafc* has been matched to the RubyGems project *acts_as_flux_capacitor* based on their URL, and that they also share a relationship between the RubyForge developer lists. Their names are quite different, as demonstrated by the different Soundex scores and the high name Levenshtein value. Still, just with the URL matches and the shared developer list, we have pretty good evidence that these are the same project.

At this point, it is time to evaluate our overall candidate match list and decide whether our procedure works well enough or not. Overall, did we find good matches? Here are some ways to consider this question.

How many entity matches did we find?

Our procedure produced around 5,800 matches. Is this a good number? Consider that we started with just over 9,600 RubyForge projects, and our ideal goal would be to find a match on RubyGems for as many of those projects as we can. The total 5,800 might seem like a really high number, but remember that RubyForge is a project hosting facility, whereas RubyGems is a gem, or library, hosting facility. On RubyForge, one project could be made up of many files and libraries, but they all lived under a single name. On RubyGems, each gem is listed separately. Therefore, many gems could share the same URL. As evidence of this, consider that there are 72 gems that listed their URL as some form of `http://rubyonrails.org/`. Rails is a huge project with many, many gems in it. On RubyForge those lived under one umbrella project, but on RubyGems they are all listed separately.

So, a single RubyForge project might be listed alongside several RubyGems projects. Therefore, we need a query that will tell us how many actual RubyForge projects we were able to find matches for in RubyGems:

```
SELECT count(DISTINCT rf_project_name)
FROM book_entity_matches;
+----------------------------------+
| count(DISTINCT rf_project_name)  |
+----------------------------------+
|                            4252  |
+----------------------------------+
1 row in set (0.01 sec)
```

That query yields 4,252 distinct RubyForge projects that were matched to RubyGems projects. That means that our simple URL and name matching procedure was able to find at least one match for 44% of the projects in our set. While we might want these numbers to be higher, let's take a moment for a reality check.

First, remember why we are looking for matches to begin with. We stated that we wanted to find matches so we could build complete project histories for software projects. A total of 4,252 project histories is a lot of material to work with, and that is certainly more matches than we would have been able to build in a reasonable time by hand.

Second, RubyForge was begun in 2003, and finally shut down in 2014. RubyGems started in 2009 and was named the official gem host in 2010. It is a distinct possibility that many of the RubyForge projects simply did not want to move to RubyGems. Maybe the projects became defunct or had lost their team leaders. Or, if they did move they may have changed URLs, names, and project teams so significantly that we will not be able to find them without a lot of additional manual procedures and domain knowledge about the project anyway.

When we think about it this way, finding possible matches for 4,252 projects is not bad!

How good are the pairs we found?

This is also a good question. Let's consider it in terms of false positives first. To attempt to ferret out false positives, we would look for two main categories of incorrect matches.

First, we want to identify pairs that had matching URLs but nothing else was good, for example, no shared developers, no RubyForge word stems in the RubyGems name or URL, high distance Levenshtein values on names, or nonmatching Soundex on names. We will call these Type 1 False Positives, or FP1 for short. To find these FP1 errors, we can run the following query against our match table:

```
SELECT rf.url, bme.*
FROM book_entity_matches bme
INNER JOIN book_rf_entities rf
  ON bme.rf_project_name = rf.project_name
WHERE url_levenshtein = 0
AND rf_name_soundex <> rg_name_soundex
AND name_levenshtein > 0
AND rf_name_in_rg_name = 0
AND rf_name_in_rg_url = 0
AND rf_dev_in_rg_dev = 0;
```

This query yields 123 projects, 42 of which have to do with the `rails` project alone. We can confirm this by adding the clause and `rf.url` like `%rubyonrails%` to the end of the query. Another handful are RubyGems libraries that are part of either the `will-paginate` or `muravey` projects, both of which had dozens of subprojects, but which all shared a common project name on RubyForge, and the same common parent URL. They were flagged as false positives because the name segment was either punctuated differently or had changed names over time, or because a patched library on RubyGems was given the prefix of a developer, but it still used the generic URL to the main project.

Another set of potential false positives are the pairs that share a common name but the URLs are different; they do not share a common developer, and the RubyForge project name is not found inside the URL either. We can call these Type 2 False Positives (or FP2). Here is a query we can use to identify these possible FP2 errors:

```
SELECT rf.url, rg.url, bme . *
FROM book_entity_matches bme
INNER JOIN book_rf_entities rf
 ON bme.rf_project_name = rf.project_name
INNER JOIN book_rg_entities rg
 ON bme.rg_project_name = rg.project_name
WHERE name_levenshtein =0
AND url_levenshtein > 0
AND rf_name_in_rg_url =0
AND rf_dev_in_rg_dev =0;
```

This query yields 121 results. These are potentially more problematic than the FP1 errors we found previously because in order to determine whether they are truly false positives, we will need to read the textual description of the projects, or if that does not yield any results, we will have to go manually to each project page and determine whether these are the same. It seems likely that projects with very unusual names are probably the same (two projects named *hatenagraphup* for example) but what about the projects named *helloworld* and *index*?

True positives (TP) are an easier story: 100% matches are easily found with this query, which looks for projects that have a matching name, matching URL, and three matching Booleans, including at least one developer in common:

```
SELECT rf.url, rg.url, bme . *
FROM book_entity_matches bme
INNER JOIN book_rf_entities rf
 ON bme.rf_project_name = rf.project_name
INNER JOIN book_rg_entities rg
 ON bme.rg_project_name = rg.project_name
```

```
WHERE name_levenshtein =0
AND url_levenshtein =0
AND rf_name_in_rg_url =1
AND rf_dev_in_rg_dev =1
AND rf_name_in_rg_name =1;
```

This yields 1,082 matches, dwarfing the FP1 and FP2 errors combined. The remaining matches are those somewhere between suspicious and certain. These are ones that are probably matches, but one or more of the Booleans was set to zero. To summarize we have:

- 5,796 total matches
- 4,252 distinct RubyForge projects that have been matched
- 1,082 positive matches
- 4,470 probably positive matches
- 123 possibly false FP1 matches
- 121 possibly false FP2 matches

Even if we declare the FP1 and FP2 categories to be entirely false, this still yields a precision value of 96%:

```
precision = 5552/(5796)
96%
```

But let's not get too excited with a 96% precision value just yet. There are plenty of reasons to be less than thrilled with our results. First, remember that we still have 3,807 RubyForge projects that we did *not* find any matches for at all. Second, and more important, we have no counts for negatives, either false or true. The reason for this is that since the beginning our matching procedure was loaded with only projects that either matched on URL or name, and no other projects were included. We also have no master list or pre-labeled training set for showing true negatives. Not having negatives means we cannot easily calculate recall or F-measure.

Still, if our goal is to find matching projects for further study of software evolution over time, I think we have succeeded in this. We now have a list of between 1,082 and 5,552 projects that we can connect, with some confidence. We can track these projects as they jumped from one hosting facility to another. Finding matches by URL was fairly successful, but by adding in some more complex matching by names, URLs, and developers allowed us to increase the number of matches we found, and differentiate between them based on how accurate the matches were.

Summary

In this chapter, we learned how to connect entities even when there is no common identifier for them. This task, called entity matching, is broadly applicable to many domains, and is one of the oldest tasks in data processing. Once we have matched entities, we are able to perform data mining on sets that were previously unconnected.

To do so, we tackled common strategies for entity matching, attribute-based, disjoint sets, and context-based. We learned several techniques for estimating whether strings are similar, including edit distances like Hamming and Levenshtein, and phonetic encodings such as Soundex, and we learned how to use blocking techniques to reduce or eliminate pairwise testing. Since it is important to evaluate the effectiveness of our entity matching methods, we learned how to calculate false positive and false negative rates. Finally, we tested our knowledge by designing an entity matching procedure for a real-world problem using data from two separate collections of data about free, libre, and open source software (FLOSS) projects. Using attributes they had in common and some simple string metrics, we were able to construct a list of several thousand projects that had moved from one hosting site to the other.

In the next chapter, we will continue to work with the RubyForge project data, dipping our toes into the deep water of social network analysis. Rather than focusing on the projects as entities, we will turn our attention to the software developers themselves. How did they self-organize to work on the different projects, and how did the developer network change over time?

4
Network Analysis

Humans are very social creatures, and our ability to find connections – with each other and with other things in our lives – is one of our strongest impulses. We naturally love to connect with others, we distinguish our connections with different names or levels (friend, spouse, acquaintance, lover, enemy, BFF, frenemy, boss, employee, stranger, co-worker, neighbor), and we sometimes keep these connections for years or decades. We are fascinated by seeing people from our network appearing in other, seemingly unconnected networks. We love the notion that there might be only six (or four, or three) degrees of separation between any two people on Earth. The *small world* phenomenon reminds us that we are more closely connected to each other than it may appear.

So far in this book, we have experimented a lot with finding connections between things, first by finding items that are commonly associated, and then by finding entities that appear different but are really the same. In this chapter, we will continue to explore how things are connected, but we will focus on data that can be represented as a network. We will learn:

- The basics of network theory, including how to measure a network
- Why the different shapes that we find in a network are interesting
- How to organize some real-world data into a structure that will let us analyze it as a network
- How to find and interpret patterns in this real-world data using Python and NetworkX
- How to compare multiple versions of a network to see how the network has changed over time

What is a network?

Networks are all around us. We use the word **network** to refer to many different types of connected things: multiple computers hooked together, a system of cities connected by small roads and large highways, a group of people who all work in the same industry, a series of television stations that broadcast common programming. In common usage, the word network can refer to almost any set of interconnected entities.

From a data mining perspective, however, our use of the word network is more precise. We use the word network to refer to a system that can be represented by a **graph** made up of nodes and links. In our specialized vocabulary, **nodes** are the things being connected, and the **links** are the relationships between the nodes. The collection of all the nodes and links is called a graph. Note that we are using the word graph in its mathematical sense, not in the sense of a visualization, like a bar graph or a line graph. In graph theory vocabulary, nodes are also called **vertices**, and links are also called **edges**. Figure 1 shows some of these terms we use for a graph or network:

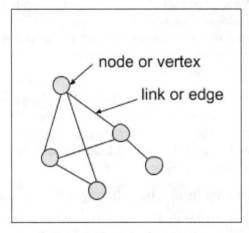

Figure 1. The parts of a network

Many times we describe the network in terms of the **direction** of the edges. A network can be either directed or undirected. An **undirected** network is one in which all the links are symmetrical, and the relationship between nodes goes in both directions. A common example of an undirected social network is Facebook. Both nodes in a Facebook friend relationship must confirm the link. **Directed** networks are when the links are not symmetrical. An example of a directed social network is Twitter. You can follow someone on Twitter but not have that person follow you back. Figure 2 shows the difference between an undirected and directed graph:

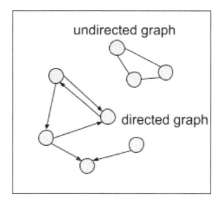

Figure 2. Directed and undirected graphs

In network mining, we may sometimes be interested in the **attributes of the nodes**. For instance, in the cities-and-roads network, we might keep track of how many people live in each city, or who the current mayor of the city is. But unlike in traditional entity-oriented data mining, in network mining we are also very interested in the **attributes of the edges**. How many people drove from Smallville to Anytown using Highway 1? How many people went the other way, from Anytown to Smallville? What is the minimum number of roads we would need to take to get from Anytown to Big City?

A **weighted network** is where one of the attributes of the links is expressed as a number. For example, in a network of airports, where the links are direct flights between airports, one weight could be how many flights there are per day. Another weight for this network could be number of passengers that fly between those airports per day. An unweighted network simply shows the relationship or link between the nodes, with no additional information about how *heavy* that link is. Figure 3 shows different combinations of weighted, unweighted, directed, and undirected graphs:

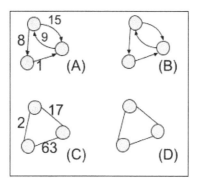

Figure 3. Graph (A) is directed, weighted. (B) is directed, unweighted. (C) is undirected, weighted. (D) is undirected, unweighted.

Here are some ways of expressing real-world networks as graphs:

- An e-mail network: The nodes could be people, and the links could represent *sent an e-mail to*. This would be a directed graph, since there is no rule that if Person A e-mails Person B, that e-mail will be answered. This graph could be weighted with the number of e-mails sent in that direction.

- The Web: The vertices could be web pages, and the edges could represent *includes a URL to*. This would be a directed graph. It could be weighted, if we were interested in how many links Page A included for Page B. If we did not include this information, it would be an unweighted, directed graph.

- Facebook likes: The nodes could be people, and the edges could be *clicked like on something posted by*. This could be a directed, weighted graph.

- Facebook friends: The nodes could be people, and the edges could be *are friends with*. Since Facebook friendship is a two-way street, this could be an undirected, unweighted graph. If we wanted to weight it, we could add a value to the link, such as *number of friends in common*.

- Shopping basket items: The nodes could be the items, and the edges could be *shared a shopping basket with*. This could be an undirected graph and the number of times these items appeared in the basket together could be the weight.

You might think that the last example of shopping baskets sounds awfully familiar to what we did with frequent itemsets and association rules in *Chapter 2, Association Rule Mining*. Should we go back and revise that chapter now that we have another way to find frequent itemsets? Maybe, but we still have a lot to learn first. First, we would need to express the entire set of items and transactions as a weighted graph. Then we will need to learn how to find the frequent subgraphs, which would be the equivalent of our frequent itemset mining.. Doing this requires that we learn how to measure the network and traverse, or walk, the graph. So let's learn those things next.

Measuring a network

Much of the analysis of a network is actually just measuring its various parts and pieces. How many nodes does it have? How are those nodes connected to each other? How many links does it have and how many ways can we traverse those edges? In this section, we will learn many of the common ways to measure a network.

Degree of a network

One way to describe a network is through its degree distribution. The **degree** of a node is the number of its connected edges. In an undirected graph, the degree of a node is the count of all the edges coming out of it. The degree distribution tells us how many nodes had a degree of 0, how many had a degree of 1, then 2, and so on. Figure 4 shows a histogram of the degree distribution for a simple undirected graph. Two of the nodes have a degree of three, two of the nodes have a degree of two, and one node has a degree of one:

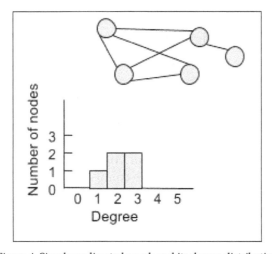

Figure 4. Simple undirected graph and its degree distribution

Figure 5 shows some alternative shapes for degree distributions that you might encounter in the wild. If every node in an undirected network had the same degree, its degree distribution histogram would look like a single bar with a very high count. Other common degree distributions include the normal bell curve shape and the long tail distribution:

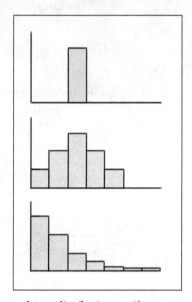

Figure 5. Common degree distributions: uniform, normal, and long tail

These examples were appropriate for undirected graphs, but how do we measure the degree of a directed graph? In a directed graph, we must use two numbers to describe the count of edges: one for the count of inbound edges to a node, and one for the count of outbound edges. These counts are called the **in-degree** and **out-degree**, and to show the graph distribution, we will have to make both an in-degree distribution and an out-degree distribution. If we add the in-degree and out-degree for nodes on a directed graph, we get the overall node degree.

Diameter of a network

Another way to measure or describe a network is in terms of its diameter. The **diameter** of a network is the maximum distance between any two nodes in the network. How do we measure the distance between any two nodes? Well, the **distance** between two points is the minimum number of hops needed to connect them. Since the distance is the shortest path between two points, but the diameter is the longest path between any two points on the graph, sometimes the diameter is called *the longest shortest path*.

Consider the undirected, unweighted graph shown in Figure 6. The distance between most of the nodes in this graph is either 1 or 2. For example, the distance between A and B is 1, and the distance between C and E is 2. However to get from node D to node E (or vice versa) will take a minimum of 3 hops. There are no other distances longer than the one from D to E, therefore, the graph diameter is 3:

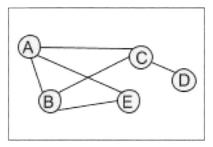

Figure 6. A simple graph for learning to measure diameter

If the graph has weights or direction, the diameter and distances might change. For instance, suppose the weight of an edge were equivalent to a monetary or physical cost to traverse that edge. This would be the case, for example, in a highway system where some of the roads between towns include tolls. Or, consider a runner who is trying to complete a five kilometer route by avoiding certain roads that have big hills. In a weighted network, the weights of the traversed edges must be taken into account in calculating the distance between every two nodes, and subsequently, these weights should affect the diameter.

Similarly, the direction of a graph will also change the way its distances are measured. Sometimes when we are calculating the diameter of a directed graph, a connection between every two points may not exist! Consider Figure 7, where there is no path from A to D (or vice versa):

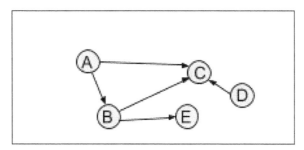

Figure 7. A directed graph diameter is affected by unreachable nodes

Walks, paths, and trails in a network

One of the handy things we sometimes want to do with networks is measure how long it takes to get from one node to another, and we might want to place restrictions on how many times a node or edge can be used to accomplish that.

A graph **walk** is when we just traverse links between nodes. In a walk, we might use all the nodes or only some, and we might traverse the same nodes or links multiple times. We can specify the length of a walk by counting the number of links that we have traversed, and if we traverse a link more than once, we count it accordingly. These assumptions hold true for any simple graph in which there is only one line between nodes going in a particular direction.

A graph **trail** is when we traverse a graph using its links at most one time each, but nodes can be used multiple times. A **path** through a graph is when neither the nodes nor the links are reused in the traversal. As with a walk, the length of a trail or path is just the number of links that were traversed.

There are many other specific types of walks, trails, and paths, for example those that declare which nodes to start or end with, or those that declare that every link must be visited exactly once (a Eulerian path). A **closed path** is one in which the start and end node is the same.

Walks, trails, and paths are interesting and important because they help us describe the features of the graph, including the number of links that we need to get from one place to another.

Components of a network

If every node is able to be reached from every other node, the graph is considered **connected**. A graph that has multiple unconnected subgraphs, where we cannot trace a path from one node to some other node, is said to be made up of multiple **components**. These component subgraphs are part of the overall supergraph, but they are missing edges that would connect them to the other components in the supergraph. In Figure 8, we can see a single graph that has three different subgraph components. We can tell that these are subgraphs because there is no path between the nodes labeled A, B, and C:

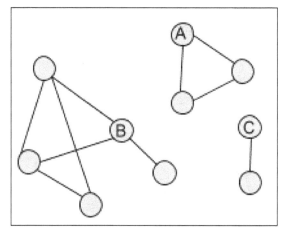

Figure 8. This graph has three component subgraphs

Components that consist of only a single node are called **isolates**. These nodes have a degree of 0. Depending on the purpose of your graph, you may be more or less interested in isolates. For example, if you are interested in tracking disconnected community members, perhaps to take corrective action, locating isolates will be important. However, if you want to reduce the size of a network to focus only on the most highly connected subgraphs, then you may wish to prune isolates from an otherwise very busy graph.

Centrality of a network

Whether we have a bunch of subgraph components or just one giant, connected supergraph, we will often want to find the nodes that serve as the most important players. Many times these are nodes that seem to be in the center of things, rather than hanging out on the periphery. In this section, we discuss various ways to measure the center of a network.

Closeness centrality

One way to find the center of a network would be to locate the nodes that are conveniently close to a bunch of other nodes. To find these nodes, we use a measure called **closeness centrality**. Closeness centrality is calculated by figuring out three things. First, figure out the shortest path distances between every pair of nodes in the network. Next, for each node, take the sum of those distances to all other nodes. Finally, divide that number into the minimum possible distance of the network, or the number of nodes minus one.

To make this clearer, let's look at an example. Figure 9 shows a network in which node A is only one or two hops from every other node on the network, except for node C, which is three hops from A. Node B, on the other hand, is also very well connected, with only three hops from node D. Which node is considered more central?

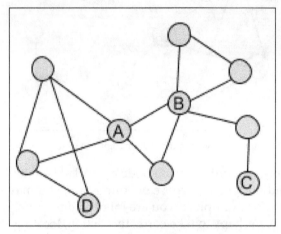

Figure 9. Does node A or node B measure higher on closeness centrality?

The total lowest number of hops from node A to every other node is 15. The minimum possible nearness for this graph is 9. The closeness centrality of node A is 9/15, or 0.60. The total lowest number of hops from node B to every other node is 14. Therefore the closeness centrality of node B is 9/14, or 0.64. Node B scores higher on closeness centrality (0.60 for node A, versus 0.64 for node B).

Degree centrality

It is important to see that closeness centrality is distinct from simple **degree centrality**. Degree centrality just measures how many nodes a given node connects to, taking into account the overall size of the network. To measure degree centrality for a node we calculate its degree, or number of edges, divided by the overall number of nodes in the network. In Figure 9, node A has a degree of four and a degree centrality of 0.40 (4/10), and node B has a degree of five and a degree centrality of 0.50 (5/10).

Betweenness centrality

In addition to degree centrality and closeness centrality, we might also want to know whether there are nodes that are indispensable to the network, in that their removal would result in a disconnected graph. Sometimes these important nodes are called bridges, bottlenecks, gatekeepers, boundary spanners, or brokers, depending on the metaphor being used by the speaker and the purpose of the network they are describing.

Figure 10 shows an example where the removal of the node marked A would result in two disconnected graphs:

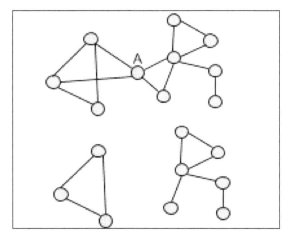

Figure 10. The removal of node A in the top graph results in two disconnected subgraphs

To find this type of important node, we use a measure called **betweenness centrality**. Nodes that exhibit higher betweenness centrality are more critical to the smooth functioning of the graph. If a node with high betweenness centrality is removed or compromised, then the traffic that used that node to get to other nodes will be stopped or slowed.

To calculate betweenness for the nodes in a network, first calculate the shortest path between every pair of nodes on the network. Then, calculate for each node, how many of the network's shortest paths include that node, but do not start or end with that node. Finally, divide that number by the sum of the number of pairs, or:

```
((number of nodes-1)*(number of nodes -2))/2
```

Figure 11 shows a small network with five nodes. We can see right away that nodes A, D, and E will not appear on any shortest path list without also being one of the end points. Removing any of these nodes A, D, or E will not break the rest of the graph at all. So we can state that their betweenness will be zero. Nodes B and C are more interesting. Which one has a higher betweenness score?

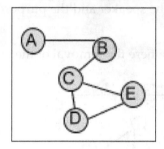

Figure 11. A small network with five nodes. Which node has the highest betweenness measure?

Node B is found inside the following shortest paths: A-B-C, A-B-C-D, and A-B-C-E. Node C is found inside the following shortest paths: A-B-C-D, A-B-C-E, B-C-D, B-C-E:

```
Node B betweenness centrality is: 3/(((5-1)(5-2))/2) = 3/6 = .5
Node C betweenness centrality is: 4/(((5-1)(5-2))/2) = 4/6 = .67
```

Therefore, in terms of betweenness centrality, node C is considered more important to this network than node B. If we think about it, this makes perfect sense. If we removed B from the network, there is only one node that becomes unreachable. However, if we removed C from the network, then there are two nodes on each subgraph that are affected.

Other measures of centrality

There are many other ways of measuring the centrality of a node on a network. For example, another way to measure centrality is to give more weight to those nodes that are connected to more central nodes. In other words, what if we calculated every node's centrality, then calculated the eigenvector centrality as the sum of the centralities of each node. This is like giving extra credit to any node that had really popular neighbors. A variant of this type of centrality measure is the famous Google PageRank algorithm. If we view web pages as nodes, then they can be conceptually linked together in a graph structure where the importance of a web page is based in part on the popularity of its inbound links.

When we do our full project at the end of this chapter, we will learn how NetworkX can easily calculate the various types of centrality for hundreds of nodes in a very complex network, thus allowing us to rank the nodes and find the most interesting ones.

But first, in order to start figuring out how to find and analyze graphs of real data, we need to understand how to represent our graph as a data structure. The next section will get us started in organizing our data so we can later analyze it in NetworkX.

Representing graph data

The theoretical aspects of networks are important, but in order to be able to apply these ideas to a real-world problem, we have to first transform our data into a format that a network analysis program can understand. In this section, we will discover the common formats for representing data in a network-friendly way.

Adjacency matrix

An **adjacency matrix** is a convenient way to represent graph data. To construct an adjacency matrix for an undirected, unweighted graph, we can create a grid that has all the nodes listed across the top as columns, and also down the side of the grid as rows. Then we use a 1 or 0 to indicate whether there is a link between those two nodes. Consider the unweighted, undirected graph shown in Figure 12:

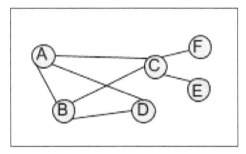

Figure 12. A simple unweighted, undirected graph

The adjacency matrix for the Figure 12 graph can be written like this:

```
  A B C D E F
A 0 1 1 1 0 0
B 1 0 1 1 0 0
C 1 1 0 0 1 1
D 1 1 0 0 0 0
E 0 0 1 0 0 0
F 0 0 1 0 0 0
```

A few things jump out right away about this adjacency matrix. First, all the A-A and B-B links are zero. Second, the value for an A-B link is the same as the value for the B-A link. This means that if we draw a diagonal line down the middle of the matrix, the bottom is exactly the same as the top.

Another important feature of the adjacency matrix as shown is that it has more 0 values than 1 values. The ratio of actual links to non-existent links is called the **density** of the graph. We can calculate density like this for any undirected simple graph:

```
(2*NumEdges)/(NumNodes*(NumNodes-1))
```

For the Figure 12 graph, this resolves as follows:

```
(2*7)/(6*(6-1)) = 14/30 = 0.46666667
```

Another version of this formula is sometimes shown as:

```
numEdges/((NumNodes*(NumNodes-1))/2)
```

Again, for Figure 12, this works out to:

```
7/((6*(6-1))/2) = 7/(30/2) = 7/15 = 0.46666667
```

A graph in which every node is connected to every other node will have a perfect density of 100%. A very disconnected graph where there are a lot of nodes and very few connections between them will have a density closer to 0.

At a programming level, an adjacency matrix can be represented as a multi-dimensional array. However, a very low graph density means that the array will have a lot of zero values. If we have a large, sparse network to analyze, an adjacency matrix stored as an array could be too large to be practical.

Edge lists and adjacency lists

Because of the potential for very sparse graphs to create too-large adjacency matrices, we can consider an **edge** list instead. Representing the same graph in Figure 12 as an edge list will look like this:

```
A,B
A,C
A,D
B,A
B,C
B,D
C,A
C,B
C,E
C,F
D,A
D,B
E,C
F,C
```

Another option would be to encapsulate the values into a structure called an **adjacency list**. An adjacency list shows that relationship X *is connected to Y and Z* as X:(Y,Z):

```
A:(B,C,D)
B:(A,C,D)
C:(A,B,E,F)
D:(A,B)
E:(C)
F:(C)
```

In this structure, we only need to keep track of the node and the other nodes it connects to. This can be implemented as a hashmap, or in Python as a dictionary structure, or in JSON as a set of key-value pairs.

Differences between graph data structures

We mentioned that the adjacency matrix is inefficient when the network graph is extremely sparse. If the adjacency matrix is stored as an array of arrays, that is an awful lot of zero values to keep track of. Are there other choices we should take into account when considering the implementation of the network as a data structure?

For all these choices – adjacency matrix, edge list, and adjacency list – simple operations such as finding the degree of a node will be constant. No matter which data structure is chosen, to count the nodes connected to node D, for example, will be straightforward. In an adjacency matrix or adjacency list, we would find the item with the key of D in our data structure, and count the elements of its value. In an edge list, we would just count all the items with D on the left.

Asking the question of whether, in Figure 12, graph node C is connected to node B is a little harder with an unsorted adjacency list. For example, in our adjacency list above, we find the row for C as: `C->(A,B,E,F)`. If this were represented as a hashmap, we would begin searching through the C item to see if B is there. If the value portion of the hashmap is unsorted, it will take longer.

As we will see later when we begin to implement our real-world project, some of this concern is simply academic. The reason for that is that we will be working with the Python NetworkX package to perform our network analyses in this chapter. The NetworkX package allows us to create graphs using lists of nodes and edges, and no matter whether we want to express that graph as an adjacency matrix, edge list, or adjacency list, there are built-in functions for doing those things. Internally though, NetworkX does store its graph as an adjacency list, using the Python dictionary data structure to do so.

Importing data into a graph structure

Of course, if we ever expect to work on real-world data, we should acknowledge that it is very likely that this data is probably not stored in a native graph format such as an adjacency list. Rather, our data could be stored in a relational database or in flat files. So no matter what kind of project we are working on, we will definitely need to save time with a pre-processing step where we will transform our data into a format that can be read by a network analysis software package, such as NetworkX. The network analysis software will then transform that data into its own internal representation of a graph structure.

To do this pre-processing step, we need to know what the different possibilities are for storing graph data as text files. The package we will be using, NetworkX, supports nearly a dozen different file formats, so we can be sure to find at least one that we can use for our data.

Adjacency list format

We discussed the idea of an adjacency list earlier, but now we consider it as a file format. NetworkX can read adjacency list files in two main flavors: a single-line version and a multi-line version. To create a file in the single-line version, we need to put each node combination on one line, starting with the source node. To express the graph from Figure 12 as a single-line adjacency list, we would need to create a file with lines as follows:

```
A  B  C  D
B  A  C  D
C  A  B  E  F
D  A  B
E  C
F  C
```

A multi-line adjacency list format should show the source node first, followed by the degree of that node, then each attached node on a subsequent line. For example, for nodes A and B in Figure 12, we would write:

```
A  3
B
C
D
B  3
A
C
D
```

For space reasons, we only showed two nodes in the multi-line adjacency file format.

Edge list format

NetworkX can also read an edge list directly from a file. The Figure 12 network in edge list format will look familiar. Notice that in an undirected graph, each pair only has to be entered once:

```
A  B
A  C
A  D
B  C
B  D
C  E
C  F
```

To add weights to the edge list, we simply add a weight number at the end of the list as shown here:

```
A B 3
A C 5
A D 2
B C 1
B D 8
C E 2
C F 1
```

Since Figure 12 did not actually have any weights on it, the weights shown in this edge list are for demonstration purposes only. Later in our real-world project for this chapter, we will use the simple edge list format for some weighted data.

GEXF and GraphML

These are both XML-based formats that NetworkX can read. Because they are similar, we will only show an example in GraphML. To express our Figure 12 graph in GraphML format, we would create a file like this:

```
<?xml version="1.0" encoding="UTF-8"?>
<graphml xmlns="http://graphml.graphdrawing.org/xmlns"
    xmlns:xsi="http://www.w3.org/2001/XMLSchema-instance"
    xsi:schemaLocation="http://graphml.graphdrawing.org/xmlns/1.0/
graphml.xsd">
  <graph id="G" edgedefault="undirected">
    <node id="A"/>
    <node id="B"/>
    <node id="C"/>
    <node id="D"/>
    <node id="E"/>
    <node id="F"/>
    <edge id="e1" source="A" target="B"/>
    <edge id="e2" source="A" target="C"/>
    <edge id="e3" source="A" target="D"/>
    <edge id="e4" source="B" target="C"/>
    <edge id="e5" source="B" target="D"/>
    <edge id="e6" source="C" target="E"/>
    <edge id="e7" source="C" target="F"/>
  </graph>
</graphml>
```

The format above is for an undirected graph, like the one in Figure 12. To make a directed type, change the value of edgedefault to directed. In GEXF, the layout is similar but some of the attributes are different, for example edgedefault becomes defaultedgetype. It is always a good idea to check the latest NetworkX documentation on all the various formats to ensure that nothing has changed since this was written.

GDF

GDF, or Graph Data Format, is a format that separates the file into two sections: nodes and edges. Figure 12 would be defined in GDF format like this:

```
nodedef>name VARCHAR,label VARCHAR
A,node A
B,node B
C,node C
D,node D
E,node E
F,node F
edgedef>node1 VARCHAR,node2 VARCHAR
A,B
A,C
A,D
B,C
B,D
C,E
C,F
```

The label for the nodes (*node A*) is optional. Notice how there are data types for each of the node names and labels; for example, both our nodes and edges are set to be VARCHAR data. You can also add weights to the network and other types of labels. These can be of the standard data types: Boolean, Decimal, Double, and so on.

 GDF is a fairly common graph file format and you might see it in various online tutorials for analyzing social networks in visual tools such as Gephi or D3. There is more information on the GDF format on the Gephi website: https://gephi.org/users/supported-graph-formats/gdf-format/.

Python pickle

A pickle is a Python object that has been serialized, or written to disk. With the pickling technique, we could write any Python object or series of objects to disk, and then ask NetworkX to read it in as a node or series of nodes. This would be useful if we did not want to make nodes in our graphs out of simple text or integers, or we if we did not want to put the nodes in a file. When would that happen? Perhaps we have a situation where we are creating a graph in real time, or where the values of nodes can change based on streaming information. In a case like this, we could pickle each Python object and read it in as a node. Also, we can pickle an entire graph in Python and read it back into NetworkX later. Be aware that the pickled version of a Python object creates quite a large file, as it includes everything Python would need to get the object back exactly as it was. So, make sure you have sufficient disk space if you are working with networks with hundreds of millions of nodes and you want to pickle them.

The NetworkX pickle documentation says in no uncertain terms that pickles themselves can be read in as nodes in a graph. So now I am wondering if we can create a graph of graphs where each node in the new graph is itself a graph. Is this really interesting or terrifying? If any readers have tried this out, I would love to hear about it.

JSON

Speaking of serialized objects that can be read into a graph, NetworkX also supports the **JavaScript Serialized Object Notation (JSON)** format both as a list of nodes and links, and as a tree structure. We will go through both of these JSON formats separately.

JSON node and link series

We can express our Figure 12 network in JSON as a series of nodes and links like this:

```
{
  "nodes":[
    {"name":"A"},
    {"name":"B"},
    {"name":"C"},
    {"name":"D"},
    {"name":"E"},
    {"name":"F"}
  ],
```

```
"links":[
    {"source":0,"target":1},
    {"source":0,"target":2},
    {"source":0,"target":3},
    {"source":1,"target":2},
    {"source":1,"target":3},
    {"source":2,"target":4},
    {"source":2,"target":5}
  ]
}
```

In this layout, the links (edges) are defined using the numeric index of the node in the node list. Node A becomes 0, node B becomes 1, and so on. Since the Figure 12 graph is undirected, we only need to show the node and edge combination once. Directed graph options are available in NetworkX as well.

JSON trees

NetworkX will also read JSON-formatted graphs that have a tree structure. A **tree** is a type of graph where each pair of nodes is connected by only one path. Our example in Figure 12 is not one of these, but you can see an example of a tree in Figure 13:

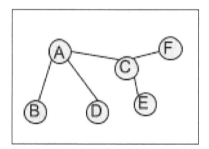

Figure 13. A graph that has a tree structure

In this graph, A is the parent of B, C, and D, and C is the parent of E and F. We can express a tree-style network in JSON like this:

```
{
 "name": "A",
 "children":
 [
   {
     "name": "B",
     "children": [ ]
   },
   {
```

```
        "name": "C",
        "children":
        [
          {
            "name": "E",
            "children": [ ]
          },
          {
            "name": "F",
            "children": [ ]
          }
        ]
      },
      {
        "name": "D",
        "children": [ ]
      }
    ]
  }
```

This format can support many nested levels in the tree, and NetworkX can read in this file type easily.

Pajek format

The final NetworkX-friendly format we want to discuss is called the Pajek format. Pajek means *spider* in Slovenian, which makes much more sense when you know that the Pajek format was invented at the University of Ljubljana in Slovenia. The basic Pajek format describes the six nodes and links from our Figure 12 graph as follows:

```
*Vertices 6
1 "A"
2 "B"
3 "C"
4 "D"
5 "E"
6 "F"
*arcs
1 2
1 3
1 4
2 3
2 4
3 5
3 6
```

In this version of the Pajek notation, nodes are called `vertices` and links are called `arcs`. There is also another version of Pajek, which they call the `edgeslist` version. It looks like this:

```
*Vertices 6
1 "A"
2 "B"
3 "C"
4 "D"
5 "E"
6 "F"
*edgeslist
1 2 3 4
2 3 4
3 5 6
```

If the nodes have no labels, it is not necessary to list them individually in the `Vertices` section. This stands to reason because it would just be a list of numbers! In a case like that, simply use the start line `*Vertices 6`, and that is sufficient.

We now have a great selection of file formats for our network data. NetworkX also supports some formats that were not shown in this list. The latest documentation for the full selection of NetworkX file formats is available at `https://networkx.github.io/documentation/latest/reference/readwrite.html`. At this time, they support 13 different file formats, and here we have described nine of the most important ones that we are most likely to run into during a project.

We are now ready build upon these theoretical concepts about graphs and networks by actually completing a project to answer an authentic network analysis question using real-world data.

A real project

To put our new knowledge about graphs and social networks to use, we will use data about the software developers working on free, libre, and open source (FLOSS) projects developed using the Ruby programming language. As we learned in *Chapter 3, Entity Matching* when we tackled entity matching between projects, many Ruby programmers used the website RubyForge.org between 2003 and 2013 to create projects and collaborate. In this chapter, we are going to use this same data to learn how the social structure of this community changed over those ten years.

RubyForge developers can be placed into a social network where the developers themselves are the nodes or vertices, and the fact that they worked on a project together represents the edge or link between the nodes. We could also count how many projects they worked on together to create a weight for the link. If two developers only worked together once, the link is weaker than if the two developers worked together on dozens of projects. This network will be undirected, since we can assume the relationship between the developers working on a project is symmetrical.

Exploring the data

The data we will need for this project includes a listing of projects and developers, as well as the timestamp of when that relationship was observed. To get these data points, we will use the FLOSSmole.org collection of RubyForge data. FLOSSmole is a collaborative project that provides data about how open source software is made. All of the raw data is available for anyone to download at `http://flossmole.org`, but to make our job easier here, I have created some data files just for this book chapter that have a lot of the unnecessary information stripped out. Those cleaned files are available on the GitHub site for this project at `https://github.com/megansquire/masteringDM/tree/master/ch4/data`.

It is certainly possible to complete this project without installing this data into a database. To do so, simply skip ahead to the next section called *Generating the network files* and just download the text files in `edgelist` format. But for those who are more interested in exploring the underlying data, I have provided a range of database queries here.

First, Figure 14 shows the entity relationship diagram for the data we will be working with in this section:

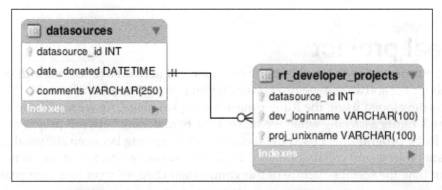

Figure 14. The two tables of data for the RubyForge project in this chapter

The following table summarizes the purpose of each column in the `datasources` table:

Datasources table	
`Datasource_id`	This column is a unique number given to every data set donated to the FLOSSmole project. This number is different for each time we collect the data.
`Date_donated`	This column holds the date and time that the data was donated to the FLOSSmole project. In the case of RubyForge data, this happens to be the same date that the collection was begun. For most of the RubyForge collections, the data was collected within one day, sometimes two days.
`Comments`	A short textual description of the data collection, for example *RubyForge collection from May, 2011*.

Figure 15 shows the first few sample rows from the datasources table for RubyForge:

datasource_id	date_donated	comments
24	2006-07-01 00:00:00	This is the July 2006 Rubyforge run.
30	2006-08-01 00:00:00	Rubyforge August 2006 run
31	2006-09-01 10:35:00	This is the September Rubyforge run.
35	2006-10-02 00:00:00	This is the October Rubyforge run
39	2006-12-01 00:00:00	This is the December 2006 Rubyforge run.
43	2007-01-01 00:00:00	Rubyforge, January 2007
48	2007-02-01 00:00:00	February 1, 2007 Rubyforge run
53	2007-03-01 00:00:00	This is the March 2007 Rubyforge data.
59	2007-04-01 00:00:00	April 2007 Rubyforge run
64	2007-05-02 00:00:00	Rubyforge May 2007 run
70	2007-06-01 00:00:00	2007 June Rubyforge
76	2007-07-01 00:00:00	2007 July Rubyforge run
82	2007-08-01 00:00:00	2007 August RF run

Figure 15. A few sample rows from the datasources table, showing the various collections of RubyForge data

The following table summarizes the purpose of each column in the `rf_developer_projects` table:

Rf_developer_projects table	
`Datasource_id`	This is a foreign key back to the datasources table. This is the unique collection number. Since multiple collections can go in a single table, this column helps make up the primary key for the table.
`Dev_loginname`	This is the login name for the developer working on a given project during the collection window represented by the `datasource_id`. Since a developer can be in this table more than once in a given timestamp window, this helps make up part of the composite primary key, along with the project name and datasource timestamp.
`Proj_unixname`	This is the short name for a given project. Since a project can be in this table more than once in a given timestamp window, this helps make up part of the composite primary key, along with the developer name and datasource timestamp.

Figure 16 shows the first few sample rows from the `rf_developer_projects` table:

←T→				dev_loginname	proj_unixname	datasource_id
☐	Edit	Copy	Delete	airportyh	aaa-openid	82
☐	Edit	Copy	Delete	airportyh	aaa-openid	88
☐	Edit	Copy	Delete	airportyh	aaa-openid	95
☐	Edit	Copy	Delete	airportyh	aaa-openid	100
☐	Edit	Copy	Delete	airportyh	aaa-openid	105
☐	Edit	Copy	Delete	airportyh	aaa-openid	108

Figure 16. First few rows from the rf_developer_projects table, showing which developer worked on which project during which time window

At this point, we have a giant database table of developers and projects and who worked on what project at what time. Now we can construct a few queries that tell us about the data we have, so that we can make an accurate and interesting network later.

First, how many data collection attempts do we have for RubyForge?

```
SELECT COUNT(DISTINCT (datasource_id))
FROM rf_developer_projects;
```

The results of this query indicate that we have data from 57 different collections of RubyForge data, ranging from 2006-2013. Next, how many unique developers and unique projects do we have for each of those collections?

```
SELECT datasource_id, COUNT(DISTINCT dev_loginname), COUNT( DISTINCT
proj_unixname)
FROM rf_developer_projects
GROUP BY 1
ORDER BY 1;
```

To see the growth of RubyForge as a whole over time, we can take the results of that query and graph them:

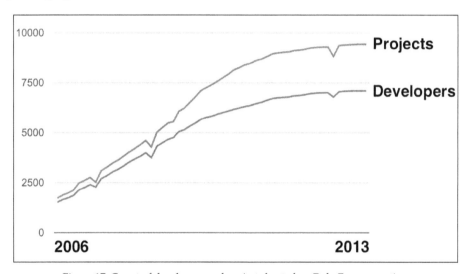

Figure 17. Count of developers and projects hosted on RubyForge over time

The figure shows that there was continual growth in both the number of developers and number of projects for many years, but eventually that growth tapered off as competing services such as RubyGems and GitHub began to flourish around 2009.

Now, given a particular timestamp, can we list the projects and all the developer pairs on it? The following query selects out the project name, and every developer pair working on that project at that time. As a sample, we used randomly selected collection number 266 (which happens to be the collection from May 2011), which is shown on line 5 of the following SQL:

```
SELECT a.proj_unixname, a.dev_loginname, b.dev_loginname
FROM rf_developer_projects a
INNER JOIN rf_developer_projects b
 ON a.proj_unixname=b.proj_unixname
WHERE a.datasource_id = 266 AND b.datasource_id = 266
AND a.dev_loginname != b.dev_loginname
AND a.dev_loginname < b.dev_loginname;
```

The first few results of this query are shown in Figure 18. Note that projects with only a single developer are excluded here:

proj_unixname	dev_loginname	dev_loginname
aafc	jimcropcho	tobinibot
accra	dolphin	jbrown
accra	dolphin	justinperkins
accra	dolphin	rauschuber
accra	dolphin	syarak
accra	dolphin	thinknot
accra	jbrown	justinperkins
accra	jbrown	rauschuber
accra	jbrown	syarak

Figure 18. For each project, there are one or more developer pairs

If we want to find out the degree for each node, or how many other nodes were connected to it, we can run a query like this:

```
SELECT a.dev_loginname, COUNT(b.dev_loginname)
FROM rf_developer_projects a
INNER JOIN rf_developer_projects b
  ON a.proj_unixname = b.proj_unixname
WHERE a.datasource_id = 266
```

```
AND b.datasource_id = 266
AND a.dev_loginname != b.dev_loginname
AND a.dev_loginname < b.dev_loginname
GROUP BY 1
ORDER BY 2 DESC;
```

This yields the result set shown in Figure 19. We show only the first few results, and these are sorted by the highest count first:

dev_loginname	COUNT(b.dev_loginname)
btakita	72
drbrain	69
arto	67
ezmobius	63
aaronp	62
chadfowler	47
alexch	44
bhuga	43
alexeyv	42
bernerdschaefer	42

Figure 19. Developers and how many other developers they worked with in a given timeframe.

From these query results, we can see that, for example, during collection 266, user `btakita` worked with 72 other people on various projects. To find out who those people are, we can run the following query to just pull out the people that `btakita` worked with:

```
SELECT a.proj_unixname, a.dev_loginname, b.dev_loginname
FROM rf_developer_projects a
INNER JOIN rf_developer_projects b
 ON a.proj_unixname=b.proj_unixname
WHERE a.datasource_id = 266 AND b.datasource_id = 266
AND a.dev_loginname != b.dev_loginname
AND a.dev_loginname < b.dev_loginname
and a.dev_loginname = 'btakita';
```

The first few results from `btakita`'s 72 rows are shown in Figure 20. To read the first row of these results, we can say that user `btakita` worked with `joemoore` on the project called `desert`:

proj_unixname	dev_loginname	dev_loginname
desert	btakita	joemoore
desert	btakita	joshsusser
desert	btakita	nathansobo
desert	btakita	nwilmes
desert	btakita	parkert
desert	btakita	thewoolleyman
erector	btakita	coreyti
erector	btakita	da3mon
erector	btakita	grafton
erector	btakita	imf
erector	btakita	jkingdon
erector	btakita	joshsusser
erector	btakita	nathansobo
erector	btakita	nkallen
erector	btakita	thewoolleyman

Figure 20. Projects and developer pairs for a specific developer

To construct a social network though from this data, we really just need a list of nodes and the links between them. The following query gets rid of the project name, since we do not need it, and instead we simply count how many times that collaboration occurs during data collection 266 (during May of 2011):

```
SELECT a.dev_loginname, b.dev_loginname, count(a.proj_unixname)
FROM rf_developer_projects a
INNER JOIN rf_developer_projects b ON a.proj_unixname=b.proj_unixname
WHERE a.datasource_id = 266 AND b.datasource_id = 266
AND a.dev_loginname != b.dev_loginname
AND a.dev_loginname < b.dev_loginname
GROUP BY 1,2
ORDER BY 3 DESC;
```

Figure 21 shows a sample of the result set from running this query:

dev_loginname	dev_loginname	count(a.proj_unixname)
arto	bhuga	23
bhuga	macbert	19
arto	macbert	19
mhatakeyama	zdavatz	16
jbasdf	oxtralite	14
drbrain	zenspider	13
bhuga	jhuckabee	12
arto	jhuckabee	12
bhuga	disturbyte	11
arto	disturbyte	11
jhuckabee	macbert	11
disturbyte	macbert	11
disturbyte	jhuckabee	10

Figure 21. How many times did each developer pair work together in a given time frame?

Keep in mind that because the number of developers and projects grew over the life of the RubyForge site, the lower collection numbers will have fewer results, and the high collection numbers will have more results. For example, collection number 24 yields only 1519 developer pairs, but collection 266 yields 8600 pairs. Already we can see that our network of developer collaborations becomes much more complicated and dense over time.

Generating the network files

Since the RubyForge data we have is so simple, just a list of nodes and a weight for the link between them, we can easily export delimited edge lists to represent each of our networks.

How many networks do we need to generate? Unfortunately, we do not have collections from the site for every single month during the 10-year period that it was in existence, but starting with the first collection in July 2006, we can set up a *roughly once a year* schedule like this:

datasource_id (collection number)	Month and Year
24	July 2006 (first collection)
64	May 2007
125	May 2008
169	May 2009
219	May 2010
266	May 2011
307	May 2012
382	June 2013
12987	May 2014 (final collection)

We will run the last query shown above, once for each of the nine collections, generating nine different edge lists. This work has been done for you, and the datafiles are available on the GitHub link for this book at `https://github.com/megansquire/masteringDM/tree/master/ch4/data`.

Now that we have our `edgelist` files, we can read them into NetworkX and begin to understand the structure of each version of the network, and compare the evolution of the network over time.

Understanding our data as a network

We have transformed what was once just a list of developers and projects into network edge lists that can be understood as an evolving social network. In this section, we will learn as much as we can about this social network of Ruby developers, and we will use the NetworkX library to help us out.

If you remember, in *Chapter 1*, *Expanding Your Data Mining Toolbox* we installed the NetworkX library into our Anaconda Python environment, so these libraries should already be ready and available for you at this point. However, if you have not done that step, take a moment and revisit that section so you can be ready to go with NetworkX. Or, if you installed NetworkX but it has been a while since you checked to see whether your version is current, you can always open a console in Anaconda and type:

```
pip install networkx --upgrade
```

This command will ensure that you have the latest version of NetworkX. To get comfortable with the features of NetworkX, we will use the first and smallest of our network data sets, the one which we named `edgelist24.csv` and which holds data from July 2006. After we get a sense of what we can do with the program, we will work on evaluating the larger, newer networks.

Generating simple network metrics

As we saw in the preceding section, when I am working with a brand new database, the first thing I like to do is run a few simple queries, such as counts, so I can get a sense of the database and what is in it. Similarly, when faced with a brand new social network, the first thing we are going to want to do with it is calculate a few simple metrics, such as finding out how big the network is, what it looks like, what its structure is, and which nodes are most important or interesting. The code for this section is available on the GitHub site for this book, at `https://github.com/megansquire/masteringDM/tree/master/ch4`.

In Anaconda, open a new file and import the NetworkX package and one other library that will allow us to generate these basic metrics, as follows:

```
import networkx as nx
import operator
```

Then, we will read in our smallest `edgelist` file, and store it as a graph variable. My `edgelists` were stored in a `data | directory` inside my working directory, as shown here:

```
g = nx.read_weighted_edgelist('data/edgelist24.csv')
```

Next, we can generate a Python dictionary where the element is a node and its degree:

```
degree = nx.degree(g)
```

Now we can calculate some basic facts about the network, such as the number of nodes, number of edges in the network, the smallest degree, and largest degree:

```
numNodes = nx.number_of_nodes(g)
numEdges = nx.number_of_edges(g)
minDegree = min(degree.values())
maxDegree = max(degree.values())

print('numNodes:', numNodes)
print('numEdges:', numEdges)
print('minDegree:', minDegree)
print('maxDegree:', maxDegree)
```

The output for this step looks like this:

```
numNodes: 719
numEdges: 1519
minDegree: 1
maxDegree: 30
```

To interpret these results, we can say that we have 719 nodes in the network, and 1519 edges or links between those nodes. The smallest degree is 1 and the largest degree is 30. To learn more about these high-degree nodes, we can sort the degree dictionary by highest degrees and print out the top ten nodes with the highest degrees:

```
degreeSorted = sorted(degree.items(), key=operator.itemgetter(1),
reverse=True)
print(degreeSorted[0:9])
```

The result is a sorted list, as follows:

```
[('rich', 30), ('curthibbs', 28), ('chadfowler', 21), ('kapheine',
20), ('mneumann', 19), ('lrz', 19), ('zenspider', 18), ('karlinfox',
18), ('cmcmahon', 17)]
```

This tells us that the user called *rich* is the highest degree individual in this network. Indeed, that makes a lot of sense, especially if we know that Rich Kilmer was the founder of RubyForge, and this is his profile!

If we are curious what the network looks like, we can print it out with this simple code:

```
nx.draw(g)
```

This yields a picture of the network, shown in Figure 22:

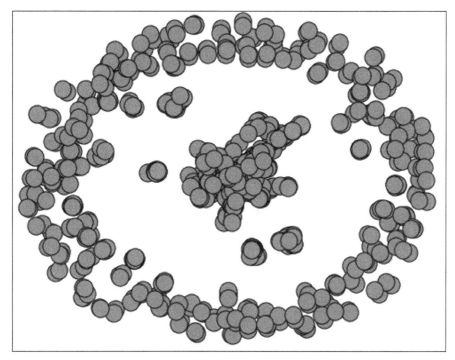

Figure 22. Basic network drawing for collection #24 (July 2006)

The most obvious thing about this network diagram is that it is very crowded and hard to read. The edges are nearly impossible to see, but nonetheless some structure is apparent in that there are many unconnected clusters of users. Some of the clusters are large, and some are small.

In the next few pages, we will take various steps to make the network diagram more meaningful and more readable, but in the meantime, my version of Anaconda has a few controls that will let us zoom in to inspect portions of the drawing more closely. To do this, use your mouse to select the **Zoom** tool (as shown in Figure 23), and then draw a rectangle around the portion of the diagram to inspect:

Figure 23. The zoom tool can help us see parts of the network more clearly

I chose to zoom in on a few of the uppermost nodes in the outer ring, and Figure 24 shows what I see now:

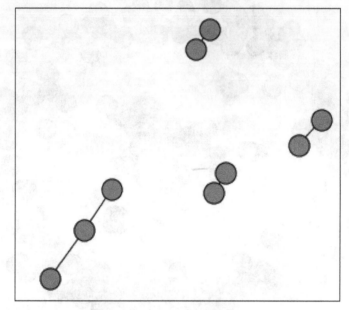

Figure 24. A zoomed-in view of some of the smaller pieces of our network

Playing with the parameters of a network

The network we drew previously is accurate, but it is not very readable. How can we make the network easier to understand and more effective, visually?

One way we can do this is to make the network more readable by reducing its size. To do so, we can remove nodes that only have one connection, which are called **pendant** nodes. This will shrink the size of the drawing. If we do not like the results, we can always bring the pendant nodes back.

First, make a copy of our graph variable, and for each node, if the degree is one or less, remove that node from the network. The code for this routine is shown below, or you can download it from https://github.com/megansquire/masteringDM/blob/master/ch4/basicNetworkMetrics2.py:

```
g = nx.read_weighted_edgelist('data/edgelist24.csv')
degree = nx.degree(g)
g2 = g.copy()
d2 = nx.degree(g2)
for n in g2.nodes():
    if d2[n] <= 1:
        g2.remove_node(n)
```

How has that action affected the number of nodes and edges in our network? We can print out the sizes of both and see that they are smaller:

```
g2numNodes = nx.number_of_nodes(g2)
g2numEdges = nx.number_of_edges(g2)
print('g2numNodes:', g2numNodes)
print('g2numEdges:', g2numEdges)
```

In fact, the results indicate that the network is about half as big now, in terms of nodes:

```
g2numNodes: 476
g2numEdges: 1370
```

Another way we can add meaning to the drawing and make it more effective is to fiddle with the nodes themselves. Can we make the less important ones smaller? Here we add some parameters to the draw() function to scale the size of the node to its degree. In this scheme, high-degree nodes will be drawn bigger on screen:

```
nx.draw(g2, node_size=[v * 10 for v in d2.values()])
```

The result is shown in Figure 25:

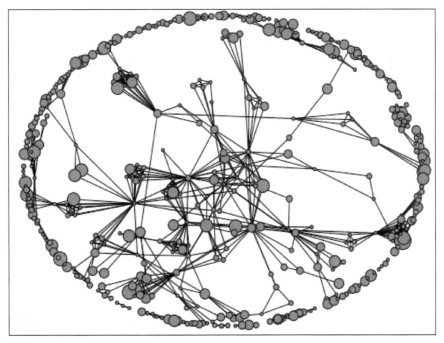

Figure 25. This version of the network shows only high degree nodes with no pendants, and the size of the node is scaled to its degree

Once again we can use the Zoom tool if we want to inspect areas more closely. When I do that, I see a few subgraphs that are large and highly connected, and I also see many graphs that are small and disconnected from the main network.

Analyzing subgraphs

What if, instead of trying to reduce the size of the network as shown previously, we wanted to investigate subgraphs? Here we show how to find out if the network is fully connected, and how to find the biggest subgraphs to look at. This code is available at https://github.com/megansquire/masteringDM/blob/master/ch4/basicNetworkMetrics3.py.

To find out whether our original graph (called g) is fully connected, we can run:

```
print(nx.is_connected(g))
```

This yields False as the answer, which we already suspected from using our Zoom tool on the network. We saw many small subgraphs of two or three nodes, so we knew that it was definitely not fully connected. To see how many subgraphs are actually in this network, we can run:

```
print(nx.number_connected_components(g))
```

Here we see that there are 154 separate graphs. Which are the most interesting ones to study? We can pull out each of these connected component subgraphs and sort them by the number of nodes in them. The largest component subgraphs might be interesting to study, so here we print the number of nodes in the five largest:

```
graphs = list(nx.connected_component_subgraphs(g))
graphsSorted = sorted(graphs, key=len, reverse=True)
for graph in graphsSorted[0:5]:
    print("num nodes:",nx.number_of_nodes(graph))
```

This yields the following result:

```
num nodes: 235
num nodes: 21
num nodes: 21
num nodes: 18
num nodes: 15
```

We now see that there is one giant connected network of 235 nodes, and then several smaller ones. If we are interested in smaller subgraphs, we can adjust the number of connected component subgraphs that we show by changing the n in the graphSorted[0:n] line.

At this point, we can also print out the degree for each component subgraph inside the **for loop** if we are interested in its members and how well connected they are. This code below will do the trick; however, be aware that it does print out a lot of information, which we will show more effectively in a moment:

```
graphDegree = nx.degree(graph)
print("degree:",graphDegree)
```

For the 18-node subgraph, the results look like this:

```
num nodes: 18
degree: {'hisnice': 3, 'shen': 3, 'erikdoe': 8, 'demetriusnunes':
2, 'christkv': 3, 'objo': 11, 'obie': 10, 'tirsen': 11, 'bjanakir':
8, 'mlee': 3, 'cowboyd': 8, 'stillflame': 1, 'duelin_markers': 3,
'sl4mmy': 8, 'asong': 3, 'stellsmi': 8, 'cvillela': 2, 'ged': 9}
```

What we might like to do is print out a drawing of each of these subgraphs separately, and since many of these graphs are a more manageable size, we can add text labels for the nodes. To do this, we will add a line to include the plotting package matplotlib at the top of our program:

```
import matplotlib.pyplot as plt
```

Then we will modify our for loop as shown below. We will add a simple loop counter, which we will use to create two new files saved to disk each time we go through the loop. One file will be for a subgraph drawing without name labels, and one will be for a subgraph drawing with name labels:

```
i = 0;
for graph in graphsSorted[0:5]:
    i += 1
    print("num nodes in graph",i,":",nx.number_of_nodes(graph))
    graphDegree = nx.degree(graph)

    # draw one set with name labels
    f1 = plt.figure()
    nx.draw(graph,
            node_size=[v * 10 for v in graphDegree.values()],
            with_labels=True,
            font_size=8)
    filename1 = 'graphLabels'+ str(i) + '.png'
    f1.savefig(filename1)
```

```
# draw one set without name labels
f2 = plt.figure()
nx.draw(graph,
        node_size=[v * 10 for v in graphDegree.values()])
filename2 = 'graph'+ str(i) + '.png'
f2.savefig(filename2)
```

One of the labeled subgraph component networks is shown in Figure 26. This is network #4, the 18-node network:

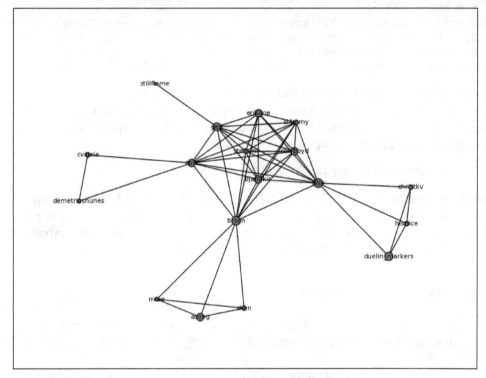

Figure 26. Subgraph #4 with labels

Remember that you can always use your Zoom tool to explore particular interesting pieces of the subgraphs. Also, since you now have copies of the network with and without labels, you can look at whichever one gives you more information or is easier to read.

Analyzing cliques and centrality in the subgraphs

In this section, we tackle the problem of how to find the most interesting nodes in a subgraph. If we remember our earlier discussion of centrality and cliques, we know that some nodes are positioned such that they serve as hubs for the flow of information through a network. Or in the case of a RubyForge network, these highly central nodes may serve as important bridges between otherwise disconnected work groups. The code for this section is available at `https://github.com/megansquire/masteringDM/blob/master/ch4/basicNetworkMetrics4.py`, and here we walk through step by step how we identify the cliques in a subgraph and the bridge nodes between them.

Inside the same for loop as we used in the previous section, we can use the `find_cliques()` function to find nodes that are tightly tied to each other. We can also use the `eigenvector_centrality_numpy()` functions to locate the most central nodes, as defined by the eigenvector closeness metric that we studied earlier.

The new `for` loop looks like this:

```
i = 0
for graph in graphsSorted[0:5]:
    i += 1
    print(nx.number_of_nodes(graph))
    graphDegree = nx.degree(graph)

    # find cliques
    cliques = list(nx.find_cliques(graph))
    print('cliques for graph' + str(i))
    print(cliques)

    # calculate eigenvector centrality
    ev = nx.eigenvector_centrality_numpy(graph)
    evSorted = sorted(ev.items(), key=operator.itemgetter(1),
reverse=True)
    for key,val in evSorted:
        print(key,str(round(val,2)))
```

This prints the results for all five of the biggest subgraphs. Here we will look more closely at the results for subgraph #4, our 18-node component. The cliques and eigenvector centralities are shown as follows:

```
cliques for graph4
[['shen', 'tirsen', 'mlee', 'asong'], ['demetriusnunes', 'obie',
'cvillela'], ['objo', 'hisnice', 'duelin_markers', 'christkv'],
['objo', 'erikdoe', 'bjanakir', 'tirsen', 'cowboyd', 'stellsmi',
'obie', 'ged', 'sl4mmy']], ['stillflame', 'ged']]
obie 0.36
ged 0.35
tirsen 0.34
objo 0.33
erikdoe 0.31
stellsmi 0.31
bjanakir 0.31
cowboyd 0.31
sl4mmy 0.31
shen 0.1
mlee 0.06
asong 0.06
christkv 0.05
hisnice 0.05
duelin_markers 0.05
demetriusnunes 0.05
cvillela 0.05
stillflame 0.04
```

How do we interpret these numbers? To show how the cliques overlay on top of the network, I have taken the original diagram for subgraph #4 and superimposed circles for each clique on it in Figure 27:

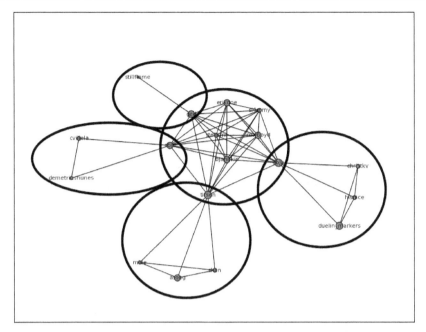

Figure 27. Subgraph #4 shown with its five cliques circled

To help describe the eigenvector centralities, the same subgraph component diagram is shown in Figure 28 with the five most central players labeled in rank order:

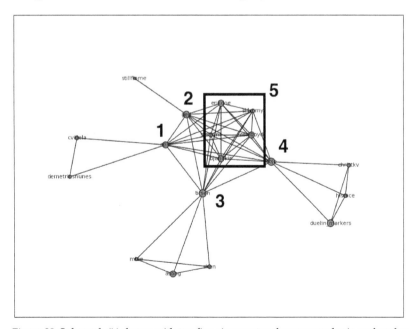

Figure 28. Subgraph #4 shown with top five eigenvector closeness nodes in rank order

The nodes ranked 1-4 are the most central because they all link to each other, and to the other items in the main cluster. Nodes in the box labeled 5 are all tied with each other. The nodes in the box all have eigenvalue centrality values of .31. These five nodes are all equally linked to the important nodes 1-4, so there are no big surprises there.

Looking for change over time

To find change over time, suppose we completed the previous procedures on all the other collections of RubyForge data, drawing networks for each of them. We might expect to find that some subgraphs (or cliques within a subgraph) have grown to include both the original members and new members, and that each subgraph just gets larger and larger. In fact, in this particular data set, we do find evidence of that sort of growth, but we also find a lot of shrinkage as community members leave. In some cases, the community members that leave are the most central nodes!

One useful way that we can arrange to see some of the evolution of our network over time is to concentrate on one particular interesting subgraph, and watch that piece grow and shift over time. In other words, in talking about centrality, we focused on subgraph #4, so perhaps we are curious about what happens to that component network after 2006. We want to show whether this subgraph #4 ended up joining onto any other component graph to create a larger one, whether any new nodes joined it, or whether any nodes left the subgraph.

First let's identify nodes that were in the 2006 subgraph and show where they are in the 2007 graph. Are these people still connected to the same collaborators as they were in 2006?

Recall that there were 18 nodes in the Figure 26-28 graphs. By 2007 (collection number 64), six of those nodes have dropped out of the network entirely. The following code redraws the new network, with the remaining 12 nodes shown in green. For visibility's sake, we also show these 12 nodes with a larger diameter. This code is available at https://github.com/megansquire/masteringDM/blob/master/ch4/basicNetworkMetrics5.py:

```
import networkx as nx
g = nx.read_weighted_edgelist('data/edgelist64.csv')
graphDegree = nx.degree(g)
pos=nx.spring_layout(g)
nx.draw(g,
        pos,
        node_size=[v * 10 for v in graphDegree.values()],
        with_labels=False,
        font_size=8)
```

```
nx.draw_networkx_nodes(g,
                       pos,
                       nodelist=['tirsen',
                       'shen',
                       'mlee',
                       'ged',
                       'objo',
                       'stellsmi',
                       'cowboyd',
                       'asong',
                       'christkv',
                       'hisnice',
                       'duelin_markers',
                       'stillflame'],
                       node_size=300,
                       node_color='g')
```

The result of running this code is shown in Figure 29:

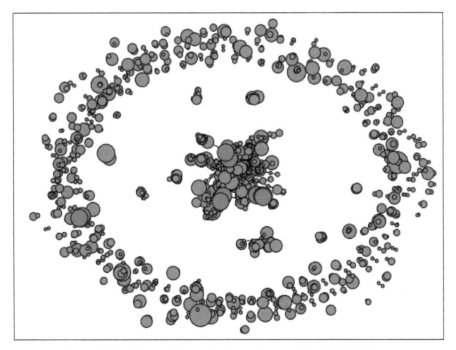

Figure 29. The 12 remaining nodes from subgraph #4 in July 2006 shown
as they appear in the May 2007 network

Right away we can see that our formerly connected subgraph is no longer connected at all. It is split across two component subgraphs, and even though there appear to be three cliques still attached in the main component in the middle, they do not appear to be closely connected to each other anymore either!

We can zoom in to look at close-ups of these portions of the network to confirm this, as Figure 30 shows:

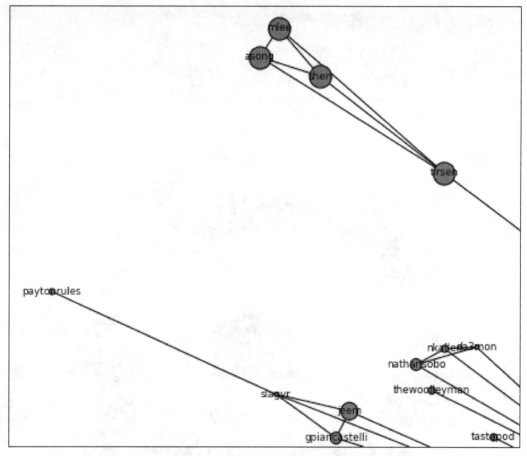

Figure 30. The user called tirsen still has a clique, but in 2007 it is no longer connected in the same way that it was in 2006

The clique headed by the user *tirsen* in 2006 still exists, but it is no longer connected in the same way. Highly-connected users *obie* and *bjanakir* have left, and *tirsen's* relationship with *objo* has also broken off. The *tirsen* clique is now connected to the main subgraph via a new connection to a user called *aslak_hellesoy*. That user was in the largest 2006 component subgraph (subgraph #1).

The 2006 clique headed by *objo* still exists, and still contains *duellin_markers*, *hisnice*, and *christkv*; however, it is no longer connected to any other nodes, and actually has become its own component subgraph of just those four nodes, as Figure 31 shows:

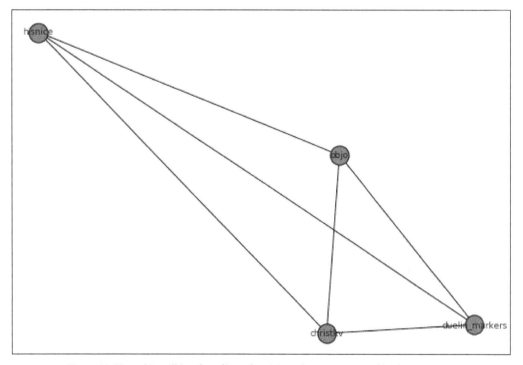

Figure 31. User objo still heads a clique, but it is no longer connected in the same way

The relationship between users *stillflame* and *ged* still exists; however, *ged* is no longer connected to the same people as in 2006, as Figure 32 shows:

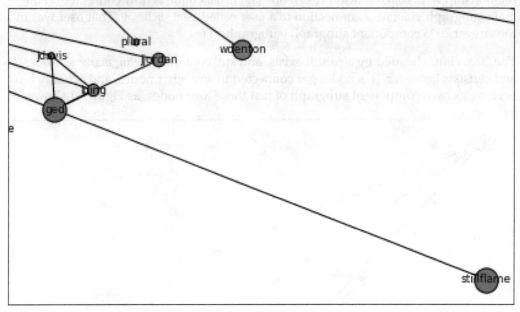

Figure 32. User ged is still connected to stillflame, but not to the rest of the subgraph from 2006

A similar thing happened to the remaining members of the ['objo', 'erikdoe', 'bjanakir', 'tirsen', 'cowboyd', 'stellsmi', 'obie', 'ged', 'sl4mmy'] clique. With four members of this clique dropped, and ties to *tirsen* and *ged* severed, only *cowboyd* and *stellsmi* are still connected from this clique.

The 2006 clique containing ['demetriusnunes', 'obie', 'cvillela'] has been completely removed from the 2007 network; none of these people exist any more.

Showing social network change over time can be challenging if there is a risk that nodes will disappear entirely, especially if those nodes are very central to the network.

For a different perspective, we will now learn how to center our study on a single node from the 2006 subgraph, creating a structure called an **ego network**. We will use this ego network as a way of reducing the number of nodes, so we can focus on the change in one particular part of the network.

We might surmise that building an ego network out of the most well-connected node in a component subgraph would be a smart move. This strategy would ensure that we see as many connected nodes as possible. However, recall that in the 2006 version of the network, in subgraph #4 the most central node (using eigenvector centrality) was *obie*, with a .36 score, and in 2007 *obie* is no longer in the network at all. Users *ged*, *tirsen*, and *objo* are still in the network though. The following code builds a graph using the 2007 data (edgelist64.csv) but with the focus on user *tirsen*. We set a range limit of showing any node that is connected up to three hops away from *tirsen*. This code is available at https://github.com/megansquire/masteringDM/blob/master/ch4/basicNetworkMetrics6.py:

```
import networkx as nx
g = nx.read_weighted_edgelist('data/edgelist64.csv')
graphs = list(nx.connected_component_subgraphs(g))
conncomp = graphs[0]
ego = nx.Graph(nx.ego_graph(conncomp, 'tirsen', radius=3))
graphDegree = nx.degree(ego)
pos=nx.spring_layout(ego)
nx.draw(ego,
        pos,
        node_size=[v * 10 for v in graphDegree.values()],
        with_labels=True,
        font_size=8)
nx.draw_networkx_nodes(ego,
                       pos,
                       nodelist=['tirsen'],
                       node_size=300,
                       node_color='g')
```

Figure 33 shows the ego network that is generated, showing *tirsen* in green, along with all nodes connected by three or fewer edges:

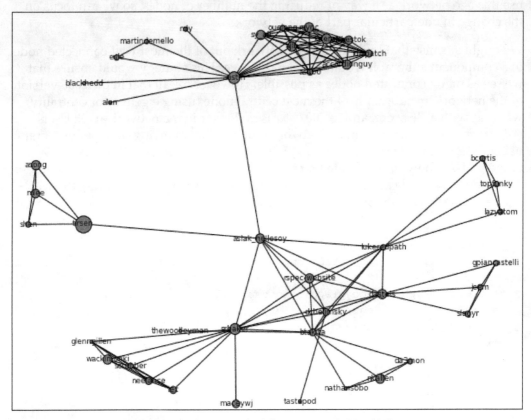

Figure 33. The ego network for user tirsen in May 2007

What has happened to *tirsen* and the associated clique by 2013? By 2013, the network has grown a lot. There are now dozens of subgraphs that have hundreds if not thousands of nodes in each. We can modify our code a bit to find the component subgraph that has *tirsen* in it. To do so, we simply loop through the component subgraphs until we find the one with that user in it, then print out that graph. This code is available at https://github.com/megansquire/masteringDM/blob/master/ch4/basicNetworkMetrics7.py:

```
import networkx as nx
g = nx.read_weighted_edgelist('data/edgelist12987.csv')
graphs = list(nx.connected_component_subgraphs(g))
for graph in graphs:
```

```
if graph.has_node('tirsen'):
    graphDegree = nx.degree(graph)
    pos=nx.spring_layout(graph)
    nx.draw(graph,
        pos,
        node_size=[v * 10 for v in graphDegree.values()],
        with_labels=False,
        font_size=8)
    nx.draw_networkx_nodes(graph,
                            pos,
                            nodelist=['tirsen'],
                            node_size=300,
                            node_color='g')
```

The resulting network is quite dense, as shown in Figure 34, but we have colored our node of interest (*tirsen*) in green and the rest of the component nodes in red:

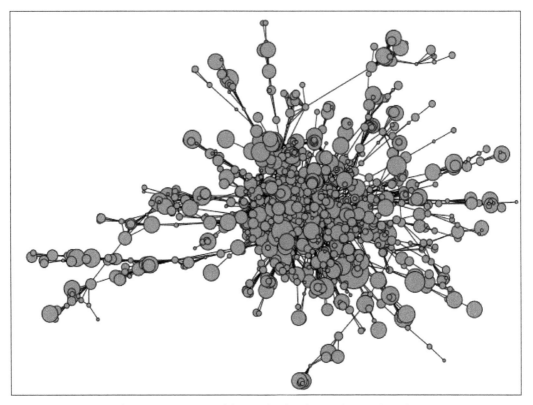

Figure 34. The user tirsen is one of thousands of nodes in a dense subgraph component

If we decide to draw just *tirsen's* ego network with a radius of 1 or 2, we just modify that `if` statement a little as follows:

```
if graph.has_node('tirsen'):
        ego = nx.Graph(nx.ego_graph(graph, 'tirsen', radius=2))
        graphDegree = nx.degree(ego)
```

Then we can point to the `ego` variable instead of `graph` in the rest of the code. The 1-radius and 2-radius ego networks are shown in Figures 35 and 36:

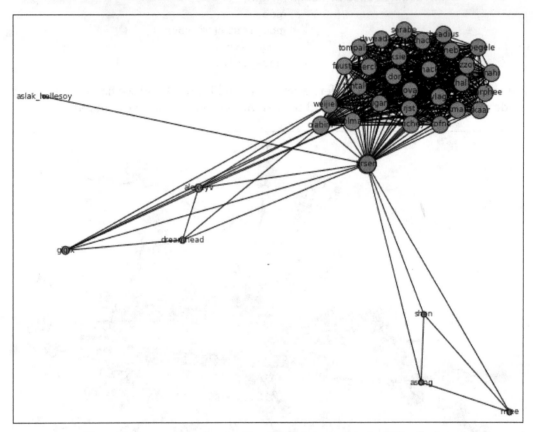

Figure 35. The user tirsen shown with a 1-radius ego graph in the 2013 collection

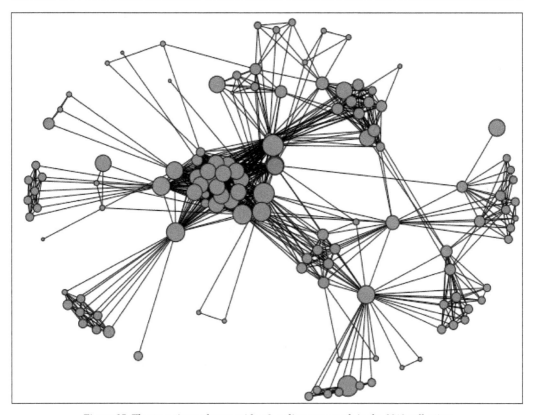

Figure 35. The user tirsen shown with a 2-radius ego graph in the 2013 collection

We knew the RubyForge developer network had grown and changed a lot, but to see it visually in terms of a single developer can be quite instructive. If we construct a 1-radius ego network once for each data collection 2006-2013, we can take snapshots of how that piece of the network grows and changes:

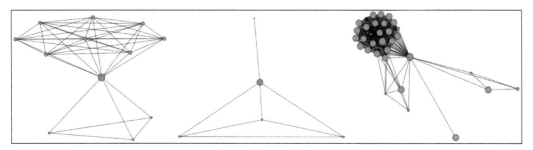

Figure 37. 2006, 2007, and 2009 examples of tirsen's ego network (1-radius)

Figure 37 shows three snapshots of the *tirsen* ego network over time. Even though we have nine snapshots, I decided to omit some of the later snapshot drawings because after a while, *tirsen's* network did not really change its appearance much, only the degree of the connected nodes got bigger. Between 2006 and 2007, the ego network got smaller, as some key players dropped out of the system altogether. By the following year, however, the network shows that this developer had rejoined a group that was very highly connected. Throughout this process, the original clique with users *shen*, *mlee*, and *asong* stays intact.

Summary

In this chapter, we learned the basics of network analysis and graph theory, including how to measure a network and describe its properties. We learned why the degree, distance, and centrality of a network are important. We also investigated the various graph data formats that are used in network analysis, and considered which ones are most effective for which types of graphs. Finally, we implemented a real-world project where we build networks of software developers that had worked together in the RubyForge ecosystem. We learned various techniques for exploring the networks, including how to build smaller and more detailed networks, and how to explore component subgraphs. We discovered a few techniques for focusing on a single node and building out ego networks, and eventually we implemented those ego networks into a view of a component and its change over time.

In the next few chapters, we will turn our attention to text mining. Specifically, in *Chapter 5*, *Sentiment Analysis in Text*, we will learn how to perform sentiment analysis on text. Sentiment analysis attempts to identify the mood or feeling found in a text or a collection of texts. Now that we understand the social structure of a group of developers, can we learn how they talk and how they feel?

5
Sentiment Analysis in Text

One of the most powerful skills we can master in data mining is learning how to deal with large amounts of unstructured or semi-structured textual data. Textual data, sometimes just called text, is important because it is everywhere, and because it conveys so much detail about the human experience in so many formats: books, news media, journals, government reports, case law, e-mail messages, chat logs, product reviews, and so on. We also find text data in places we might not expect. For example, when the spoken word is written down it also becomes text, as do song lyrics and video transcripts. When we look at the code that makes up web pages and computer programs, we find text. When we need a computer to leave a record of what activities have transpired, we have it create a text log file. When we need a common, universally interoperable medium for communicating between devices, we often use plain text to do so.

Over the next few chapters, we will be exploring some of the ways that we can find patterns in text data, and in particular, we will look for patterns in natural human language text. First, in this chapter, we will learn how to detect the opinions or sentiments expressed in a text. This task, called sentiment analysis, helps us understand texts better by discerning the mood or tone of the human who wrote the text. We will learn:

- What sentiment analysis is, and why we might care about it
- How to understand some of the most common techniques for finding the sentiment in a text, and what software tools are available to implement these techniques
- How to apply sentiment analysis to two real-world collections of text

What is sentiment analysis?

Many texts contain language that can be described as emotional. Whether to express the feelings of the writer, or to inspire a particular feeling in the reader, human language can convey anger, disappointment, disgust, joy, happiness, amusement, and so on. Discovering this type of emotional content can tell us a great deal about the writer, including what the writer's intention was and the expected response of the reader. Even noticing the absence of emotional content in a text can be interesting. Once we understand how to discern the emotional content of a text, or lack thereof, we can compare texts and writers to each other in terms of the emotional content, we can compare emotional content over time, and we can sometimes even predict how a reader will respond to a particular text.

Analyzing a text for its emotional content can take many forms. In this chapter, we will be primarily concerned with **sentiment analysis**, sometimes called **opinion mining**. Sentiment analysis looks for the subjective feelings presented in text by the writer, and attempts to label a text accordingly.

Common application areas for sentiment mining are product reviews (*how do shoppers feel about this product?*), and political pulse-taking (*how do the voters feel about this candidate's position on an issue?*). We can extract these feelings from texts of different lengths, for example from news articles, movie reviews, product reviews, tweets, e-mails, and text messages. Many sentiment analysis applications attempt to create a summary, or tally, of feelings, described in terms of polarity, such as positive/negative or like/dislike. Examples of summarized sentiment described in terms of polarity are:

- 60% of tweets are positive about the candidate's speech on Issue X
- 9 out of 10 reviews of this movie are negative
- The users of chat room A used more negative language than the users of chat room B when discussing Issue X

Some of the difficulties we have with sentiment analysis are the same ones that humans have in communicating with each other. People use words differently, and often in unexpected ways. The meaning of words can change in subtle ways, which is both a blessing and a curse for communication. Words, sentences, and entire documents can certainly express multiple complex feelings, sometimes contradicting each other or negating and confirming each other in the same sentence. Training a computer program to detect the subtleties of language is a tricky task indeed.

There is a growing body of work describing the research and theory of sentiment analysis, but much of it is found in the academic literature and is quite dense. However, if you need more information on any of the concepts in this chapter, two of the classic references that I would recommend are Bo Pang and Lillian Lee's 2008 paper called *Opinion mining and sentiment analysis* (available on the second author's website at `http://www.cs.cornell.edu/home/llee/omsa/omsa.pdf`) and Bing Liu's 2012 paper called *Sentiment analysis and opinion mining* (available at the author's site at `https://www.cs.uic.edu/~liub/FBS/SentimentAnalysis-and-OpinionMining.pdf`). Both of these papers are considered classics in the field, and have been cited hundreds of times each. As survey papers, they both provide many links to other papers upon which this research field is based.

The basics of sentiment analysis

To begin a sentiment mining project, we first need to understand how opinions are structured in text so we can find the best way to train the computer to deal with them. Opinion mining and sentiment analysis are considered sub-problems of the much larger field of **natural language processing** (**NLP**), and as such, are subject to many of the same unsolved issues in trying to account for all the quirks of human communication. However, sentiment mining is restricted in an important way, namely that its goal is not to *understand* the statements made by people, but rather to just figure out their tone. As we will see later, any one strategy for finding the sentiment of any given text may not be perfect, but this may not matter much if the amount of data is high and the stakes are comparatively low.

The structure of an opinion

Each opinion typically has a **target**. If we read the sentence, "*This was the worst movie I ever saw,*" the target of that opinion is *the movie*. In the sentiment analysis literature, the opinion target is sometimes called an **entity**. Each entity present in an opinion can also have **components**, or sub-parts, and **attributes**, or descriptors for the entity or component. If we see an opinion like "*The amateurish ending of the plot was the worst part of the movie,*" the overall target of the opinion is still the *movie*, but we notice that there are additional components: the movie has a *plot*, which itself had an *ending*, which was described as being *amateurish*. These components and attributes are generically called **aspects** of the opinion.

The writer may express an opinion about entities, components, and aspects either implicitly or explicitly. The following sentences demonstrate the difference in an **explicit** and **implicit** expression of an opinion about the entity, `movie`:

- Case 1: "That was the worst movie I ever saw"
- Case 2: "Well that movie was a total waste of $10"

In the first case, we identified an entity, *movie*, and the sentence clearly describes that entity as *the worst*. In the second case, a negative opinion can be inferred from the statement that the movie was a *waste* of money. Understanding that this is a negative opinion requires understanding that movies cost $10, and that this person views wasting money as a bad thing. Teaching a computer to understand implicit opinions can be difficult. As we will find later, supervised machine learning techniques based on pre-classified training samples can come in handy here.

Sarcastic, idiomatic, and conditional statements are also challenges in automatically discerning the sentiment in an opinion. Consider statements like the following:

- "You should go see *The Little Mermaid* if you have nothing better to do on a Saturday night, but you might be better off washing your hair or re-organizing your sock drawer"
- "Has anyone else used the *The Little Mermaid* script to line a bird cage?"

These statements make sense if you know that washing your hair or re-organizing your sock drawer are considered boring activities, and lining a bird cage is what you do with worthless papers. The conditional statement *"you should go"* sounds positive, but is immediately offset by the *"but"* in the next clause. Sometimes questions are assumed to be neutral, in that they are designed to elicit information, but in this case, the second question is definitely meant to be negative.

Another wrinkle we must account for in sentiment analysis is when opinions are comparative in nature. A comparative opinion is one that tries to distinguish two or more items based on their shared characteristics. Consider the following comparative opinions:

- Statement 1: "The songs in *Beauty and the Beast* were better than *The Little Mermaid*"
- Statement 2: "*Beauty and the Beast* and *The Little Mermaid* both had some good music"
- Statement 3: "*The Little Mermaid* has the best soundtrack of any animated film"
- Statement 4: "*Beauty and the Beast* was funnier, but *The Little Mermaid* had better music"

Statement 1 is a direct comparison of the two movies in terms of the songs present in each, and one movie is considered superior to the other. Notice that the reviewer stops short of saying that the songs were good or bad, rather the two sets of songs are simply compared to each other and one came out on top.

Statement 2 compares the two movies to each other on the same "music" aspect, and finds that they are equally good.

Statement 3 finds that one movie is better than all other movies on the "soundtrack" aspect.

Statement 4 compares the two entities on two different aspects.

Both comparisons and implicit opinions are difficult to account for in sentiment analysis work. If we read a sentence like "The ugly fact is that *Beauty and the Beast* is nothing like the festering boil that was *The Little Mermaid* and I would really like to see it again three or four times," we quickly determine that many of the words in the sentence are negative; however the comparison and implicit opinion both indicate that this person really liked the movie, *Beauty and the Beast*. Therefore, comparisons, implicit language, and idioms are very important for us to consider because they are common, and if we find ways to handle them, our sentiment mining will be more accurate.

Document-level and sentence-level analysis

We can analyze opinions either at a document level or at a sentence level. At the **document level**, for example in a movie review or a chat log, the sentiment analysis task is to summarize an overall feeling about the item in question. This could include aggregating sentiment values, for example aggregating the feelings of multiple people or multiple sentences by the same person. Is this chat room a positive, happy place or is it a negative, toxic environment? Is this speaker in the chat room generally positive or mostly negative? In this movie review, did this writer generally like the movie or is the review mostly negative?

Some sentiment analysis research focuses on first identifying and removing non-subjective sentences, since those may not be relevant to the overall sentiment determination. This task of determining whether a sentence has enough subjective material in it to be considered an opinion is called **subjectivity classification**, and this is a whole subfield of research. In this chapter, we will focus mostly on document-level sentiment analysis.

Important features of opinions

To perform a sentiment analysis on a text, we will need to consider the various features of the text that imply its sentiment. Typically, the most important feature will be the **terms** used in the text. Terms include words and phrases, but could also include punctuation, emojis, and emoticons as those can also imply mood or feeling. Words that we determine indicate positive or negative sentiment are called **sentiment words**, or **opinion words**. Examples of sentiment words are *good, bad, hate, gross, garbage, love, adore,* and so on. Lately, in social media text, emojis are becoming an important term type in their own right. Whether a term – and especially a sentiment word – is used in the text, and how much it is used, is the most important feature we can use to determine sentiment.

We should keep in mind that not every domain will treat the same words in the same way, and words that imply strong sentiment in one domain may have no meaning in another domain. A common example in the literature is the word *unpredictable* which, when used in a movie review could be a positive descriptor (*unpredictable* plot), but when used in a car review could be a negative comment (*unpredictable* steering).

Aside from sentiment words, other features of a text that can indicate sentiment include:

- The rarity of a word used. Some research has shown that a rare word, or *Hapax legomenon*, abbreviated **hapax**, could be an indicator of sentiment if it is used for emphasis or as a marker for subjectivity.

- The **position** of a word in the text. Typically the words in a text are treated as a **bag of words**, with no regard to their positions. However, some studies have shown that whether a word appears with other words (as a two- or three-word phrase, for example) or in certain positions in a sentence could change its sentiment.

- The presence of **negation words** and other so-called **opinion shifters**. The impact of the simple addition of *not* can be significant and obvious, as we see in the difference between *I do like this movie* and *I do not like this movie*. There are many other more subtle words and phrases that are used to shift an opinion, for example, *This movie could have a better plot and the dialogue is hardly intelligent*. The addition of *could have* and *hardly* change the sentiment in important ways.

- The **parts of speech** present in a text. Some studies have found that the presence of adjectives and adverbs is indicative of subjectivity in text, and thus might be relevant for finding text that is particularly opinionated.

Sentiment analysis algorithms

Supposing we wanted to broadly classify the sentiment of a text as positive or negative, we may choose to model the opinion mining task as a classification problem, such as could be solved with supervised machine learning techniques like a Naïve Bayes classifier (NBC). Given a set of positive text features and negative text features, an NBC strategy will allow us to take a new text and classify it as being more positive or more negative given the observations about other similar texts we have made in the past. The machine learning literature is replete with examples of supervised classification, and it is a very reliable approach for certain types of problems.

The trick of course with this type of classification scheme is being able to count on the observations we have made in the past as reliable indicators of future observations. These **training examples** are critically important and are the basis for the success of the entire scheme. After all, if we choose training examples that are too generic or irrelevant to our domain, the system will not be able to correctly classify future cases. On the other hand, if we train a system too closely, we risk **overfitting**, or generating a classifier that only works with one specific set of data.

In the case of sentiment analysis of movie reviews for example, suppose the training examples are 1,000 old movie reviews that have been pre-divided roughly equal groups of positive and negative reviews. An NBC approach would learn which features were most important about these original reviews and look for these same features in the new reviews, giving each new review a percentage chance of being positive or negative. Some **feature engineering** is usually expected as well with a supervised classification scheme, for example, directing the classifier to take into account the particular language of the domain in question, or to pay more attention to parts of speech or word positions or frequency of certain words or phrases. Earlier we mentioned that the word *unpredictable* might be a positive word in movie reviews, so we could explicitly engineer that feature accordingly.

Some of the general-purpose tools available for sentiment mining already have the classification scheme baked in, so they are ready for us to feed in sentences. In our example at the end of this chapter, we use some of the built-in sentiment classifiers that have been pre-trained with positive and negative words. In the next section, we will take a look at some of these pre-collected and pre-classified sentiment collections.

General-purpose data collections

The sentiment classification systems described previously rely on training examples in order to learn what kind of text is positive or negative. These training examples can be manually classified (a task sometimes called **coding**) by humans into positive and negative, or whatever the intended classes are. Once coded, the training set can be reused over and over again to train other classifiers. Therefore, this training process and the resulting classified word lists are very important to the overall sentiment analysis process as they save a lot of time and also let us compare results to each other. But where do the training examples come from? There are many lists of sentiment-classified words online, and even some canned datasets that we can use to test a classifier. Three of the more commonly used word lists, or lexicons, are described here.

Hu and Liu's sentiment analysis lexicon

Minqing Hu and Bing Liu's list of 6,800 words is one of the first sentiment lexicons that was made available for public use. The lexicon is still available on Liu's university website at `https://www.cs.uic.edu/~liub/FBS/sentiment-analysis.html#lexicon`. This site also has a handful of datasets of product reviews that can be used to test your classifier. When uncompressed from RAR format, the word list is divided into two text files, `positive.txt` and `negative.txt`. Each file contains a simple list of words. There are about 4,800 negative words provided and the remaining 2,000 words appear in the positive list. The first 10 positive words are shown in the following example:

```
a+
abound
abounds
abundance
abundant
accessable
accessible
acclaim
acclaimed
acclamation
```

The authors point out that they have included many words that are commonly misspelled on social media, for example the misspelling *accessable* appears in the preceding list for this reason. In contrast to the next two lexicon samples, there is no scale or ranking for the sentiment of each word. The words are stated to be either positive or negative, without gradients or comparisons to each other.

SentiWordNet

SentiWordNet is another list of words that have been coded as positive or negative. The file is available for download, and as of writing this is a `gzipped` file of about 13 MB. It is available at: `http://sentiwordnet.isti.cnr.it`. There are approximately 117,000 words, scores, and definitions (called **glosses**) in the file.

The header row and first two entries look like this:

```
# POS   ID   PosScore   NegScore   SynsetTerms   Gloss

a  00001740  0.125  0  able#1  (usually followed by `to') having the
necessary means or skill or know-how or authority to do something;
"able to swim"; "she was able to program her computer"; "we were at
last able to buy a car"; "able to get a grant for the project"

a  00002098  0  0.75  unable#1  (usually followed by `to') not having
the necessary means or skill or know-how; "unable to get to town
without a car"; "unable to obtain funds"
```

The first word in the file shown previously is `able`. This word is given a unique number, `00001740`, and is marked `a` for its POS, or part of speech, which is an adjective. This word has a positive score of `.125` and a negative score of `0`. The second word is *unable*, hich has a positive score of `0` and a negative score of `.75`. The SentiWordNet documentation also explains how to calculate a score for each the objectivity of each word. The **objectivity score** is the sum of the positive and negative scores for a word, subtracted from 1. This score measures how **neutral** the word is. Words that have low scores for both positivity and negativity will end up scoring high on objectivity.

Vader sentiment

The Vader sentiment tool, created by C.J. Hutto and Eric Gilbert at Georgia Tech, includes a lexicon and many test files. Vader is especially tuned for social media data, and in particular microblogging data such as tweets. As such, it includes many emoticons, such as *:-)*, and acronyms, such as *lol* and *wtf*. The project is available on GitHub at `https://github.com/cjhutto/vaderSentiment` and the specific lexicon is available inside that project at the following URL: `https://github.com/cjhutto/vaderSentiment/blob/master/vaderSentiment/vader_sentiment_lexicon.txt`.

Vader is also one of the built-in classifiers that comes with the Python Natural Language ToolKit (NLTK) and is therefore found in many sample projects online. When we look inside the `vader_sentiment_lexicon.txt` file, we see that a typical set of lines looks like this:

```
burdens     -1.5   0.5      [-2, -2, -1, -1, -2, -1, -1, -1, -2, -2]
burdensome  -1.8   0.9798    [-1, -1, -3, -2, -1, -2, -2, -1, -4, -1]
bwahaha      0.4   1.0198    [0, 1, 0, 1, 0, 2, -1, -1, 2, 0]
bwahahah     2.5   0.92195  [3, 4, 2, 2, 2, 3, 1, 2, 2, 4]
calm         1.3   0.78102  [1, 1, 0, 1, 2, 3, 2, 1, 1, 1]
calmative    1.1   0.9434    [3, 2, -1, 1, 1, 1, 1, 1, 1, 1]
```

The word appears first, followed by its mean rating or score, the population standard deviation (calculated as `stdevp`), and a bracketed list of the individual ratings of 10 independent scorers. The Vader sentiment documentation explains the scoring:

> *"Features were rated on a scale from "[–4] Extremely Negative" to "[4] Extremely Positive", with allowance for "[0] Neutral (or Neither, N/A)".... We kept every lexical feature that had a non-zero mean rating, and whose standard deviation was less than 2.5 as determined by the aggregate of ten independent raters."*

The result is a list of about 7,500 words, each of which is scored both on polarity, or whether it is a positive or negative word, along with the **sentiment intensity**, or how positive or how negative the word is.

In the next section, we will begin to construct a sentiment analysis application. We will learn how to use the NLTK Python package and the Vader tool to sentiment analyze a set of texts. We will walk through a typical sentiment analysis project, comparing results and various options for improving it.

Sentiment mining application

In this section, we will look at building an application to do sentiment analysis on text using the NLTK tools. There are several different options for how to direct NLTK to do sentiment analysis on text, so our experiments with these various methods will teach us a bit about what is going on inside NLTK and also about how sentiment analysis works.

You might recall that we installed and tested NLTK in *Chapter 1, Expanding Your Data Mining Toolbox*, and we used NLTK for entity matching back in *Chapter 3, Entity Matching*, so if you skipped those chapters, you may need to install or upgrade NLTK now. To do this from within Anaconda, open the **Tools** menu, select **Open a terminal**, and type:

```
conda upgrade nltk
```

This will fetch all the relevant NLTK packages and upgrade your Anaconda installation.

Motivating the project

With this housekeeping task finished, we are ready to start thinking about what kind of sentiment analysis we want to experiment with. Throughout this book, we have been using data from free, libre, and open source software (FLOSS) development teams. Here, we will analyze some of their chat archives and e-mails for sentiment.

One nice thing about FLOSS development teams is that most, if not all, of their work is done in public. That includes posting source code and reporting bugs, but also most project chat and decision-making communication is done publicly as well. The reason is that the discussion and decision making that goes into writing and fixing the software is critical to understanding how the software works, and for getting new team members up to speed quickly. So, traditionally the communication channels in FLOSS development have been transparent, just like the code. This means that e-mail mailing lists are archived and posted publicly, Internet Relay Chat (IRC) discussion channels are archived and the logs made public, and so on. In fact, using Twitter or other so-called *walled garden* social media channels for conducting important discussions has been discouraged in some projects, as it tends to make archiving more difficult.

If we are able to collect and analyze the archived communications from some of these projects, we might be able to answer simple sentiment-oriented questions. Examples of sentiment-oriented questions would include whether the mood or tone of the developer-oriented chats differs from the tone observed in the user-oriented chats, whether some of the team members have a particular positive or negative speech style, or whether certain days, times, or topics elicit more emotional language. Are there any differences in the emotional level of developer and user IRC chat?

Data preparation

Our first step in completing such a project will be to construct two giant lists of sentences, one from a developer chat and one from an associated user chat. For the sake of running a coherent and manageable test, we will collect these chats from the same project, and we will limit ourselves to comparing chats from just one single day, at least for the time being. We will only use chat data from a project with publicly posted archives of the chat logs.

In the Ubuntu project, IRC chat dialogue is archived and available at `http://irclogs.ubuntu.com`. From that site, we chose Monday, April 4, 2016 as our target date. On this day, the `#ubuntu-devel` developers channel shows 516 lines in the archive file, including both 503 dialogue messages and 13 system status messages. For comparison, the channel for general users, known simply as `#ubuntu`, contains 1,717 lines, of which 84 are system messages and 1,633 are dialogue. The following table summarizes the differences between these two channels:

	Developer Channel	General User Channel
URL for text archive	`http://irclogs.ubuntu.com/2016/04/04/%23ubuntu-devel.txt`	`http://irclogs.ubuntu.com/2016/04/04/%23ubuntu.txt`
Lines in file (2016-04-04)	516	1717
Number of system messages	13	84
Number of dialogue messages	503	1633

To begin to analyze the sentiment of these two groups of messages, we first have to do some rudimentary data cleaning. To see why, consider this snippet of a few lines from the `#ubuntu-devel` archive file:

```
[06:27] <dholbach> good morning
[07:18] <mwhudson> yay https://launchpad.net/ubuntu/+source/docker.
io/1.10.3-0ubuntu4
=== seb128_ is now known as seb128
[09:38] <mardy> Mirv: hi! ping ping :-)
[09:52] <Mirv> mardy: pong pong
[09:52] <mardy> Mirv: red alert :-) Do you think we can get this fixed
by 16.04? bug 1564767
```

The line that is preceded with `===` is a system message. These include no real valuable information for this project, and so we will remove these from the final data collection. Next, the timestamps are not relevant for our purposes here, and so these can also be removed. Likewise, the usernames that appear between `<>` indicate the speaker of the line, and so these can also be removed.

One convention on IRC is to direct your comments to a particular user by using their name and a colon, like this line in which the user `Mirv` is addressing another user `mardy` by name:

```
[09:52] <Mirv> mardy: pong pong
```

If we were worried that a person had a username like Happy, or Joy, or Ecstasy, we may give some thought to removing all usernames so as not to unintentionally bias the sentiment analyzer. However, in analyzing this particular set of IRC logs, I do not see enough of these types of names to worry. The vast, vast majority of usernames in the Ubuntu IRC channels are not even words, much less happy or sad words. One user is called *infinity* on the `#ubuntu-devel` channel and another user is called *exalt* on the `#ubuntu` channel. Other than these, the rest of the usernames are not dictionary words at all.

We can quickly and easily clean these files in a simple text editor or programmer's editor such as Text Wrangler. In Text Wrangler, the **Find | Replace** dialogue can be used with a `grep` expression to replace all timestamps and name prefixes. For example, we will want to remove beginnings of lines like this:

```
[09:52] <Mirv>
```

By leaving the **Replace** box empty, matching strings will be replaced with nothing. The `grep` string can be entered into Text Wrangler as shown in Figure 1. This regular expression finds lines that start with the `[` character and removes everything from there to the first space following the `>` character.

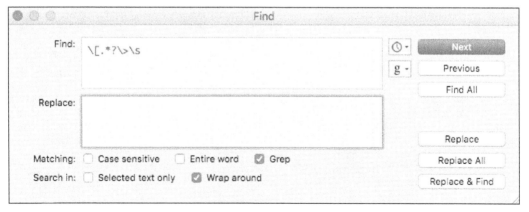

Figure 1. Text Wrangler regular expression to remove line prefixes

Following the removal of the line prefixes, we also need to remove the system messages. This can also be accomplished with the `grep` box in Text Wrangler as shown in Figure 2. This regular expression finds lines that start with three = characters and removes everything to the end of the line, plus any subsequent whitespace character.

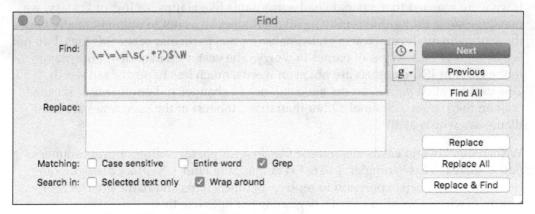

Figure 2. Text Wrangler regular expression to remove system messages

We should also remove the names that are found at the start of some of the lines. These are used to direct a message toward a particular reader, but these names do not really help us here since they are not part of the text that conveys sentiment. Figure 3 shows a regular expression to remove non-whitespace starting at the front of a line, followed by a colon and a space:

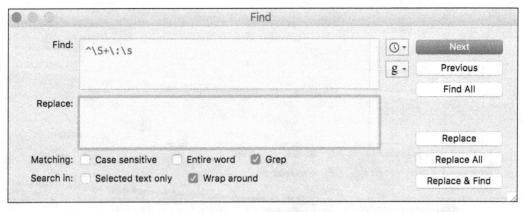

Figure 3. Text Wrangler regular expression to remove names and colon at front of line

We can also accomplish these same cleaning tasks in Anaconda Spyder if you are more comfortable working in that editor. First, read in the log file as a `.txt` file using the **File | Open dialog**, and then use the **Search | Replace Text** dialogue with the same regular expressions, as follows:

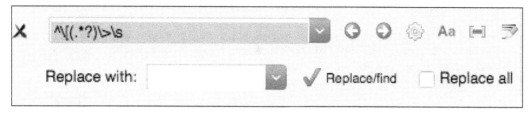

Figure 4. Spyder regular expression dialog box

To ensure that you are working in regular expression mode in the **Replace** dialogue box, make sure that you click the wheel icon to the right of the text box on the top line, shown in Figure 4.

Once you have completed these cleaning steps, you will have two files, consisting of dialogue from two different chat channels on the same day. Just in case you did not want to clean the data yourself, I have uploaded these files to the GitHub site for this book, available at `https://github.com/megansquire/masteringDM/tree/master/ch5/data`.

Data analysis of chat messages

One thing to keep in mind before we get started in earnest with this project is that in sentiment analysis, the text is usually analyzed at the sentence level. However, most chat dialogue is not very well-punctuated, and may contain many partial sentences and many run-on sentences. Also, text tokenizers will split paragraphs into sentences based on the period character ('.'), but chat dialogue is replete with periods used in other ways, and many sentences do not even end in periods at all. This all means that dealing with chat text can be challenging.

For example, consider the following lines from the `#ubuntu-devel` chat:

```
maybe look through http://code.qt.io/cgit/qt/qtbase.git/ log/src/
plugins/platforms/xcb/qxcbwindow.cpp too if there's something to
backport instead of your patch
but are they still interested in Qt 5.5?
no, they'd be interested in 5.6 though if it's affected by the same
bug
and most likely 5.6 branch is the best place to offer a fix too in,
they merge from there to 5.7 and dev.
I'll now test 5.6, but looking at their code, I believe they've
already fixed it
```

```
the problem is, it's not just one patch to backport, but many
ok, to me it'd look like the line of code in question is still
unchanged, just a variable name changed. but maybe it was fixed
elsewhere?
we actually have a lot of XCB fixes already in, in order to try to fix
multi-monitor issues that plagued 5.5 still (and maybe even 5.6 still
too).
but at this point I'd tend to agree that if it's yet another multiple
patches, it would be better to take your two-liner patch instead
yes, that function is still there in Qt 5.6, but
handleConfigureNotifyEvent() doesn't call that method anymore :-)
```

Some of the challenging parts of this text are:

- Only one of the lines is punctuated by a period, and one by a question mark
- Capitalization does not necessarily indicate a start of a sentence
- There is a URL, which contains many periods, and several version numbers, which also contain periods
- There is a function name that uses parentheses, but also a parenthetical expression, and an emoticon smiley that uses a right parenthesis

The best sentiment techniques available now will try to take parts of speech and sentence placement into account, as well as punctuation. For example, the Vader tool discussed earlier gives the following examples in its documentation:

```
VADER is smart, handsome, and funny.
compound: 0.8316, neg: 0.0, neu: 0.254, pos: 0.746,
VADER is smart, handsome, and funny!
compound: 0.8439, neg: 0.0, neu: 0.248, pos: 0.752,
```

Positive, negative, and neutral scores are given as percentages that add up to 1. The first sentence is scored as 74.6% positive and 25.4% neutral, but the second one, with the addition of an exclamation point, is scored slightly higher, at 75.2% positive. The compound score is the normalized sum of the positive and negative scores after punctuation emphasis points have been added and scores amplified accordingly. In the Vader source code, the compound is calculated on these scores as:

```
compound = score/math.sqrt((score*score) + alpha)
```

The alpha value is set to 15 in the Vader code. Alpha is described as a value that *approximates the max expected value.*

So, if we are considering using an off-the-shelf, pre-trained sentiment analyzer such as Vader, we will need to make the executive decision about how to handle our lines with weird punctuation and incomplete sentences. We can treat each line as a separate sentence, but we need to know that the shortcoming of this is that the sentences might not be grammatically correct and still may contain many URLs and strange words, acronyms, usernames, function names, code snippets, and so forth. Remember that most pre-trained sentiment analyzers, such as Vader, have been trained on tweets, or on English sentences such as in movie or product reviews. These pre-trained sentiment analyzers also use part-of-speech information and punctuation to help decide whether a string is positive or negative. Depending on how similar our dialogue lines are to the training dialogue, Vader may interpret our sentences differently from what we are expecting.

There is only one way to find out whether Vader will work with our data. It is time to run some experiments with NLTK and Vader a bit and see what it does with our chat data.

Let's write a short program to read in one of our files of chat text, and for the first few lines, determine the sentiment score (positive, negative, and neutral), as well as what the compound value is for that line. The code for this program is available on the GitHub site for this book at `https://github.com/megansquire/masteringDM/blob/master/ch5/scoreSentences.py`:

```
from nltk.sentiment.vader import SentimentIntensityAnalyzer

with open('ubuntu.txt', encoding='utf-8') as ubuntu:
    ubuntuLines = [line.strip() for line in ubuntu.readlines()]
ubuntu.close()

sid = SentimentIntensityAnalyzer()
finalScore = 0

# just print the first 20 lines of the chat log & scores
for line in ubuntuLines[0:20]:
    print(line)
    ss = sid.polarity_scores(line)
    for k in sorted(ss):
        print(' {0}: {1}\n'.format(k,ss[k]), end='')
    print()
```

From this set of lines, we can see that the majority of sentences are scored as 100% neutral. Some examples of neutral scoring lines that occur near the beginning of the file are:

```
which ubuntu release?
compound: 0.0
neg: 0.0
neu: 1.0
pos: 0.0

Hi! Is there any software on Ubuntu that can replace Itunes for
syncing files on the Ipod?
compound: 0.0
neg: 0.0
neu: 1.0
pos: 0.0
```

Not nearly as many lines are scored on the negative side, for example these:

```
no its not
compound: -0.296
neg: 0.524
neu: 0.476
pos: 0.0

this is so ridiculous
compound: -0.5009
neg: 0.519
neu: 0.481
pos: 0.0
```

There are a few clearly positive comments, which are scored accordingly:

```
that would be awesome, really
compound: 0.6249
neg: 0.0
neu: 0.494
pos: 0.506

different people like different support media
compound: 0.6369
neg: 0.0
neu: 0.435
pos: 0.565

ok thanks
```

```
compound: 0.6249
neg: 0.0
neu: 0.0
pos: 1.0
```

We should remember that the compound score is normalized using only the sum of the positive and negative scores, so the compound score can occasionally be calculated as higher than a positive score, or lower than a negative score. In the case of the sentence different people like different support media, the compound score ended up being .6369 while the positive score was only .5650.

If we wanted to test whether the general #ubuntu chat channel was more negative or positive on that day than the #ubuntu-devel chat channel, we could calculate sentiment for all the lines in each, sum the compound scores, and divide by the number of messages. The code for the following example is available at https://github.com/megansquire/masteringDM/blob/master/ch5/sumCompounds.py:

```python
from nltk.sentiment.vader import SentimentIntensityAnalyzer

with open('ubuntu.txt', encoding='utf-8') as ubuntu:
    ubuntuLines = [line.strip() for line in ubuntu.readlines()]
ubuntu.close()

with open('ubuntu-devel.txt', encoding='utf-8') as ubuntuDevel:
    ubuntuDevelLines = [line.strip() for line in \ ubuntuDevel.
readlines()]
ubuntuDevel.close()

listOfChannels = [ubuntuLines,ubuntuDevelLines]
sid = SentimentIntensityAnalyzer()
for channel in listOfChannels:
    finalScore = 0
    for line in channel:
        ss = sid.polarity_scores(line)
        score = ss['compound']
        finalScore = finalScore + score
        roundedFinalScore = round(finalScore/len(channel),4)
    print("Score", roundedFinalScore)
```

The results print a score for the #ubuntu and #ubuntu-devel channels in turn:

```
Score 0.0774
Score 0.1012
```

We should be cautious about trying to read too much into these results or any results of sentiment analysis, actually since we already determined that our pre-trained examples are from a different domain. At the very least, we should be straightforward about the limitations of this approach. From these results, it appears that the `#ubuntu-devel` channel reached a slightly higher score, or a marginally more positive score, than the general chat channel did.

Data analysis of e-mail messages

Another interesting test for sentiment analysis would be to see how it handles e-mail messages. E-mails tend to be longer and have more text in them than IRC chat messages. Another difference with e-mail messages is that they typically tend to include punctuation, whereas IRC messages may not, and the punctuation in e-mails is used in a more predictable way. Since systems like Vader do use punctuation to infer emphasis, we may find that it performs differently on e-mails than it does on chat.

To test our sentiment analysis technique on e-mails, we decided to look at a single e-mail user who is known for his very emotionally charged speech style: Linus Torvalds, the eponymous leader of the Linux project. Torvalds started Linux as a free (and later, open source) operating system in the early 1990s, and has been its leader since. The development of this project has been conducted entirely on an e-mail mailing list called the **Linux Kernel Mailing List** (**LKML**). In its 20-plus-year history, the LKML has amassed millions of messages from tens of thousands of users and developers. Torvalds himself writes and responds to thousands of messages per year, and his brash writing style in these messages has been the subject of many news articles. The website, Reddit even has an entire section devoted to his rants, called **linusrants**, available at `https://www.reddit.com/r/linusrants`.

Since Torvalds' e-mails are longer than chat text, highly emotive, and usually properly punctuated, it will be an interesting test for the sentiment analyzer to see if it can score these e-mails more easily than the chat messages. Can the sentiment analyzer help us find the most brash, forceful, or strident e-mails that Torvalds wrote? To do this, we will first need a text collection of Torvalds' public e-mails sent to the LKML. Luckily for us, one of my former students, Daniel Schneider, built a very large collection of LKML e-mails which he donated to the FLOSSmole project for research purposes. One particular advantage of this e-mail collection is that all the messages have been cleaned thoroughly to support text mining. Specifically, he removed as many reply texts, signature lines, and source code lines from the e-mails as possible, leaving us with a collection that includes only the words written by the e-mail sender.

For our purposes in this chapter, I have extracted a small selection of e-mails from the collection, namely the e-mails from Linus Torvalds that were sent to the LKML during the month of January 2016. There are 78 e-mails in this subset. The following code will CREATE a simple MySQL table to hold the e-mails, and both the CREATE and INSERT statements are available at https://github.com/megansquire/masteringDM/tree/master/ch5/data/lkmlLT2016-01:

```
CREATE TABLE IF NOT EXISTS `lkml_ch5` (
`url` varchar(200) COLLATE utf8_unicode_ci NOT NULL DEFAULT '',
`sender` varchar(100) COLLATE utf8_unicode_ci NOT NULL,
`datesent` datetime NOT NULL,
`body` text COLLATE utf8_unicode_ci NOT NULL,
`sentiment_score` decimal(6,4) DEFAULT NULL,
`max_pos_score` decimal(6,4) DEFAULT NULL,
`max_neg_score` decimal(6,4) DEFAULT NULL,
PRIMARY KEY (`url`))
 ENGINE=MyISAM DEFAULT CHARSET=utf8 COLLATE=utf8_unicode_ci;
```

The url column is the primary key for this table, and points to the original link to that e-mail message at the Indiana University LKML archive. In this small collection of 78 e-mails, the sender column will only ever include one person, Linus Torvalds. The datesent column holds the original date and time from the e-mail message. The body of the e-mail holds the remaining text after the reply text, source code, and signatures have been removed. We also stripped out carriage returns and newlines from this text, as well as any HTML artifacts that were left in the message from when we downloaded it from the Indiana University web archive.

The remaining three columns are calculated fields whose values will come from our sentiment analysis process. Recall that Vader calculates a percent positive, percent negative, and percent neutral sentiment score for each sentence, as well as a compound, adjusted score for each sentence. Since these e-mails are made up of many sentences, we elected to calculate and store three values at the e-mail level:

- We calculate an average compound score for each e-mail
- We store the highest positive score for any sentence in the e-mail
- We store the highest negative score for any sentence in the e-mail

Storing all of these values ensures that an e-mail with one highly negative sentence can still be detected and evaluated, even if the average compound scores for the e-mail were unremarkable.

The following is the code to sentiment analyze the Torvalds e-mails. We begin by importing our required libraries and connecting to the database.

```
from nltk.sentiment.vader import SentimentIntensityAnalyzer
from nltk import tokenize
import pymysql
import sys

password = sys.argv[1]
db = pymysql.connect(host='localhost',
                     db='test',
                     user='megan',
                     passwd=password,
                     port=3306,
                     charset='utf8mb4')
selectCursor = db.cursor()
updateCursor = db.cursor()
```

We then set up our SELECT and UPDATE queries. We run the SELECT query and fetch all the records:

```
selectEmailQuery = "SELECT url, body FROM lkml_ch5"

updateScoreQuery = "UPDATE lkml_ch5 \
                    SET sentiment_score = %s, \
                    max_pos_score = %s, \
                    max_neg_score = %s \
                    WHERE url = %s"
selectCursor.execute(selectEmailQuery)
emails = selectCursor.fetchall()
```

Next we start a loop through each of the e-mails returned from the SELECT:

```
for email in emails:
    url = email[0]
    body = email[1]

    # variables to hold overall average compound score for message
    finalScore = 0
    roundedFinalScore = 0

    # variables to hold the highest positive score in the message
    # and highest negative score in the message
    maxPosScore = 0
    maxNegScore = 0
```

The next bit of code sets up the Vader sentiment analyzer, tokenizes each e-mail into sentences, and for each sentence, figures out the polarity of that sentence. The code then builds a final score comprised of the compound sentence scores, and keeps track of the highest positive and negative score for any sentence in the e-mail:

```
print("===")
sid = SentimentIntensityAnalyzer()
emailLines = tokenize.sent_tokenize(body)
for line in emailLines:
    ss = sid.polarity_scores(line)
    line = line.replace('\n', ' ').replace('\r', '')
    print(line)
    for k in sorted(ss):
        print(' {0}: {1}\n'.format(k,ss[k]), end='')
    lineCompoundScore = ss['compound']
    finalScore += lineCompoundScore

    if ss['pos'] > maxPosScore:
        maxPosScore = ss['pos']
    elif ss['neg'] > maxNegScore:
        maxNegScore = ss['neg']
```

The final portion of the code just calculates the average compound score by dividing the sum of all the compounds by how many sentences were in the e-mail. We print the scores, update the database, and close our database connection:

```
# calculate avg compound score for the entire message
roundedFinalScore = round(finalScore/len(emailLines),4)
print("***Final Email Score", roundedFinalScore)
print("Most Positive Sentence Score:", maxPosScore)
print("Most Negative Sentence Score:", maxNegScore)

# update table with calculated fields
try:
    updateCursor.execute(updateScoreQuery,(roundedFinalScore,
maxPosScore, maxNegScore, url))
    db.commit()
except:
    db.rollback()
db.close()
```

When this code runs, it updates the database table with the three values we are most interested in: the overall average sentiment compound score for each e-mail, as well as the highest negative score and highest positive score for every e-mail.

From the 78 e-mails and their scores then, how do we determine the most interesting e-mails to look at, from a sentiment point of view? For instance, what if we wanted to find the messages that were the most negative? If we sort by the sentiment score alone, we might miss some messages that have one or two really negative sentences, but on the whole appear to have a mediocre negativity score. Alternatively, if we sort only by the `max_neg_score` column, we will see a lot of messages that have the word `No.` in them, but all the remaining text could be fairly innocuous.

One approach would be to find messages that scored low (negative) on an average compound e-mail score, *and* which also have one or more highly negative sentences. To do this, first we need to create a set of e-mails with the lowest (most negative) sentiment score. Then, we need a set of e-mails which have at least one very negative sentence. The intersection of these two sets represents a group of messages that should be very interesting in their negativity. If we limit our search to the top 20 in both sets, which messages appear in both lists?

Since MySQL does not have the INTERSECT keyword, but does support a UNION ALL with a subquery, we can construct a clunky-but-functional SQL command to return the intersection of the top 20 messages in both sets as follows:

```
SELECT a.url, a.body, a.sentiment_score, a.max_neg_score, COUNT(*)
FROM (
    (SELECT b.url, b.body, b.sentiment_score, b.max_neg_score
    FROM `lkml_stripped_torvalds_2016_01` AS b
    ORDER BY b.sentiment_score ASC
    LIMIT 20)

    UNION ALL

    (SELECT c.url, c.body, c.sentiment_score, c.max_neg_score
    FROM `lkml_stripped_torvalds_2016_01` AS c
    ORDER BY c.max_neg_score DESC
    LIMIT 20)) AS a
GROUP BY 1,2,3,4
HAVING COUNT(*) > 1;
```

This query finds the top 20 in one set and the top 20 from the other set, and shows that there are 10 messages that appear in both sets. Figure 5 shows a screen capture of the results from this query, as displayed in the PhpMyAdmin query tool. For space reasons, I truncated the URL column to only show the rightmost 10 characters:

right(a.url,10)	body	sentiment_score	max_neg_score
00934.html	This seems sad for two reasons: - it adds unnec...	-0.2402	0.4250
01231.html	No. This is much too late for this kind of hackery...	-0.1588	1.0000
02704.html	On Tue, Jan 26, 2016 at 12:10 PM, Paul E. McKenney...	-0.2068	0.7560
02745.html	So I think this is ridiculously ugly. AIO is a h...	-0.0877	0.5880
02857.html	Hmm. Is it really called for to rename all the doc...	-0.2117	0.4540
03596.html	Nope. No can do. I get a build error: driver...	-0.1280	0.5240
03741.html	I suspect it could go either way. You want a small...	-0.1182	0.4870
03964.html	I don't think there are *any* architectural guaran...	-0.1537	0.4440
04404.html	It just doesn't look very legible. Also, how cou...	-0.1867	0.4070
04414.html	Ugh. I guess that makes sense, but it's still very...	-0.0837	1.0000

Figure 5. The 10 records in both the top 20 sentiment_score and the top 20 max_neg_score

When these 10 messages are sorted by the overall sentiment score, the *most negative* message is `934.html`, which has a **sentiment_score** of `-0.2402` and a **max_neg_score** of `0.4250` (or one sentence that scored 42.5% negative). Here is the text of the message:

```
This seems sad for two reasons: - it adds unnecessary overhead on
non-pcid setups (32-bit being an example of that) - on pcid setups,
wouldn't invpcid_flush_single_context() be better? So on the whole I
hate it.Why isn't this something like And yes, that means that we'd
require X86_FEATURE_INVPCID in order to use X86_FEATURE_PCID, but that
seems fine. Or is there some reason you wanted the odd flags version?
If so, that should be documented.
```

The sentence that scored the 42.5% negative was *So on the whole I hate it*. One sentence appears to be incomplete due to removing source code (*Why isn't this something like...*) It is interesting that the most negative sentence in that e-mail only scores a 42.5% and this is still high enough to make the top 20 list. When we look at the second-highest scoring message, sorted by the sentiment score, we see that this one happened to score a perfect 100% for **max_neg_score**. Why? The text of that message is as follows:

```
No. This is much too late for this kind of hackery. That second patch
in particular is both subtle and ugly, and is messing with lockdep.
No way will I take something like this the last fay [sic] before a
release. It's not even a regression, nor did you send me anything at
all for this release. Trying to sneak something in just before 4.4 is
not ok.
```

This one had a **sentiment_score** of -0.1588. The **max_neg_score** of 100% was for the sentence *No*.

At this point we have the ability to analyze the sentiment of various types of text, including short bursts of chat text and longer e-mail messages. We have a good understanding of what the scores mean, how to compare them, and how to figure out what the interesting messages are. So far we have only used the Vader sentiment intensity analyzer that came with NLTK, but if we wanted to continue this experiment with other sentiment tools, I would recommend looking at the NLTK documentation to see what other options are available and how to use them. The documentation page about sentiment is a great place to start: `http://www.nltk.org/api/nltk.sentiment.html`.

Summary

After finishing this chapter, we now have a functional understanding of how sentiment analysis works, and we have compared many different strategies that the mainstream sentiment analysis tools use to accomplish this goal. We paid special attention to the Vader tool which comes as standard with the Python NLTK, since it is well-tested and straightforward to use. To learn how to use its sentiment intensity scoring system, we calculated the sentiment for a few different real-world datasets, both messy chat data and somewhat more structured e-mail data.

In the next chapter, we will continue to hone our skills in text mining, but instead of looking at the emotion conveyed by an entire sentence, we will focus our attention on locating entities within sentences. This task, called named entity recognition, is slightly related to the entity matching task we looked at in *Chapter 3, Entity Matching*, in that in both cases we are working with entities such as people or organizations. However, in our next chapter we add a text mining twist: how can we identify the entities in a text without knowing what we are looking for in advance?

6
Named Entity Recognition in Text

The next text mining tool we are going to add to our toolbox is actually from the domain of information extraction. When we talk about **information extraction**, we typically mean text mining techniques that use natural language processing to pull out key pieces of desired information from a large amount of unstructured text. I like to think of information extraction as being like a gold miner's sifting pan. Using these tools, we extract only the good stuff - the gold nuggets - and let the rest of the dirt fall away. In this chapter, the gold nuggets we will be sifting for are called named entities. Given a semi-structured or unstructured body of text, can we locate and extract all the **named entities**, such as people, places, or organizations, and leave the rest of the text behind?

In this chapter, we will learn:

- What named entities are and why they are useful to search for
- What the different techniques are for finding named entities, and what the benefits are of each
- How to find the named entities in text, including how to differentiate them from other tagged parts of speech
- How to apply these named entity recognition techniques using real data
- How to determine whether our named entity recognition was successful or not

Why look for named entities?

Named Entity Recognition (**NER**) is the act of locating certain people, places, and things in a larger body of text. Finding the specific entities that are being discussed in a text is a critical task for creating better chatbots, for creating better **Question Answering** (**QA**) systems, or for helping speech recognition systems do a better job. When I am preparing dinner in my kitchen, if I ask Amazon Echo to *tell me about meatloaf*, will I get a description of the food, or of Meatloaf the musician? (For those who are wondering, I tried this at home and Echo responded with a description of the musician!)

> Named entity recognition should not be confused with the tasks we performed in *Chapter 3, Entity Matching*, earlier in this book. The two tasks are similar in that they both deal with nouns, called entities, but the comparison ends there. While NER tries to locate the entities in text, EM tries to figure out whether two entities are the same thing.

Named entity recognition can also be used to identify nouns that are particularly interesting or which we want to highlight in some way. For example, on a website we could choose to automatically link to corporate home pages each time a particular company is mentioned. Or, we could automatically add stock ticker symbols for company names we recognize. Other uses for NER are to add links to the Wikipedia pages for famous people, or to provide a Google Maps link when we detect a place name.

Figure 1 shows an example from a *Wall Street Journal* online news article that has highlighted *Apple* and *Tim Cook* as named entities. Since the *WSJ* has their own descriptive pages on its site for both people and corporations, these links provide the user with the additional information they need on these particular entities without requiring them to leave the site to conduct those searches:

Apple Inc. sold twice as many Watches as iPhones in each device's debut year. Yet the smartwatch is dogged by a perception that seems premature given the history of Apple's most popular devices: disappointment.

As the Watch marks its first anniversary on Sunday—two days before Apple's quarterly earnings announcement—the product's fate is critical to the company. It is Apple's first all-new product since the iPad and a test of its ability to innovate under Chief Executive Tim Cook, when sales of iPhones are slowing.

Figure 1. The Wall St. Journal recognizing and providing links for two named entities: Apple and Tim Cook

However, in the *WSJ* example, the task of highlighting those two named entities is very simplistic, and could probably be more accurately achieved with simple pattern matching rather than true NER. The most obvious reason for this is that they could simply just scour each article for mentions of companies or people with pages already created in their system. True NER should attempt to find named entities that we are not already looking for.

The news article also includes the named entities *Watch*, *iPhone*, and *iPad*, and although those are not highlighted in the *WSJ* example, we can easily imagine a different type of website where we would indeed want these words highlighted, such as an affiliate shopping site with product links. Additionally, if we were developing an e-mail-to-calendar application, we would want to identify the word *Sunday* and perhaps also the event called *first anniversary* that appears in the text just before it.

Named entity recognition is definitely driven by the purpose of the application. If the number and type of entities you need to display are very small, you may be able to get away with simple pattern matching where you compare capitalized words to a constrained vocabulary, or list of words, representing the entities in your system. On the other hand, more ambitious NER applications will attempt to extract the named entities without only relying on a preset list of known entities.

Sometimes these pre-constructed lists of words are called gazettes, or gazetteers. Traditionally, a **gazetteer** is a list of places and other facts used to build a map or atlas. In NER, it refers to a constrained vocabulary of proper nouns.

Another challenge for NER is in extracting named entities without necessarily knowing the boundaries of the entity. For example, can multi-word entities exist? Can entities exist inside of other entities? Consider a sentence like:

Pirates of the Caribbean thrilled audiences worldwide.

Without the italicized clue that this is the title of a movie, the sentence is somewhat ambiguous. Is the NER smart enough to know that *Pirates of the Caribbean* is a named entity, or will it assume the word *Pirates* is just a plural noun, capitalized because it is at the start of a sentence? If so, our named entity recognizer might decide that *Caribbean* is a named place entity rather than part of a movie title.

For this reason, extracting named entities requires leveraging codified knowledge of some particular domain. For example, the NER could use the code word audience from the sentence *Pirates of the Caribbean thrilled audiences worldwide* to deduce that this sentence is about a movie. Or, the NER could be given lists of movies as a sort of gazetteer approach. Or, the NER could be trained to know about the particular spelling or capitalization rules of a domain that indicate named entities. The movie title above is italicized, which is a big clue that the words go together. Similarly, in biology, species names are often written in Latin and italicized, for example *Homo sapiens*.

In the technology domain, with products or company names we find frequent use of acronyms, numbers inside words, plays on words, nonsense words, punctuation, and medial capitalization. Medial capitals are where there are capital letters inside the word, sometimes called **InterCaps** or **CamelCase**. Examples of products or business names that use some of these unconventional spellings include OSX, C++, Yahoo!, Eat24, Xbox, Apple][c, and enTourage eDGe. An ambitious NER designed to learn technology product names will need to understand these variations and more.

Thus, it seems clear that developing a named entity recognition system is going to be a little more complicated than simply looking for capitalized nouns. In the next section, we will get more specific about the techniques that we can use to accurately recognize and extract named entities from text.

Techniques for named entity recognition

Before we tackle the strategies for named entity recognition, we should differentiate between some similar terms that we will come across when doing this work. Usually, when English-speakers first begin to think about named entities, they assume named entities are just proper nouns. What is a proper noun? **Proper nouns** are typically capitalized in English, and refer to a specific named person, place, or thing. **Proper names** can include proper nouns as well as noun phrases. Alaska, Barack Obama, January, and The Grateful Dead are all proper names. Are all proper nouns and names capitalized? Not necessarily, as we saw with iPhone and iPad, and also eBay, and the author bell hooks. Are all capitalized nouns proper? No. For example, we write the *Englishman came around for tea*, where Englishman is capitalized, yet Englishman is a common noun in English.

NER is considerably more interesting than just recognizing nouns, or proper nouns. In a linguistic sense, named entities are sometimes defined more strictly to only include those for which there must be no ambiguity about what noun is being discussed. For example, *Barack Obama* is an unambiguous name for a specific person, so we call this name a **rigid designator**, and it would qualify as a named entity (and a proper name). On the other hand, the phrase *The President of the United States* is called a **flaccid designator** because, even though it is a proper name and refers to an actual person – who happens to be named Barack Obama at the moment – the actual physical entity that this name refers to will change. Other examples of rigid and flaccid designators would be the difference between *Wednesday* and *tomorrow*, or *Mastering Data Mining with Python* and *the best book ever written*. Some proper nouns are rigid designators and others are not, and some named entities are proper nouns and some are not.

Even though a flaccid designator may be capitalized or may refer to the same thing as a rigid designator in popular usage, the job of NER is to filter out the true named entities from the impostors. So the presence of capital letters on a word that has been also identified as a noun can be a good clue that the thing is a named entity. However, that logic would dictate that *The President of the United States* is necessarily a named entity, yet a strict definition of named entities as rigid designators would suggest that it should not be a named entity. Consider also the following sentences:

- I am starting my new project on Monday.

  Here, *Monday* is a proper noun and a rigid designator, since it refers to one particular Monday in time.

- Monday is the best day to start any new project.

  In this sentence, *Monday* is also a proper noun, but it is being used generically, so it is a flaccid designator.

- The new Watch by Apple is very expensive, but it plays my iTunes.

  Here, the brand name *Watch* is a named entity, as is *Apple* and *iTunes*. All three are also proper nouns, but only the first two follow traditional capitalization rules.

- Watch me buy this EDM song on the iTunes store.

  In this example, *Watch* is the first word of the sentence, so it is capitalized, but not a named entity. It is being used as a verb rather than a noun. *EDM* is an acronym for Electronic Dance Music, so it is capitalized.

From all these examples, we can see that while imperfect, both capitalization and parts of speech are pretty good indicators of which word or phrases could be considered named entities in a text. Capitalization is easy enough to spot by just observing the case of the characters in a word. Even medial caps can be included if we want to recognize words such as *iPhone* and *iTunes*. However, as we have shown, capitalization alone is not sufficient to indicate whether a word or phrase is a named entity or not. The next critical step will be to find nouns and noun phrases, which are great indicators of named entities.

Tagging parts of speech

To find the **Part of Speech (POS)** for each word in a sentence, we can use a type of software called a POS tagger. A POS tagger first splits texts into sentences, then assigns each word, or token, in the sentence a part of speech. The combination of a token and its part of speech is called a tuple. A tuple looks like this:

```
('dog', NN)
```

Sometimes the assigned part of speech is easy to guess, such as NN for noun, but other times the POS tagger will recognize the word as a more exotic part of speech; for example, the NLTK tagger finds the word *dogs* is a plural noun and *dog's* is a possessive noun:

```
('dogs', NNP)
("dog's", NN$)
```

The second word, *dog's*, is surrounded by double quotes since it has a single quotation mark inside of itself.

How does the POS tagger know the part of speech for every word, especially considering that some words will change their part of speech depending on how the word is used in a sentence? To answer this question, we must first understand the concept of a corpus. A **corpus** is a collection of texts, and an **annotated corpus** is one that has been tagged, for example with the correct POS for each word. Once we have a POS tagged corpus that we are confident is correct, we can use that to determine the parts of speech for all the tokens in new documents that we have not yet seen.

There are many well-known corpora that are used over and over again to tag new documents. One of the most famous is called the **Brown Corpus**, after Brown University. This corpus was created in 1961. It consists of 500 documents, each approximately 2000 words, for a total of about a million tagged tokens. The documents are all from native speakers of American English. The original documentation for this corpus can be found at http://www.hit.uib.no/icame/brown/bcm.html.

Today, the Brown Corpus is just one of many, many corpora available to be used as a model by a POS tagger. Some, like Brown, consist of a variety of text types, such as fiction, news articles, and religious books. Other corpora focus on specific text types, such as news. Still other corpora are tagged for different languages or different dialects, or have been updated with newer words that did not exist in 1961 when the Brown Corpus was created.

As we will see in our project later in the chapter, an off-the-shelf POS tagger, such as the one that comes with NLTK, can be directed to use different corpora. The default corpus that is used by NLTK is called the Penn Treebank tagger. The Penn Treebank list of abbreviations for parts of speech is quite extensive, and can be found at `https://www.ling.upenn.edu/courses/Fall_2003/ling001/penn_treebank_pos.html`.

For example, the different noun abbreviations in Penn are:

- **NN**: Noun, singular or mass (I see a *dog*.)
- **NNS**: Noun, plural (I see many *dogs*.)
- **NNP**: Proper noun, singular (My dog is named *Fido*.)
- **NNPS**: Proper noun, plural (There are many *Fidos* in the park.)

There are many other abbreviations for parts of speech but since we are focused on named entity recognition in this chapter, we will mostly be working with nouns.

Classes of named entities

If NER were as simple as just identifying proper nouns, it would not be nearly as much fun. In addition to POS tagging, we can also use a tagger to attempt to deduce what kind of named entity we have found. Common classes for the named entities include: PERSON, ORGANIZATION, GPE (for geopolitical entity, or place), and so on. It is true that these are very large, general classes for the nouns, but they still do serve as one additional layer of granularity. With these classes, Fido may be classified as a canine PERSON, *Pirates of the Caribbean* should be classified as an ORGANIZATION, and the partial match *Caribbean* would likely be classified as a place or GPE.

Now that we know more about the NER goals of identifying each named entity and specifying its class, it is time to start looking at techniques that can help us achieve these goals with real data.

Building and evaluating NER systems

Based on our discussion so far in this chapter, we know that building an NER system will start with the following steps:

1. Separate our document into sentences.
2. Separate our sentences into tokens.
3. Tag each token with a part of speech.
4. Identify named entities from this tagged token set.
5. Identify the class of each named entity.

To help us correctly find tokens at step 2, separate the real named entities from the impostors at step 4, and to ensure that the entities are placed into the correct class at step 5, it is common to leverage a machine learning approach, similar to what NLTK and its sentiment mining functions did for us in *Chapter 5, Sentiment Analysis in Text*. Relying on a large set of pre-classified examples will help us work out some of the more complicated issues we introduced above for recognizing named entities, for example, choosing the correct boundary in multi-word noun phrases, or recognizing novel approaches to capitalization, or knowing what kind of named entity it is.

But even with a flexible machine learning approach, the vagaries and oddities of written language remind us to be careful; some legitimate named entities may slip through the cracks, while other tokens may be called named entities when they really are not. With so many exceptions to the *rules* for how to find named entities, the risk of generating false positives or false negatives is high. Therefore, just as with earlier chapters, we will need an evaluation plan for whatever machine learning-based NER system we end up choosing.

NER and partial matches

Because of the potential for NER systems to over- or under-classify words as named entities, we will need to use the kind of false positive and false negative calculations that we first saw in *Chapter 3, Entity Matching*. However, the calculations will be slightly different with NER due to partial matches. **Partial matches** happen when our NER system catches, for example, *Caribbean* but not *Pirates of the Caribbean*. These are sometimes called boundary errors, since the NER system found some of the token, but messed up its boundaries by being too short or too long. An NER system may also misidentify the entity into the wrong class. For example, it may recognize *Fido* but call it a GPE rather than a PERSON.

With these kinds of partial matches, we have three choices for how to handle them:

- Strict Scoring: We can score the partial match as both a false positive (because *Caribbean* is not a correct guess) and a false negative (because *Pirates of the Caribbean* was also missing).

- Lenient Scoring: We can score the partial match as a true positive. No penalties are given for false negatives or false positives, and we just assume that *Caribbean* is good enough.

- Partial Scoring: We can come up with rules that give some credit for matches that are partially correct, for example, finding *Caribbean* instead of *Pirates of the Caribbean*.

Strict and lenient scoring are straightforward to understand, but partial credit scoring needs a bit more explanation. How does it work?

Handling partial matches

One system for handling partial matches came out of the **Message Understanding Conference** (**MUC**) series. This seven-conference series was held by the US Government agency DARPA in the late 1980s and 1990s to encourage researchers to devise new techniques for information extraction. One of the outcomes of the sixth iteration of this conference was to begin to piece together a scoring system for named entities that would handle partial matches on either the phrase itself or the assigned class. With a comprehensive rule scoring system, it is possible to evaluate proposed NER matchers to determine whether they are as good as human NER systems. So how does MUC scoring work?

The MUC scoring system works by computing two scores: one for finding the correct entity terms, and another score for classifying them correctly into their category of PERSON, GPE, and so on. The class is scored as correct, as long as some part of the entity term was also found. These two scores are then fed into a precision and recall calculation, similar to what we saw earlier in *Chapter 3, Entity Matching*.

To show how this works, the table below shows the expected and guessed results from a sample NER system. PERSON, ORGANIZATION, and GPE have been abbreviated as PER, ORG, and GPE, respectively:

Item	Expected named entity	Guessed named entity	Boundaries correct?	Class correct?
1	Pirates of the Caribbean / ORG	Caribbean / GPE	No	No
2	Fido / PER	Fido / GPE	Yes	No
3	Microsoft Windows / ORG	Microsoft / ORG	No	Yes
4	Captain America / PER	Captain America/ PER	Yes	Yes
5	Great Bend / GPE	-	-	-
6	-	Marvel / ORG	No	No
7	Shaker Heights / GPE	Shaker Heights / GPE	Yes	Yes

Note that on line 3, the correct class was guessed even though only the text boundary was only partially correct. On line 5, there was an expected named entity that was skipped by the system. On line 6, the system found an entity where none was expected.

To figure out the precision and recall, we keep track of the following:

- **CORRECT**: Number of correct guesses for both the boundaries and the class
- **GUESSED**: Number of actual answers for both boundaries and class
- **POSSIBLE**: Number of possible answers for both boundaries and class

We can use the example above to calculate each of these measures:

- **CORRECT**: The NER system guessed three correct boundaries and three correct classes, so CORRECT = 6.
- **GUESSED**: The NER system guessed a total of six boundaries (it missed one on line 5), and a total of six classes (again, missing the one on line 5), so GUESSED = 12.
- **POSSIBLE**: The number of possible guesses for text boundaries should be six (lines 1-5, and 7), and the number of possible class guesses is also six, so POSSIBLE = 12.

To calculate the MUC precision and recall for a NER system we apply these measures as follows:

```
MUC_Precision = CORRECT / GUESSED
              = 6/12
              = 50%
MUC_Recall = CORRECT / POSSIBLE
           = 6/12
           = 50%
```

We can also calculate the F1-measure as the harmonic mean of precision and recall as follows:

```
F1 = 2*((MUC_Precision * MUC_Recall) / (MUC_Precision + MUC_Recall))
   = 2*(.5 * .5) / (.5 + .5))
   = 50%
```

If we were operating under a strict scoring protocol, there are only two named entities that were guessed totally correctly in that system example: the ones on lines 4 and 7. However, there were six guesses by the NER system, and six total possible guesses. This yields:

```
Strict_Precision = CORRECT / GUESSED = 2/6 (30%)
Srict_Recall = CORRECT / POSSIBLE = 2/6 (30%)
```

Whether a partial or strict scoring protocol is used depends on the objectives of the work. How important are precise boundaries and classes in that domain? Your answer may vary depending on what you are working on. For example, if you are more interested in counting the named entities that appear in a text, it may be sufficient just to account for partial matches.

In the next section, we will devise a named entity recognition system and calculate the associated accuracy scores for a project using real data.

Named entity recognition project

In this set of small projects, we will try our NER techniques on a variety of different types of text that we have seen already in prior chapters, as well as some new text. For variety, will look for named entities in e-mail texts, board meeting minutes, IRC chat dialogue, and human-created summaries of IRC chat dialogue. With these different types of data sources, we will be able to see how writing style and content both affect the accuracy of the NER system.

A simple NER tool

Our first step is to write a simple named entity recognition program that will allow us to find and extract named entities from a text sample. We will take this program and point it at several different text samples in turn. The code and text files for this project are all available on the GitHub site for this book, at https://github.com/megansquire/masteringDM/tree/master/ch6.

The code we will write is a short Python program that uses the same NLTK library we introduced in *Chapter 3*, *Entity Matching*, and *Chapter 5*, *Sentiment Analysis in Text*. We will also import a pretty printer library so that the output of this program will be easier to understand:

```
import nltk
import pprint
```

Next we will set up five different files, and just comment out the ones we are not working with at the moment. After we describe the rest of the code, we will describe each of these files in turn, where they came from, and what the NER results were:

```
# sample files that we use in this chapter
filename = 'apacheMeetingMinutes.txt'
#filename = 'djangoIRCchat.txt'
#filename = 'gnueIRCsummary.txt'
#filename = 'lkmlEmails.txt'
#filename = 'lkmlEmailsReduced.txt'
```

The next section of code describes our simple NER routine. First, we open each file and read it into the `text` object:

```
with open(filename, 'r', encoding='utf8') as sampleFile:
    text=sampleFile.read()
```

Next, we load a tokenizer that will read through each line in the text and look for sentences. It is important to look at sentences instead of just looking at lines because, depending on the type of text we are working with, there could be multiple sentences per line. For example, most IRC chat will be one sentence per line, but most e-mail will have multiple sentences per line:

```
en = {}
try:
    sent_detector = nltk.data.load('tokenizers/punkt/english.pickle')
    sentences = sent_detector.tokenize(text.strip())
```

For each sentence we find, we are going to figure out the part of speech for every word in the sentence. The ne_chunk() function takes the collection of words and tags, and finds the most likely candidates for named entities, storing these in the variable chunked:

```
for sentence in sentences:
    tokenized = nltk.word_tokenize(sentence)
    tagged = nltk.pos_tag(tokenized)
    chunked = nltk.ne_chunk(tagged)
```

Next we will examine each item in chunked and build a dictionary entry for it and its label. Recall from our earlier discussion that a label, or class, can be one of ORGANIZATION, PERSON, GPE for location, and so on:

```
for tree in chunked:
    if hasattr(tree, 'label'):
        ne = ' '.join(c[0] for c in tree.leaves())
        en[ne] = [tree.label(), ' '.join(c[1] for c in tree.
leaves())]
except Exception as e:
    print(str(e))

pp = pprint.PrettyPrinter(indent=4)
pp.pprint(en)
```

Finally, we print the dictionary of named entities and their classes. In the next section, we describe what happens when we run this code against each of the different files shown in the beginning of the program. We also describe where we got the data for these files, and what kind of text they include.

Apache Board meeting minutes

The first text source we will use is taken from the publicly available collection of meeting minutes from the Board of Directors for the Apache project. Since 2010 the Apache Board of Directors has posted the minutes from its meetings on its website, available here: http://www.apache.org/foundation/board/calendar.html.

The text file I created for this project is taken from the February 17, 2016 minutes, specifically the President's section B. The original link for this February minutes file is https://www.apache.org/foundation/records/minutes/2016/board_minutes_2016_02_17.txt.

The final file is 33 lines long. A sample of the file is as follows:

```
I believe our Membership felt fully involved and as a result is almost
unanimous in their approval of the new design.
Well done Sally (and thanks to LucidWorks and HotWax Systems for
donating creative services).
Sally has confirmed a return of her media/analyst trainings at
ApacheCon.
```

Our NER program will be looking for words such as LucidWorks, HotWax Systems, Sally, and ApacheCon.

When we run the program against this Apache meeting minutes file, we get the results, which are as follows:

```
{'ApacheCon': ['ORGANIZATION', 'NNP'],
 'Appveyor CI': ['PERSON', 'NNP NNP'],
 'CFP': ['ORGANIZATION', 'NNP'],
 'David': ['PERSON', 'NNP'],
 'GitHub': ['ORGANIZATION', 'NNP'],
 'HotWax Systems': ['ORGANIZATION', 'NNP NNP'],
 'Huge': ['GPE', 'JJ'],
 'Infra': ['ORGANIZATION', 'NNP'],
 'LucidWorks': ['ORGANIZATION', 'NNP'],
 'Mark Thomas': ['PERSON', 'NNP NNP'],
 'Melissa': ['GPE', 'NNP'],
 'New': ['GPE', 'NNP'],
 'Remediation': ['GPE', 'NN'],
 'Sally': ['PERSON', 'NNP'],
 'TAC': ['ORGANIZATION', 'NNP'],
 'TLPs': ['ORGANIZATION', 'NNP'],
 'VP Infra': ['ORGANIZATION', 'NNP NNP'],
 'Virtual': ['PERSON', 'NNP'],
 'iTunes': ['ORGANIZATION', 'NNS']}
```

The program correctly found most items, but incorrectly found the words CFP, Huge, New, and Remediation. These words were capitalized because they were the first word in the sentence, and this undoubtedly led to them being accidentally declared as named entities by NLTK when they were actually not. The word Virtual may seem at first like it is a mistake, but in reading the text it turns out that this is the name of a company. Unfortunately, the NER tool declared it to be a PERSON. Additionally, Melissa should have been a PERSON, not GPE, and Appveyor CI should have been labeled ORGANIZATION rather than PERSON.

We did not find any false negatives with this text sample. Using the formulas from the last section, we can calculate the accuracy of our program as follows:

- **CORRECT**: The NER system guessed 15 correct boundaries and 12 correct classes, so CORRECT = 27

- **GUESSED**: The NER system guessed a total of 19 boundaries, and a total of 19 classes, so GUESSED = 38

- **POSSIBLE**: The number of possible guesses for text boundaries should be 15, and the number of possible class guesses is also 15, so POSSIBLE = 30

To calculate the MUC precision, recall, and F1 harmonic mean for our NER system, we apply these measures to our data like this:

```
MUC_Precision = CORRECT / GUESSED
    = 27/38
    = 71%
MUC_Recall = CORRECT / POSSIBLE
    = 27/30
    = 90%
F1 = 2*((MUC_Precision * MUC_Recall) / (MUC_Precision + MUC_Recall))
    = 2*(.71 * .90) / (.71 + .90))
    = 79%
```

In this case, the NER program seemed to err on the side of false positives. It made several incorrect guesses, but did not miss any named entities in the text. Next we will see how the program does with highly unstructured chat text.

Django IRC chat

The Django project has an IRC channel where the community can discuss various aspects of the project including how it works, bug fixing, and so on. The IRC logs are provided for anyone to read at `http://django-irc-logs.com`. From this collection of log files, we chose a random date, March 23, 2014, and extracted all of the IRC log messages sent on that date. We did not collect the system messages, such as users logging in or logging out. There are 677 lines of text in this sample.

One thing we notice right away about IRC chat is because of the casual nature of this communication format, most lines of text are not written with proper capitalization or punctuation. To clean the data so that it would be able to be used by the sentence tokenizer, we added a period at the end of each line to simulate a sentence structure, and we removed URLs. A few sample lines from the data set look like this:

```
is it not possible though?.
it's possible, if you write a pile of JS to do it.
to dah pls no JS.
i just want native django queryset filter things.
Maybe he wouldn't have to. Maybe you could just use AdminActions.
```

We can see that any line that already ended in a question mark now has an additional period at the end, but this will not affect our NER program. We see various differences in capitalization, for example the person typing last does use it, but the rest of the lines are more loosely capitalized.

The NER program identified 105 named entities, shown below. Examples of false positives would be generic, capitalized nouns such as the Boolean variable value False, the generic acronym API for application programming interface, and the generic acronym CA for certificate authority. True positives include FTP for the File Transfer Protocol program and South as the name of a system.

Here, the NER program is even more generous than it was with the Apache meeting minutes, with 52 false positives. The remaining 53 entities we will declare as correct, and we will give them 2 points each: 1 point for a correct boundary and 1 point for a correct class. For entities that have correct boundaries but an incorrect class, we assign 1 point. For example, marking Allauth as a PERSON rather than ORGANIZATION yields 1 point. Entities that are incorrect in boundary are given 0 points. Only the first few entries are shown, for space reasons:

```
{0   'API': ['ORGANIZATION', 'NNP'],
 0   'APIs': ['ORGANIZATION', 'NNP'],
 0   'Admin': ['PERSON', 'NNP'],
 2   'AdminActions': ['ORGANIZATION', 'NNS'],
 0   'Ahh': ['GPE', 'NNP'],
 2   'Aldryn': ['PERSON', 'NNP'],
 2   'Aleksander': ['PERSON', 'NN'],
 1   'Allauth': ['PERSON', 'NNP'],
 0   'Anyone': ['GPE', 'NN'],
 2   'Australian': ['GPE', 'JJ'],
 ...}
```

To identify false negatives, we read through the chat log, and constructed the following list of 21 named entities that should have been caught but were not. Most of these are usernames, which are rarely capitalized. Non-username false negatives include *html5* and *softlayer*, which also should have been capitalized but were not:

```
m1chael
html5
softlayer
tuxskar
comcast
gunicorn
tjsimmons
nginx
zlio
theslowl
frog3r
HowardwLo
dodobas
spoutnik16
moldy
carlfk
benwilber
erik`
apollo13
frege
dpaste
```

We can apply the same formulas:

- **CORRECT**: The NER system guessed 53 correct boundary and class pairs and 32 partially correct classes, so CORRECT = 85

- **GUESSED**: The NER system guessed a total of 105 boundaries, and a total of 105 classes, so GUESSED = 210

- **POSSIBLE**: The number of possible guesses for text boundaries should be 74 (53 found entities plus 21 false negatives), and the number of possible class guesses would also be 74, so POSSIBLE = 148

To calculate the MUC precision, recall, and F1 harmonic mean for our NER system, we apply these measures as follows:

```
MUC_Precision = CORRECT / GUESSED
    = 85/210
    = 40%
MUC_Recall = CORRECT / POSSIBLE
    = 85/148
    = 57%
F1 = 2*((MUC_Precision * MUC_Recall) / (MUC_Precision + MUC_Recall))
    = 2*(.40 * .57) / (.40 + .57))
    = 47%
```

We can see from these dismal numbers that the accuracy of the NER program is vastly reduced in an IRC chat context, when compared to the board meeting minutes context. To improve accuracy, we will need to address both false positives and false negatives.

The main issue with false negatives seems to be missing the names of the chat participants, so one way to improve those recall numbers would be to provide a better way of detecting usernames. We could find a list of chatters on the system and capitalize their names to make it more likely that the NER tool would find them. Another approach would be to teach the system what a common username protocol looks like in IRC. For example, on IRC it is common to begin a chat line by directing it towards the person you are talking to, like this:

```
tjsimmons: don't forget that people typically use nginx to serve /
static.
```

Here the person who is being addressed is called *tjsimmons*. The system could be taught that any single word at the beginning of a line followed by a colon character is probably a user's name and should be included as a named entity.

False positives seem to mostly stem from over-sensitivity to capitalized generic words such as acronyms, function names, and the like. This is a harder problem to solve, but one approach could be to provide a domain-specific context for the NER to work from. For instance, we could provide a pre-constructed vocabulary of known words to ignore or we could train the system to recognize common features of uninteresting words from this domain. An example of the latter would be the rule *if any capitalized word is followed by (), it is a function, so ignore it*. Depending on the data you have, you may need to add additional layers to your NER system so that it can become more accurate.

GnuIRC summaries

As a contrast to the Django IRC chat, which was very casual and very loosely punctuated and capitalized, we will also analyze also a formal summary of an IRC chat, written in clear prose by a human being. The GNUe project IRC channel had a human summary written each week for several years in the early 2000s. Two lines of the sample of the summary for the GNUe project are shown here:

```
Michael Dean (mdean) said that a new release (feature wise) is
probably about 3 or 4 weeks away, since the database upgrade was going
to be huge. As of this writing, he may make an interim bug fix/small
feature release to get some of the email support down.
Daniel Baumann (chillywilly) pointed out that this abstraction thingy
GComm could be confused with the GNU Comm project. But as far as Jason
Cater (jcater) was concerned, GComm is our internal package name... to
the external world, it's GNUe Common, but said that was a good point.
```

By 2015, the GNUe IRC summaries were no longer available online, but I rebuilt the data set using XML files from Archive.org, and posted it on my FLOSSmole site at the following URL: `http://flossdata.syr.edu/data/irc/GNUe/`.

The data set for this project is called `gnueIRCsummary.txt` and it is available on the GitHub site for this chapter at `https://github.com/megansquire/masteringDM/tree/master/ch6`.

This file consists of the first 10 paragraphs of the 23-27 October 2001 GNUe summary, which is a sample of about 55 lines of text.

When we run the NER program against this data set, we see many cases of partial boundaries. This data set will be a great way to test our partial MUC-style scoring protocol. The system accurately caught *Andrew Mitchell*, but seemed to split *Jeff Bailey* into two separate words. How do we score these? The system scored *Bailey* incorrectly as an ORGANIZATION but *Jeff* correctly as a PERSON, we need to score one correct and one incorrect. Here, next to each line, I have added numbers to indicate whether the item was given 0, 1, or 2 points:

- 2 points means that both the boundaries and the class are correct

- 1 point means that the class was correct but the boundary was only partial

- An incorrect boundary and incorrect class is worth 0 points

Note that no partial points were given if that entity was already found in full. So there are no points given for *Jason* when *Jason Cater* was already found. The exception to this rule is that sometimes the first name is mentioned in the text without the last name. This is the case with *Derek* and *Derek Neighbors*, both of which are used in the text. Therefore, we can score both *Derek* and *Derek Neighbors* as a 2. Only the first five rows of this result set are shown, for space reasons:

```
{2    'Andrew Mitchell': ['PERSON', 'NNP NNP'],
0     'Bailey': ['ORGANIZATION', 'NNP'],
0     'Baumann': ['ORGANIZATION', 'NNP'],
1     'Bayonne': ['PERSON', 'NNP'],
1     'Cater': ['PERSON', 'NNP'],
...}
```

False negatives for this data set include:

```
pyro
pygmy
windows
orbit
omniORB
```

It is questionable whether the missing usernames should also be considered false negatives. For instance, in this data set, the first instance of a first and last name combination is followed by a username, as in *Derek Neighbors (dneighbo)*. In the future, we may wish to train this system to find these usernames in addition to the full names. In this example, however, we elect to ignore the usernames and not penalize the system for not finding them, since it did attempt to find the full names, and those represent the same entity as the usernames.

We can apply the same formulas:

- **CORRECT**: The NER system earned a total of 41 boundaries and location points
- **GUESSED**: The NER system guessed a total of 33 boundaries, and a total of 33 classes, so GUESSED = 66
- **POSSIBLE**: The number of possible guesses for text boundaries should be 21 (all the 2 point answers plus the five false negatives), and the number of possible class guesses is also 21, so POSSIBLE = 42

To calculate the MUC precision, recall, and F1 harmonic mean for our NER system, we apply these measures as follows:

```
MUC_Precision = CORRECT / GUESSED
    = 41/66
    = 62%
MUC_Recall = CORRECT / POSSIBLE
    = 41/42
    = 98%
F1 = 2*((MUC_Precision * MUC_Recall) / (MUC_Precision + MUC_Recall))
    = 2*(.62 * .98) / (.62 + .98))
    = 76%
```

Here we see that the inclusion of partial scores for boundaries almost entirely makes up for the five false positives. If we had scored these strictly, with no partial matches allowed, there would be only 16 totally correct guesses, so the numbers would look like this:

```
MUC_Precision = CORRECT / GUESSED
    = 32/66
    = 48%
MUC_Recall = CORRECT / POSSIBLE
    = 32/42
    = 76%
F1 = 2*((MUC_Precision * MUC_Recall) / (MUC_Precision + MUC_Recall))
    = 2*(.48 * .76) / (.48 + .76))
    = 59%
```

This example shows that whether we choose a loose or strict scoring protocol will affect the presumed accuracy of our NER system. When you are presented with NER accuracy results from someone else, it is important to ask about the scoring protocol that they used.

Next we will experiment with some e-mails. These will be similar to the proper English of the GNUe IRC summaries and the Apache Board meeting minutes, but will have the same high technical content as the Django IRC chats.

LKML e-mails

In *Chapter 5, Sentiment Analysis in Text*, we used a tiny sample of the e-mail messages sent to the Linux Kernel Mailing List. Here we start with the same 77 e-mails sent by Linus Torvalds to the LKML, but for this project, I made two changes to that data set. First, I removed a few portions of a few of the lines that had boilerplate text, such as `On Fri, Jan 8, 2016 at 4:13 PM Linus Torvalds wrote:`, since these lines have nothing to do with the concepts in the text, and I did not want to risk the NER program accidentally finding words such as *On*, *Fri*, or *Jan* in the text. Second, in order to reduce the result set of named entities to a more manageable size, I decided to also remove three of the e-mails. These three e-mails were summaries of patches that had been added into the kernel that week, so each message included dozens of names in them.

> On the GitHub site for this book, you will find both files, `lkmlEmails.txt` and `lkmlEmailsReduced.txt`. The second of these is the one we will use for the remainder of this chapter, although you should feel free to test with the first file too if you like. Experimenting with the first file will produce many, many more named entities than the second one.

Running our NER program against the `lkmlEmailsReduced.txt` file yields the following named entities . Once again, I have scored each as either a 0, 1, or 2 following the example in the previous sections. Again, only the first five lines are shown for space reasons:

```
{2  'AIO': ['ORGANIZATION', 'NNP'],
 0   'Actually': ['PERSON', 'NNP'],
 1   'Al': ['GPE', 'NNP'],
 1   'Alpha': ['GPE', 'NNP'],
 2   'Andrew': ['GPE', 'NNP'],
...}
```

Once again, the NER program does find a lot of first names; however, here the last names are rarely used. (The case with the `lkmlEmails.txt` file is different. The inclusion of those three extra e-mails does mean a lot more duplicate first names.) Our program did seem to miss three named entities (perhaps more if we decided that function names or libraries were important to catch as well):

```
valgrind
mmap
github
```

To calculate precision and recall, we need to figure out the following:

- **CORRECT**: The NER system earned a total of 72 boundaries and location points

- **GUESSED**: The NER system guessed a total of 72 boundaries, and a total of 72 classes, so GUESSED =144

- **POSSIBLE**: The number of possible guesses for text boundaries should be 42 (all 39 of the correct and partially correct answers plus the 3 false negatives), and the number of possible class guesses is also 42, so POSSIBLE = 84

To calculate the MUC precision, recall, and harmonic mean F1 for this NER system, we fit our data into the formulas as follows:

```
MUC_Precision = CORRECT / GUESSED
    = 72/144
    = 50%
MUC_Recall = CORRECT / POSSIBLE
    = 72/84
    = 86%
F1 = 2*((MUC_Precision * MUC_Recall) / (MUC_Precision + MUC_Recall))
    = 2*(.5 * .86) / (.5 + .86))
    = 63%
```

Here the low number of false negatives drives up the recall rates, but precision is still fairly low due to a lot of false positives.

Having four very different types of text samples allows us to compare the strengths and weaknesses of this simple NER program against text with different characteristics. False negatives seem to result from words missing capitalization, and false positives seem to result from over-sensitivity to capitalized words at the beginning of sentences, acronyms, and boundary issues with multi-word phrases.

Summary

In this chapter, we learned about the task of **Named Entity Recognition** (**NER**) and how that works in practice. We reviewed the characteristics of a named entity, and compared many strategies for finding named entities in text and classifying found entities into their correct type. We implemented a simple NER program using NLTK and used it to detect named entities in four different types of technical communication: chat, chat summaries, e-mails, and meeting minutes. We calculated the accuracy of our NER program using precision, recall, and the F1-measure against each of these text samples, and learned how the characteristics of the text sample will affect the accuracy of the program.

One of the outcomes of this chapter was to demonstrate that text that is written in plain language with fewer technical terms will be easier to mine for named entities than very technical language with a lot of code snippets, function names, acronyms, and the like. We noticed that we got the best results from the Apache board meeting minutes and the GNUe IRC chat summaries, both of which were written in complete English sentences and had relatively little technical language compared to the IRC chat and e-mail samples.

Next, we will build on the ideas introduced with the GNUe chat summaries. Those chat summaries were written by a person, but is it possible to write a program that can summarize text? How would this program work, and how would we know if it had summarized the text correctly? Would a computer program possibly do as good a job as a human at summarizing text? In the next chapter, we will explore this idea of text summarization.

7
Automatic Text Summarization

In an era of information overload, the objective of **text summarization** is to write a program that can reduce the size of a text, while preserving the main points of its meaning. The task is somewhat similar to the way an architect might create a scale model of a building. The scale model gives the viewer a sense of the important parts about the structure, but does so with a smaller size footprint, fewer details, and without the same expense in time or materials.

Consider Reddit, a news-oriented social media site, with its thousands of news articles posted daily by users. Is it possible to generate a short summary of a news article that preserves the key facts and general meaning of the original story? A few Reddit users created summary bots to do exactly this. These so-called TLDR bots (too long; didn't read) post summaries of user-submitted news stories, usually including a link to the original story and statistics to show by what percentage they reduced the text. One of these bots is named autotldr, which has its own Reddit user page at `https://www.reddit.com/user/autotldr/`. Created in 2011, autotldr follows links to news stories and summarizes them in a comment posting. It always announces itself before its summary like this, *This is the best tl;dr I could make, original reduced by 73%. (I'm a bot)*. Users seem to enjoy the autotldr bot, and its machine-generated news summaries have been up-voted 190,000 times.

So how does this kind of text summarization actually work?

In this chapter, we will learn:

- What is automatic text summarization and why is it important?
- How can we build a naive text summarization system from scratch?
- How can we implement more sophisticated text summarizers and compare their effectiveness?

What is automatic text summarization?

In the academic literature, text summarization is often proposed as a solution to information overload, and we in the 21st century like to think that we are uniquely positioned in history in having to deal with this problem. However, even in the 1950s when automatic text summarization techniques were in their infancy, the stated goal was similar. H.P. Luhn's 1958 paper *The automatic creation of literature abstracts*, available in a number of places online, including at `http://altaplana.com/ibm-luhn58-LiteratureAbstracts.pdf`, describes a text summarization method that will save a prospective reader time and effort in finding useful information in a given article or report and that the problem of finding information is being aggravated by the ever-increasing output of technical literature.

Luhn proposed a text summarization method where the computer would read each sentence in a paper, extract the frequently occurring words, which he calls **significant words**, and then look for the sentences that had the most examples of those significant words. This is an early example of an **extractive** method of text summarization. In an extractive summarization method, the summary is composed of words, phrases, or sentences that are drawn directly from the original text. Ideally, every text will have one or more main ideas or topic sentences that can serve as summaries of some portion of the text. The extractive summarization algorithm looks for these important sentences. As long as the amount of text that is extracted is a subset of the original text, this type of summarization achieves the goal of compressing the original text into a shorter size.

Alternatively, an **abstractive** summarization attempts to distill the key ideas in a text and repackage them into a human-readable synthesis. This task is similar to paraphrasing. However, since the goal is to create a summary, abstractive methods must also reduce the length of the text and not just be a restatement of it.

For this chapter, we will focus on summarization techniques for text documents. Other researchers are also working on summarization algorithms designed for video, images, sound, and more. Some of these data types lend themselves better to extractive summarization rather than abstractive summarization; for example a video summary should probably consist of clips taken from the videos themselves. We will focus on **single-document** summaries in this chapter, but there are also summarization techniques that are designed to work with collections of documents. The idea with **multi-document** summarization is that we can scan across a number of related documents, picking out the main ideas correctly, while ensuring that the resulting summary is free of duplicates and is human-readable.

In the next section, we will review some of the currently available single-document text summarization libraries and applications.

Tools for text summarization

Since our focus in this book is data mining with Python, we will focus on understanding some of the tools, libraries, and applications designed for text summarization in a Python environment. However, if you ever find yourself in a non-Python environment, or if you have a special case where you want to use an off-the-shelf or non-Python solution, you will be glad to know that there are dozens of other text summarization tools for other programming environments, many of which require no programming at all. In fact, the autotldr bot we discussed at the beginning of this chapter uses a package called SUMMRY, which has an API that is accessible via REST and returns JSON. You can read more about SUMMRY at `http://smmry.com/api`.

Here we will discuss three Python solutions: a simple NLTK-based method, a Gensim-based method, and a Python summarization package called Sumy.

Naive text summarization using NLTK

So far in this book, we have used NLTK for a variety of tasks including sentiment mining in *Chapter 5*, *Sentiment Analysis in Text* and named entity recognition in *Chapter 6*, *Named Entity Recognition in Text*. For our purposes in this chapter, we can also use the tokenizers from NLTK to build a simple text summarizer that is based on Luhn's method that he wrote about in *The automatic creation of literature abstracts*. This basic, extractive program will first tokenize each sentence in the text sample, then choose which words occur most frequently while excluding unimportant words, called **stopwords**, and finally it will find the sentence or sentences that include the important words.

Our program will include one other subtle effect. We will construct a score for each sentence based on the aggregated scores of the words inside it. For example, suppose the word *cat* appears in a text 10 times, and the word *hat* appears three times. The sentence *The cat wears a hat* will score a 13, or the score for *cat* plus the score for *hat*. The sentence *His hat is different than her hat* will only score 3, since the score for *hat* is counted only once. This scoring system has the advantage of privileging sentences that have a variety of important words in them, while minimizing the effect of sentences that have fewer important words, even if those words are repeated multiple times. The rationale for this scoring system is that sentences with a variety of important words are more likely to be topic sentences or main ideas, and topic sentences are more relevant for building a summary.

The code for this program, `simpleTextSummaryNLTK.py`, is available on the GitHub site for this book, at `https://github.com/megansquire/masteringDM/tree/master/ch7`. This GitHub site also contains the code samples for the other two summarizers used later in the chapter as well.

First we need to include a few libraries. We have used all of these in previous chapters, but if you skipped those, you can install libraries in Anaconda with `conda install <packagename>`:

```
from nltk.tokenize import word_tokenize
from nltk.tokenize import sent_tokenize
from nltk.probability import FreqDist
from nltk.corpus import stopwords
from collections import OrderedDict
import pprint
```

Next, we need a sample of text to summarize. For the example, I decided to use the text from the first portion of this chapter. You can get the text from the GitHub site or paste in some other text sample of your choosing. Following the text variable creation, we instantiate several data structures to hold the various data structures for sentences and counts:

```
text = '' # put text here
summary_sentences = []
candidate_sentences = {}
candidate_sentence_counts = {}
```

Now we should strip any carriage returns out of the text, for easier reading when the sentences are displayed. This code replaces carriage returns in the text sample with space characters:

```
striptext = text.replace('\n\n', ' ')
striptext = striptext.replace('\n', ' ')
```

Next we will get the list of the top 20 most frequent words in this text sample. We will tokenize the text sample into words, lowercase them, making sure we throw out any stopwords and punctuation:

```
words = word_tokenize(striptext)
lowercase_words = [word.lower() for word in words
                    if word not in stopwords.words() and word.isalpha()]
```

We can use the FreqDist package to find the frequency distribution of the remaining words, and the `most_common()` function to pull out the top 20 words from this list. This list is fairly informative, so we can print it to the screen to look at it:

```
word_frequencies = FreqDist(lowercase_words)
most_frequent_words = FreqDist(lowercase_words).most_common(20)
pp = pprint.PrettyPrinter(indent=4)
pp.pprint(most_frequent_words)
```

Here, we will take the stripped text sample and tokenize it into a list of sentences. For each sentence, we will create a dictionary with the sentence itself as the key and its lowercase equivalent as the value:

```
sentences = sent_tokenize(striptext)
for sentence in sentences:
    candidate_sentences[sentence] = sentence.lower()
```

Now it is time to determine which of these sentences has the most important words in it. We iterate through the dictionary of candidate sentences, searching the lowercase version of the sentence for the important words. If we find an important word, we increment the score for that sentence by the value of the word we found. We save the original mixed-case version of the sentence, and its score, to the `candidate_sentence_counts` dictionary:

```
for long, short in candidate_sentences.items():
    count = 0
    for freq_word, frequency_score in most_frequent_words:
        if freq_word in short:
            count += frequency_score
            candidate_sentence_counts[long] = count
```

Finally we sort the sentences, placing the most important sentences first. We retain the top four most important sentences, and print them to the screen, along with their scores:

```
sorted_sentences = OrderedDict(sorted(
                    candidate_sentence_counts.items(),
                    key = lambda x: x[1],
                    reverse = True)[:4])
pp.pprint(sorted_sentences)
```

This program chooses the following words as the most significant from this chapter:

```
[   ('summarization', 15),
    ('text', 15),
    ('in', 4),
    ('extractive', 4),
    ('method', 4),
    ('summary', 4),
    ('words', 4),
    ('sentences', 4),
    ('original', 3),
    ('information', 3),
    ('documents', 3),
    ('ideas', 3),
```

```
('goal', 3),
('similar', 3),
('techniques', 3),
('literature', 3),
('early', 2),
('main', 2),
('this', 2),
('video', 2)]
```

Then, the program produces the following four-sentence summary:

> In an extractive summarization method, the summary is comprised of
> words, phrases, or sentences that are drawn directly from the original
> text. With this early work, Luhn proposed a text summarization method
> where the computer would read each sentence in a paper, extract the
> frequently occurring words, which he calls significant words, and
> then look for the sentences that had the most examples of those
> significant words. In the academic literature, text summarization is
> often proposed as a solution to information overload, and we in the
> 21st century like to think that we are uniquely positioned in history
> in having to deal with this problem. Luhn's 1958 paper "The automatic
> creation of literature abstracts," describes a text summarization
> method that will "save a prospective reader time and effort in finding
> useful information in a given article or report" and that the problem
> of finding information "is being aggravated by the ever-increasing
> output of technical literature."

If we tried to treat this as a standalone summary, like a literature abstract, it is not very effective. The summary lacks the cohesion that a human would bring to the summarization task. The sentences seem disjointed and lack a proper flow from one to the next. This method also seems to be biased towards longer sentences. This makes sense if we consider that longer sentences will end up having higher scores, if only due to the aggregation of the word counts within them. Finally, this method does not take into account the placement of the sentence within the paragraph. Some academic research has shown that the main ideas, or topic sentences, in a text are likely to appear either first or last in a paragraph. If we wanted to add any of these additional features to our program, we would need to decide how to adjust our scoring system accordingly.

Text summarization using Gensim

A slightly more sophisticated approach to text summarization is included in the Gensim topic modeling package. *Chapter 8, Topic Modeling in Text* of this book has topic modeling as its entire focus, so we will not duplicate those tasks here. However, perhaps we can peek ahead just a little bit and use one tiny part of the Gensim library for our text summarization needs.

The Gensim approach to text summarization is quite different than the naive Luhn approach we used in the last section. To understand it, we need to recall some of the concepts from *Chapter 4*, *Network Analysis*, about graph theory and network analysis. The Gensim approach to finding important sentences in a text begins with building a weighted, undirected graph, where the nodes are the sentences and the links between them are a measure of how similar the sentences are to each other. This method is called TextRank, after the similar PageRank algorithm designed finding relevant web page search results. In TextRank, similarity is defined by how many common lexical tokens are shared between the two sentences. To avoid inadvertently privileging long sentences – which was one of the weaknesses of the naive Luhn approach we experimented with earlier – TextRank normalizes the similarity score by taking into account how long the sentence is. After the graph is built, the sentences with the highest weights are extracted as representative summaries of the text as a whole.

This approach was first described in the 2004 paper *TextRank: Bringing Order into Texts* by Rada Mihalcea and Paul Tarau, available at `https://web.eecs.umich.edu/~mihalcea/papers/mihalcea.emnlp04.pdf`. This work was updated by Federico Barrios, Federico Lopez, Luis Argerich, and Rosita Wachenchauzer in 2015, with the results of their experiments in calculating better similarity scores, or weights, in the graph. The latter group has contributed to the Gensim code base, according to the Changelog at `https://github.com/RaRe-Technologies/gensim/blob/develop/CHANGELOG.txt`.

To get started with text summarization in Gensim, we will first import the library:

```
import gensim.summarization
```

If you get an error from Anaconda about not having Gensim installed, remember to use `conda install gensim` to get that library loaded into your system.

Next we will set up a text string that we want to summarize. I used the same text sample as in our naive Luhn summarizer. By using the same text string, we will more easily be able to compare the results of the two text summarizers to each other. We can also strip off end-of-line carriage returns since this text sample has sentences that extend over multiple lines:

```
text = '' # put text here
striptext = text.replace('\n\n', ' ')
striptext = striptext.replace('\n', ' ')
```

Next, we summarize and print the results:

```
summary = gensim.summarization.summarize(striptext, word_count=50)
print(summary)
```

With the `word_count` parameter, we asked for a summary of no more than 50 words. The resulting summary is:

```
Luhn's 1958 paper "The automatic creation of literature abstracts,"
describes a text summarization method that will "save a prospective
reader time and effort in finding useful information in a given
article or report" and that the problem of finding information
"is being aggravated by the ever-increasing output of technical
literature." With this early work, Luhn proposed a text summarization
method where the computer would read each sentence in a paper, extract
the frequently-occurring words, which he calls significant words,
and then look for the sentences that had the most examples of those
significant words.
```

This is actually a pretty good pairing of sentences, and reads fairly well. To see how Gensim chose those sentences, we can ask Gensim to pick out the keywords from the text sample and print them:

```
keywords = gensim.summarization.keywords(striptext)
print(keywords)
```

Gensim returns a list of the following 22 words:

```
documents
document
literature text summarization
abstracts
abstractive
ideas
idea
shorter
words
summary
summaries
information
reader
type
types
luhn
important
sentence
sentences
extract
extractive
extracted
```

Notice that the Gensim `keywords()` function does not naturally combine words that have the same stem. In other words, the keywords *extract*, *extractive*, and *extracted* could be combined into a single concept but `keywords()` does not do this.

Additionally, with Gensim summarizer, not all the keywords have to be a single word; multi-word phrases are supported. The result *literature text summarization* is an example of such a phrase. How did this rather awkward phrase get chosen? My first hypothesis was that perhaps Gensim was getting confused by the comma in the first sentence of the text sample. But I removed the comma, and it still found *literature text summarization* was a keyword. I tested the summarizer by rewording the beginning of the sentence as follows: *Text summarization is often proposed...* After doing this, the `keywords()` function returned a new list of 23 words. The lists are very similar, except that *text summarization* is now the first result, the word *size* was added, and the order of some of the words was slightly altered.

The Gensim keyword list has a few things in common with the Luhn-style list created earlier, namely the words *text* and *summarization* are in both sets, as are *extractive*, *words*, *literature*, *ideas*, *information*, *summary*, and *documents*. Between the two summarizers, that does seem to be a good list of words.

Text summarization using Sumy

There are many more methods for text summarization than just our naive Luhn-style approach and Gensim's TextRank approach. If we are not sure which one to try, or perhaps we want to try even more exotic methods, we can turn to a full-fledged text summarization library that has multiple algorithms built in. Sumy is just such a library, and it is available at `https://github.com/miso-belica/sumy`. Because it is not part of the Anaconda distribution, we will have to install it manually by running the following command inside a terminal:

```
pip install sumy
```

Once we have Sumy installed, we can set up a simple text summarizer and try out the different algorithms that are built in. The following code shows four different text summarization algorithms implemented in Sumy. We will walk through each of them in turn. Before doing so, we must first import a number of Sumy's summarizers, as well as its utility library. This code is available on the Github site for this book at `https://github.com/megansquire/masteringDM/blob/master/ch7/sumySummarize.py`:

```
from sumy.parsers.plaintext import PlaintextParser
from sumy.nlp.tokenizers import Tokenizer
```

```
from sumy.summarizers.luhn import LuhnSummarizer
from sumy.summarizers.text_rank import TextRankSummarizer
from sumy.summarizers.lsa import LsaSummarizer
from sumy.summarizers.edmundson import EdmundsonSummarizer
from sumy.nlp.stemmers import Stemmer
from sumy.utils import get_stop_words
```

Then we set up our language to be *english,* and our number of summary sentences to be four:

```
LANGUAGE = "english"
SENTENCES_COUNT = 4
```

 In addition to English, Sumy has `stopword` lists available for Czech, French, German, Portuguese, Slovak, and Spanish.

Next, we read in our sample file. Here Sumy will be directed to read `sampleText.txt`, a file that consists of the exact same text as we used in our earlier two examples:

```
parser = PlaintextParser.from_file("sampleText.txt",
Tokenizer(LANGUAGE))
stemmer = Stemmer(LANGUAGE)
```

Here the last line directs Sumy to use the built in stemmer to take care of word stems. Recall that stemming was one of the features we did not have in our previous two algorithms, but when we looked at the keyword lists and how repetitive they were, stemming seemed like a good idea.

Sumy's Luhn summarizer

Now we are ready to call four different summarization methods so that we can compare them. We separate each of the following four print statements with a line so that we can compare the results. Sumy's Luhn-based method is first:

```
print("\n====== Luhn ======")
summarizerLuhn = LuhnSummarizer(stemmer)
summarizerLuhn.stop_words = get_stop_words(LANGUAGE)
for sentenceLuhn in summarizerLuhn(parser.document, SENTENCES_COUNT):
    print(sentenceLuhn, "\n")
```

The `LuhnSummarizer()` function creates a summarizer based on the stemmed text. It requires a list of `stopwords` too, so we use Sumy's `get_stop_words()` function for an English-language list of these words.

The four sentences chosen by the Luhn summarizer are shown here. I added letters (A, B, C, and so on) before each sentence so that we can compare them across summarizers and figure out which sentences are chosen more frequently:

```
====== Luhn ======
A. However, even in the 1950s when automatic text summarization
techniques were in their infancy, the stated goal was similar.
B. Luhn's 1958 paper "The automatic creation of literature abstracts,"
describes a text summarization method that will "save a prospective
reader time and effort in finding useful information in a given
article or report" and that the problem of finding information
"is being aggravated by the ever-increasing output of technical
literature."
C. With this early work, Luhn proposed a text summarization method
where the computer would read each sentence in a paper, extract the
frequently-occurring words, which he calls significant words, and then
look for the sentences that had the most examples of those significant
words.
D. As long as the amount of text that is extracted is a subset of
the original text, this type of summarization achieves the goal of
compressing the original text into a shorter size.
```

Sumy's TextRank summarizer

Next, we set up a summarizer using `TextRank`. `TextRank` also requires a list of `stopwords`:

```
print("====== TextRank ======")
summarizerTR = TextRankSummarizer(stemmer)
summarizerTR.stop_words = get_stop_words(LANGUAGE)
for sentenceTR in summarizerTR(parser.document, SENTENCES_COUNT):
    print(sentenceTR, "\n")
```

The four sentences chosen by Sumy's implementation of `TextRank` are shown next. One sentence, labeled D, was also found in the Luhn summary. The other three sentences labeled E, F, and G are new:

```
====== TextRank ======
E. With this early work, Luhn proposed a text summarization method
where the computer would read each sentence in a paper, extract the
frequently-occurring words, which he calls significant words, and then
look for the sentences that had the most examples of those significant
words.
```

F. In an extractive summarization method, the summary is comprised of words, phrases, or sentences that are drawn directly from the original text.

D. As long as the amount of text that is extracted is a subset of the original text, this type of summarization achieves the goal of compressing the original text into a shorter size.

G. In this chapter we will focus on summarization techniques for text documents, but researchers are also working on summarization algorithms designed for video, images, sound, and more.

Sumy's LSA summarizer

The next algorithm is based on Latent Semantic Analysis, or LSA. This approach was first introduced for text summarization by Yihong Gong and Xin Liu in a 2001 paper *Generic Text Summarization Using Relevance Measure and Latent Semantic Analysis*, available at `http://www.cs.bham.ac.uk/~pxt/IDA/text_summary.pdf`. This work was enhanced in the 2004 paper *Using Latent Semantic Analysis in Text Summarization and Summary Evaluation* by Josef Steinberger and Karel Ježek, available at `http://www.kiv.zcu.cz/~jstein/publikace/isim2004.pdf`. We will tackle more of the details behind latent semantic analysis in *Chapter 8, Topic Modeling in Text*, when we learn about topic modeling, but for now, the basic idea is that the LSA technique forms a matrix of terms on the rows and sentences on the columns. The value at the intersection of row and column is how many times each term appears in each sentence. Similarity is determined by first reducing the matrix mathematically, and then the cosines of the angles of the vectors in the reduced matrix are compared to find rows that are similar. In text summarization, the most important sentences will be those that are the most similar to others:

```
print("====== LSA ======")
summarizerLSA = LsaSummarizer(stemmer)
summarizerLSA.stop_words = get_stop_words(LANGUAGE)
for sentenceLSA in summarizerLSA(parser.document, SENTENCES_COUNT):
    print(sentenceLSA, "\n")
```

The following results indicate that item B was previously found in Luhn, and item F was found in `TextRank`. Items H and I are unique to LSA:

```
====== LSA ======
B. Luhn's 1958 paper "The automatic creation of literature abstracts,"
describes a text summarization method that will "save a prospective
reader time and effort in finding useful information in a given
article or report" and that the problem of finding information
"is being aggravated by the ever-increasing output of technical
literature."
```

```
F. In an extractive summarization method, the summary is comprised of
words, phrases, or sentences that are drawn directly from the original
text.
H. Alternatively, an abstractive summarization attempts to distill
the key ideas in a text and repackage them into a human-readable, and
usually shorter, synthesis.
I. However, since the goal is to create a summary, abstractive
methods must also reduce the length of the text while focusing on only
retaining the most important concepts in it.
```

Sumy's Edmundson summarizer

Finally, we implement another more complex algorithm, named after H.P. Edmundson's 1969 paper *New Methods in Automatic Extracting*, which is available at `http://courses.ischool.berkeley.edu/i256/f06/papers/edmonson69.pdf`. The main difference with the Edmundson approach over, for example, the Luhn approach, is that he allows the analyst to inject certain words as **cues** that are highly correlated to the importance of a sentence. This cue method is *based on the hypothesis that the probable relevance of a sentence is affected by the presence of pragmatic words*. Examples of words that point to an important sentence are called **bonus words**. The opposite of these are **stigma words**, or those that negatively affect whether a sentence is important. Finally, he allows for **null words**, which are words that are neutral, or irrelevant, to the importance of a sentence.

In the Sumy implementation of Edmundson, the user is required to configure lists of bonus, stigma, and null words. Edmundson advocates for using statistical analyses of similar documents to come up with these words. In the following example, we will initialize each of these lists with the throwaway token *foo* just to get the program running, and then we will investigate what happens when we alter the bonus, stigma, and null words:

```
print("====== Edmonson ======")
summarizerEd = EdmundsonSummarizer(stemmer)
summarizerEd.bonus_words = ('foo')
summarizerEd.stigma_words = ('foo')
summarizerEd.null_words = ('foo')
for sentenceEd in summarizerEd(parser.document, SENTENCES_COUNT):
    print(sentenceEd, "\n")
```

The Edmundson results with *foo* as the cue words are shown here. Items A and B were found previously in the Luhn summarizer, but items J and K are new:

```
J. In the academic literature, text summarization is often proposed
as a solution to information overload, and we in the 21st century like
to think that we are uniquely positioned in history in having to deal
with this problem.
```

A. However, even in the 1950s when automatic text summarization techniques were in their infancy, the stated goal was similar.
B. Luhn's 1958 paper "The automatic creation of literature abstracts," describes a text summarization method that will "save a prospective reader time and effort in finding useful information in a given article or report" and that the problem of finding information "is being aggravated by the ever-increasing output of technical literature."
K. In the next section we will review some of the currently available text summarization libraries and applications.

What happens to the Edmundson summarizer when we adjust the cue words? To perform this experiment, we will first read through the text sample and find words that seem to positively correlate to what we think the topic sentences are, then do the same thing for negative, or stigma, words and null words. We can adjust the code as follows:

```
print("====== Edmonson ======")
summarizerEd = EdmundsonSummarizer(stemmer)
summarizerEd.bonus_words = ('focus', 'proposed', 'method',
'describes')
summarizerEd.stigma_words = ('example')
summarizerEd.null_words = ('literature', 'however')
for sentenceEd in summarizerEd(parser.document, SENTENCES_COUNT):
    print(sentenceEd, "\n")
```

The results are shown here. Items J and K are still in the output, just like before, but now the results show item I (also found by LSA) and item G (also found by TextRank):

J. In the academic literature, text summarization is often proposed as a solution to information overload, and we in the 21st century like to think that we are uniquely positioned in history in having to deal with this problem.
I. However, since the goal is to create a summary, abstractive methods must also reduce the length of the text while focusing on only retaining the most important concepts in it.
G. In this chapter we will focus on summarization techniques for text documents, but researchers are also working on summarization algorithms designed for video, images, sound, and more.
K. In the next section we will review some of the currently available text summarization libraries and applications.

The Edmundson technique is obviously very configurable, which could be a good thing if we had a list of cue words we felt confident about. However, if we are not really sure what to use as cue words, that same flexibility and configurability becomes a weakness.

Scanning across the four implementations, the sentences that were chosen the most are B, D, F, I, and G. Each of these sentences was chosen at least twice. We can manually organize these sentences into a single paragraph, and we get the following summary:

```
Luhn's 1958 paper "The automatic creation of literature abstracts,"
describes a text summarization method that will "save a prospective
reader time and effort in finding useful information in a given
article or report" and that the problem of finding information
"is being aggravated by the ever-increasing output of technical
literature." In an extractive summarization method, the summary is
comprised of words, phrases, or sentences that are drawn directly from
the original text. As long as the amount of text that is extracted is
a subset of the original text, this type of summarization achieves the
goal of compressing the original text into a shorter size. However,
since the goal is to create a summary, abstractive methods must
also reduce the length of the text while focusing on only retaining
the most important concepts in it. In this chapter we will focus on
summarization techniques for text documents, but researchers are also
working on summarization algorithms designed for video, images, sound,
and more.
```

This summary is a bit awkward in its style, but it does convey some of the main points of the introduction to this chapter. It is all the more impressive when we consider that it was automatically generated, based on very little domain knowledge or human intervention.

Summary

Automatic text summarization is a field that is growing in importance as the volume of data in the world increases. There are numerous approaches to text summarization, but all of them rely on the construction of mathematical representations of the words and sentences in a document, then, through extractive or abstractive methods, building a program that can reduce a document to its most important parts. We reviewed three of the common extractive summarization libraries that can be integrated into our Python code: an NLTK-based summarizer, a Gensim-based approach, and a new package called Sumy with its numerous embedded summarizers. We then compared the different approaches to text summarization by using the same text sample and passing it through different summarization algorithms to see how they differed.

It is good that in this chapter, we have begun thinking about what makes an important sentence or a *key* word. In the next chapter, we will be learning about topic modeling, which means discovering what important topics are being discussed in a text. Many of the same high-level concepts apply to both topic modeling and text summarization, so we should feel quite prepared as we move forward into *Chapter 8, Topic Modeling in Text.*

8
Topic Modeling in Text

Topic modeling in text is loosely related to the summarization techniques we explored in *Chapter 7, Automatic Text Summarization*. However, topic modeling involves a more complex mathematical foundation and it produces a different type of result. The goal of text summarization is to produce a version of a text that is reduced but still expresses common themes or concepts in a text, whereas the goal of topic modeling is to expose the underlying concepts themselves.

To extend our *Chapter 7, Automatic Text Summarization* metaphor, in which text summarization was compared to building a scale model of a house, topic modeling is like trying to describe the purpose of a set of houses based on multiple sample dwellings. For example, the topic model of one neighborhood of houses might be busy family, storage space, and low maintenance and another neighborhood could have houses described with the words social, entertaining, luxury, and showplace. These two models clearly represent two different types of houses, designed and built with two different purposes.

How does topic modeling work? Is it more sophisticated than simply counting how many times each word occurs? In this chapter, we will learn:

- What is topic modeling? What are some of the common techniques we can use to accomplish this task?

- What are the currently available libraries and tools for applying topic modeling in Python, and how do they work?

- How can we compare the effectiveness of a topic modeling approach, in terms of the results it generates?

- How do you apply topic modeling to a real-world problem?

What is topic modeling?

Just like with the keyword-based text summarization techniques we looked at in *Chapter 7, Automatic Text Summarization*, topic modeling also takes into account what words are used in a text. However, the focus of topic modeling is more about themes and concepts, and not solely about summarizing text. Topic models can be used for summarization, but they can also be used for many other goals:

- Topic models can assist with organization of documents, for example, to group news articles together into a cohesive section

- Topic models can help us make recommendations about what to read next by finding materials that have a topic list in common

- Topic models can improve search results by revealing documents that may use a mix of different keywords but are about the same idea

One critical component of the type topic modeling we will investigate in this chapter is that the analyst does not need to know what the topics or keywords are in advance. Instead, the model is created in an **unsupervised** way. In unsupervised topic modeling, the list of topics is built by the computer using probabilities to determine what the topics should be and what documents and words reference those topics.

Researchers for the social media site Facebook published an article in 2013 about how that company uses one type of topic modeling to understand the topics users post about, and more importantly, to understand how audiences respond to those postings. The article is available for download on the Facebook Research blog here: `https://research.facebook.com/publications/gender-topic-and-audience-response-an-analysis-of-user-generated-content-on-facebook/`. In the paper, the authors explain their purpose:

> *"... We examine whether male and female [social network service] users talk about different topics, and how their audience of friends and followers respond."*

They provide a list of 25 topics that they discovered are common in Facebook postings, and they list the corresponding keywords that support those topics. For example, they list the topic *Sleep* and the associated keywords *last night, wake up, bed, nap, asleep*. The topic *Food* includes keywords such as *lunch, coffee, chicken, ice cream*.

Again, the critical component of unsupervised topic modeling is that we do not need to construct a list of keywords and topics in advance. The Facebook researchers did not need to know in advance that they had a number of posts about *Sleep* using the keywords *bed*, *nap*, and *awake*. Rather, the topic lists are generated and grouped by the topic modeling program, at which point the human analysts can suggest the umbrella terms, such as *Sleep* and *Food*, which encapsulate the ideas in each topic list. In the next section, we will take a closer look at how one of these unsupervised topic modeling programs works.

You might be curious to know what the Facebook researchers found out about the differences in topics and responses between male and female users of their service. At the end of their paper they explain:

"Using topic modeling, we find that women are more likely to broadcast personal issues, while men are more likely to post philosophical topics. Although men get fewer comments than women, masculine topics receive more comments."

For more about the Facebook study, you can download the original paper and read related work in the machine learning area of their research blog, available at: `https://research.facebook.com/publications/machinelearningarea/`.

Latent Dirichlet Allocation

The most common technique currently in use for topic modeling of text, and the one that the Facebook researchers used in their 2013 paper, is called **Latent Dirichlet Allocation (LDA)**.

Many people wonder how to pronounce Dirichlet in English. The most common pronunciation I have heard is DEER-uh-shlay, and I have also heard DEER-uh-klay a few times.

LDA was first proposed for text topic extraction by David Blei, Andrew Ng, and Michael Jordan in a 2003 paper entitled simply *Latent Direchlet Allocation*, available from the *Journal of Machine Learning Research* at `http://www.jmlr.org/papers/volume3/blei03a/blei03a.pdf`. Blei also wrote a good follow-up article in 2012 for the *Communications of the ACM* about LDA and some new variants and improvements for it. This later article is written in very accessible language and is available for download at `https://www.cs.princeton.edu/~blei/papers/Blei2012.pdf`.

The first thing we should know about LDA is that it is a probabilistic topic modeling technique. In topic modeling, we assume that in any collection of related documents, each document includes some combination of topics. A collection of documents could be academic papers, e-mails, Facebook posts, and so on. With topic modeling, our main goal is to find the hidden topic structure for this collection of documents. A topic structure includes three things: the topics themselves, the statistical distribution of these topics among the documents, and the words within a document that comprise the topic.

Probabilistic topic modeling techniques such as LDA are able to work in an unsupervised way because they use conditional probabilities to derive this hidden topic structure for a given document collection. To do this, LDA assumes that each document in a collection is about some set of topics, but that these topics are distributed unevenly throughout the documents. The topic structure itself is the hidden variable that needs to be derived based on the observed variables, which are the words in the document.

The computational challenge for LDA is to calculate the probability of each possible topic structure given the words, or observations. The reason why this is challenging is that it involves calculating the probability of every observed word under every possible topic. If the number of topics and words are both large, we have a computationally intractable problem. To solve this problem for large data sets, topic modeling algorithms will attempt to reduce the number of possibilities for topics or words, similarly to how we attempted to reduce the number of candidates in our association rule mining back in *Chapter 2, Association Rule Mining*.

The implementation of LDA that we will be *using* in this book, Gensim LDA, uses a reduction technique based on the work of Matthew Hoffman, David Blei, and Francis Bach, first described in their 2010 paper *Online Learning for Latent Dirichlet Allocation* which you can download from `https://www.cs.princeton.edu/~blei/papers/HoffmanBleiBach2010b.pdf`. In the next section, we will practice using Gensim to infer a topic model from text.

Gensim for topic modeling

We used the Gensim library already in *Chapter 7, Automatic Text Summarization* for extracting keywords and summaries of text. Here we will use it for building a topic model of a collection of texts. Just as we did in earlier chapters, we will practice with a few different types of document collections and see how the results vary.

First, we will build a small test program to make sure that Gensim and LDA are installed correctly and able to generate a topic model from a collection of documents. If Gensim is not loaded into your version of Anaconda, simply run `conda install gensim` in your terminal.

We begin with importing the Gensim libraries and a **PrettyPrinter** for formatting:

```
from gensim import corpora
from gensim.models.ldamodel import LdaModel
from gensim.parsing.preprocessing import STOPWORDS
import pprint
```

We will need some variables to serve as ways of adjusting the model. As we learn how topic modeling works, we will tweak these values to see how the results change. The `num_topics` variable holds how many topics we would like the model to find. The `num_words` variable tells how many words we would like to view from each topic, if different from the default of 10. The `passes` variable indicates how many times we would like to go over the data. Generally, for a large corpus this could be set to 1, but for a small corpus might need to be set higher in order to ensure that the model does not choose weird values randomly, and that the results begin to converge on some truly representative topics:

```
num_topics = 5
num_words = 5
passes = 20
```

Next, we set up several sample files for testing. To see how the LDA model works with different types of text, we can use the same text samples we used in previous chapters, as well as several new ones, all made available for download at https://github.com/megansquire/masteringDM/tree/master/ch8.

In terms of our LDA vocabulary, each text file is considered a collection of documents, with one document per line inside the file. We can comment out any text file we are not working with at the moment:

```
filename = 'data/introSectionsToChapters.txt'
# filename = 'data/sampleTextFromCh7.txt'
# filename = 'data/gnueIRCsummary.txt'
# filename = 'data/apacheMeetingMinutes.txt'
# filename = 'data/lkmlLinusJan2016.txt'
# filename = 'data/lkmlLinusJan2006.txt'
# filename = 'data/lkmlLinusAll.txt'
```

These files are of different lengths, have different numbers of documents in them, and different purposes and tones:

- The `introSectionsToChapters.txt` file is an expanded version of the introductory text file we used in *Chapter 7, Automatic Text Summarization*. This new file contains the introductory paragraphs of each of the first eight chapters of this book, one chapter per line.

- The `sampleTextFromCh7.txt` file was the small introductory text file that we used in *Chapter 7, Automatic Text Summarization*.

- The `gnueIRCsummary.txt` and apacheMeetingMinutes.txt files were all used in *Chapter 6, Named Entity Recognition in Text*.

- The `lkmlJan2016.txt`, `lkmlJan2006.txt`, and `lkmlLinusall.txt` files are collections of e-mails sent by Linus Torvalds to the Linux Kernel Mailing list.

We can read the lines in the file into a list that we call `documents`:

```
with open(filename, encoding='utf-8') as f:
    documents = f.readlines()
```

Next, each document is turned into a list of words. Each word in the list is lowercased, then stopwords and contractions (such as *don't* and *it's*) are ignored:

```
texts = [[word for word in document.lower().split()
        if word not in STOPWORDS and word.isalnum()]
        for document in documents]
```

Next we create a Dictionary and a corpus from the lists of words:

```
dictionary = corpora.Dictionary(texts)
corpus = [dictionary.doc2bow(text) for text in texts]
```

The Dictionary object has a function called `doc2bow()`, where **bow** stands for **bag of words**. A bow just means that each word in the list is thrown in a bag where it is counted and stored. In a bag of words, the words are considered independently of their order in the original list. Each item in the annotated corpus is a tuple of the form `(word, frequency)`.

Now we are ready to create the LDA model:

```
lda = LdaModel(corpus,
            id2word=dictionary,
            num_topics=num_topics,
            passes=passes)
```

From here, we can simply print out the topics that the LDA procedure found:

```
pp = pprint.PrettyPrinter(indent=4)
pp.pprint(lda.print_topics(num_words=num_words))
```

The resulting topic list is shown below for the `introSectionsToChapters.txt` file with `num_topics=5`, `num_words=5`, and `passes=20`:

```
[
  (0, '0.050*topic + 0.036*modeling + 0.026*text + 0.026*chapter +
0.016*different'),
  (1, '0.034*text + 0.024*news + 0.020*summarization + 0.015*bots +
0.015*original'),
  (2, '0.052*data + 0.015*mining + 0.013*techniques + 0.013*frequent +
0.013*information'),
  (3, '0.019*data + 0.019*network + 0.016*finding + 0.016*text +
0.016*sentiment'),
  (4, '0.002*data + 0.002*text + 0.002*named + 0.002*information +
0.002*entity')
]
```

At first these lines seem hard to understand. We can interpret each line by saying, for topic 3, the word *data* is the most contributing word, the word *network* is the second most contributing word, and so on.

Understanding Gensim LDA topics

Gensim will build a topic list as shown previously, with the caveat that this list is user-configurable as to how many topics it includes and how many words are shown for each topic. I strongly encourage experimentation with different numbers of topics and displayed words, in order to understand how the output changes depending on how these values change.

Once we have a topic list we like, we can consider labeling the topics. In other words, if the topics Gensim reveals seem particularly coherent in terms of the words that are included, we could consider assigning them some human-friendly umbrella terms. For the example with the `introSectionsToChapters.txt` file, we might rename topics 0-4 as follows:

* **Topic modeling**: topic, modeling, text, chapter, different
* **Text summarization**: text, news, summarization, bots, original
* **General data mining**: data, mining, techniques, frequent, information

- **Network analysis and sentiment mining**: data, network, finding, text, sentiment
- **Named entity recognition, entity matching**: data, text, named, information, entity

The initial descriptors for each topic were created by me, but the list of words comprising each topic was discovered by our program.

As we play around with the number of topics and number of words, we can see that the model starts to shift and change. If we ask for num_topics=2 and num_words=10, we see the following:

```
[
  (0,'0.030*topic + 0.021*modeling + 0.016*text + 0.016*chapter +
0.010*different + 0.010*model + 0.010*summarization + 0.010*techniques
+ 0.007*produce + 0.007*common'),
  (1,'0.034*data + 0.015*text + 0.010*mining + 0.009*information +
0.009*named + 0.009*techniques + 0.008*entity + 0.008*patterns +
0.008*association + 0.008*finding')
  ]
```

These topics are much more generic and do not seem to capture the distinct concepts of the book chapters as well as the earlier example did. As it turns out, we had better results asking for more topics and fewer words for each. Now we can see why we had configured the number of topics and words as variables in our program. Experimentation with this part of the procedure is critical.

Understanding Gensim LDA passes

Now, we will run a few new tests with a new data set to learn about how the LDA uses randomness, and thus how the number of passes affects the data.

First, we will model the set of topics returned from lkmlLinusJan2016.txt, using num_topics=4, num_words=5 and passes=20. This is the same dataset that we first used in *Chapter 5, Sentiment Analysis in Text*, albeit with a new filename. It is a collection of 78 e-mails sent by Linus Torvalds to the Linux Kernel Mailing List during January 2016. We see the following topics emerge:

```
[
  (0, '0.015*think + 0.011*v + 0.010*read + 0.010*u + 0.008*data'),
  (1, '0.014*gpu + 0.013*think + 0.010*use + 0.010*cpu +
0.010*things'),
  (2, '0.024*think + 0.012*use + 0.012*want + 0.011*aio +
0.009*things'),
  (3, '0.016*memory + 0.014*pull + 0.011*maybe + 0.010*ordering +
0.010*gpu')
  ]
```

After observing the topics discovered, we can apply some general descriptions as follows:

- **Reading and writing data**: think, v, read, u, data
- **GPU and CPU**: gpu, think, use, cpu, things
- **Asynchronous IO (aio)**: think, use, want, aio, things
- **Memory ordering on GPU**: memory, pull, maybe, ordering, gpu

If we run the same program again, with the same variable values for number of topics, number of words, and passes, we see a slightly different set of topics emerge, but with some similarities to the first set:

```
[
  (0, '0.013*memory + 0.011*use + 0.011*think + 0.010*actually +
0.008*ordering'),
  (1, '0.017*think + 0.012*cpu + 0.011*gpu + 0.008*read + 0.008*v'),
  (2, '0.013*think + 0.012*patch + 0.012*like + 0.011*want +
0.010*actually'),
  (3, '0.023*think + 0.016*use + 0.013*things + 0.012*actually +
0.011*sector')
]
```

 In this second set of topics, *think* is still an important word, as are *cpu*, *gpu*, and *use*. *Actually* also emerges as an important word.

It may seem odd at first to consider that LDA returns different results each time we run it, until we remember our earlier discussion about how probabilistic topic models must employ some kind of strategy to minimize the number of calculations between words and topics. LDA employs randomness at a few places in its code to achieve this. At the time of writing this, the Gensim developers are working on a new feature to allow users to set the *random* number's seed, to produce the same values each time. This will help with testing and will allow for smoother reproduction of results. I look forward to this new code making it into a future release of Gensim.

In the meantime, we can experiment with increasing the number of passes over the data. By passing over the data more times, we hope to reduce the effect of that randomness for our small data set, allowing the results to converge around the most important topics. This offsets the chance of one or two less important words accidentally getting too much emphasis in a single-pass operation. Setting our `passes` variable to 100, we see the following topics emerge for the LKML data set:

```
[
  (0, '0.016*actually + 0.013*use + 0.013*memory + 0.012*people +
0.010*like'),
  (1, '0.017*think + 0.009*end + 0.009*v + 0.008*read + 0.008*use'),
  (2, '0.018*gpu + 0.015*think + 0.014*cpu + 0.013*actually +
0.010*want'),
  (3, '0.024*think + 0.013*things + 0.011*sector + 0.009*interface +
0.009*like')
]
```

With 100 passes over the data, many of the same concepts show up, and the contribution of words such as *gpu* and *actually* increases for those topics.

Applying a Gensim LDA model to new documents

Once an LDA topic model has been built, we can feed new documents into it and the model will tell us which topic best describes this new document. The next few lines of code build on top of the code we wrote in the previous section. Picking up where we left off, after just creating the LDA model and printing the topics out, we can read in a new text file consisting of a single, new e-mail. Since our original e-mail set was from January 2016, I have chosen to compare an e-mail sent on February 1. My hope is that this e-mail will closely resemble at least one of the topics we have already built:

```
unseenText = 'data/lkmlSingleNewEmail.txt'
with open(unseenText, encoding='utf-8') as fnew:
    newdoc = fnew.read()
```

Next we convert that new e-mail document into a bag of words. We need to remove `stopwords` and check for alphanumeric characters, same as before. We send our lowercase words into the `doc2bow()` function, and it returns a corpus:

```
newcorpus = dictionary.doc2bow(newword for newword in newdoc.lower().
split() if newword not in STOPWORDS and newword.isalnum())
```

We pass the new corpus into the existing LDA model, stored in the `lda` variable, and print the whole thing:

```
pp.pprint(lda[newcorpus])
```

The results will look something like this for a list of four topics:

```
[
(0, 0.79236847616482542),
(1, 0.087326122043685422),
(2, 0.016795592901994647),
(3, 0.10350980888949456)
]
```

Each item in the list is a tuple consisting of the topic number and a probability of our new document fitting into that topic. In this case, our new, unseen e-mail has a 79.2% chance of fitting best into the topic 0.

Serializing Gensim LDA objects

One weakness of our procedure so far is that each time we run our code, even with the same variable values and same data set, we get a slightly different topic model. This could be frustrating if we have a situation where we have built a model, but then want to run a new document through it some time later. We might want to save the LDA model that we built for longer-term use. To do this, we can **serialize** the model to disk and read it back any time we want. We had briefly discussed this serialization idea back in *Chapter 4*, *Network Analysis*, when we wanted to save a Networkx object as a pickle for later reuse. Here, we will apply Gensim's serialization options at different points in the code.

Serializing a dictionary

Within the LDA procedures we have set up so far, there are several places in the code where we might want to save to disk. One is after the creation of the dictionary. To do this, following the dictionary creation we can simply run the `save()` function on the dictionary object, and pass in a filename to indicate where we would like the dictionary saved:

```
dictionary = corpora.Dictionary(texts)
dictionary.save('lkml.dict')
```

To read the serialized dictionary object back into any program, use the `load()` method as follows:

```
dictionary = corpora.Dictionary.load('lkml.dict')
```

At this point you can test to see whether the dictionary was written and read correctly by simply printing it out. Printing my `1kml` dictionary with `print(dictionary)` shows the first few words of the output:

```
Dictionary(980 unique tokens: ['writes', 'day', 'implement',
'performance', 'segment']...)
```

Serializing a corpus

Next, we might want to save our corpus that we have created from the bag of words text. There are four methods built into Gensim for serializing our corpus. The first is called **Matrix Market (MM)** format.

While I was reading about Matrix Market (MM) format, I noticed that sometimes people inadvertently call it MM format on the Gensim mailing list, Stack Overflow, and other online documentation. This can be confusing and can make searches for the correct term, Matrix Market, more difficult.

But what is a **matrix market** anyway? The U.S. Government's **National Institute of Standards and Technology (NIST)** documentation for the format is available at `http://math.nist.gov/MatrixMarket/formats.html`, and the original 1996 paper *The Matrix Market Exchange Formats: Initial Design*, written by Ronald F. Boisvert, Roldan Pozo, and Karin A. Remington, describes an exchange format for matrices, and the associated marketplace to exchange the matrices, which they called a **Matrix Market**.

Since both words are about the same length, and saying them is a bit of a tongue twister, I would recommend just calling it MM format!

To serialize a corpus in the MM format, we can run the following:

```
corpus = [dictionary.doc2bow(text) for text in texts]
corpora.MmCorpus.serialize('1kml.mm', corpus)
```

To read the corpus back out of the file later, we can run:

```
corpus = corpora.MmCorpus('1kml.mm')
```

In addition to the MM format, there are three other formats for serializing the corpus, which are detailed in the Gensim documentation at `https://radimrehurek.com/gensim/tut1.html`, and which you may find useful for your purposes. It is also possible to start the LDA process using a serialized corpus that someone else has given you in one of these various formats, and you can read in one format and write out to another format.

Serializing a model

Once we have the LDA model built, we can save it to disk as well. Suppose we have used the following code to create an LDA model:

```
lda = LdaModel(corpus, id2word=dictionary, num_topics=4, passes=20)
```

To save the resulting model to disk, use its `save()` function, like this:

```
lda.save('lkml.gensim')
```

You can call the file anything you like, but the `save()` function will create two files: the one you specified and a `.state` file.

The short code snippet below creates a model, saves it, loads the previously saved model into a new object, then prints it out to show that it is the same as the original:

```
lda = LdaModel(corpus, id2word=dictionary, num_topics=4, passes=20)
pp.pprint(lda.print_topics(num_words=5))
lda.save('lkml.gensim')
newlda = LdaModel.load('lkml.gensim', mmap='r')
pp.pprint(lda.print_topics(num_words=5))
```

The useful thing about the LDA model serialization is that after we spend time creating a model that we feel is most accurate and representative of the data, we can save it, and then access it later without having to rebuild it. With a small data set like the one we have been working with, the advantages of model serialization may seem minor in terms of their time savings. However, you may find that with a project of significant size, with more documents and more words, that the serialization process becomes necessary.

Gensim LDA for a larger project

Let's learn how the LDA topic modeling process changes when we have a larger set of documents and words to work with. Suppose we extend the LKML data set to include not just the 78 e-mails from January 2016, but instead, what if we use all the e-mails Linus Torvalds has ever sent to the LKML? After cleaning the data to remove missing messages, source code, attachments, Linus' own name used as a signature, and end-of-line characters, we have a single text file containing 22,546 e-mails. This e-mail text file, called `lkmlLinusAll.txt`, is provided on the GitHub site for this chapter at `https://github.com/megansquire/masteringDM/tree/master/ch8`.

After reading these into a dictionary, our program reports that there are 26,709 unique tokens. Asking for the same four topics, five words, but asking for only one pass over this large data set yields the following topic list:

```
[
(0,'0.014*people + 0.013*think + 0.011*merge + 0.010*actually +
0.010*like'),
(1,'0.011*fix + 0.008*code + 0.008*error + 0.007*actually +
0.007*think'),
(2,'0.022*fix + 0.012*like + 0.012*think + 0.010*actually +
0.009*use'),
(3,'0.045*fix + 0.013*updates + 0.012*add + 0.012*use + 0.008*like')
]
```

The prevalence of the topic *fix* is very different than in the previous January 2016 e-mail set. In fact, the highest contribution of any word is *fix* with a 0.045 contribution to topic 3. Compare this to the earlier January-only data set, where the highest contributing word was *think* with a contribution figure of around 0.024.

When we ask for ten topics instead of four in the `lkmlLinusAll.txt` file, we observe the following result:

```
[
(0,'0.016*lock + 0.015*fix + 0.015*actually + 0.012*case +
0.011*commit'),
(1,'0.013*want + 0.012*use + 0.012*think + 0.011*memory +
0.011*actually'),
(2,'0.025*page + 0.011*memory + 0.010*like + 0.009*actually +
0.009*think'),
(3,'0.023*think + 0.017*like + 0.014*actually + 0.012*people +
0.010*things'),
(4,'0.044*fix + 0.012*patch + 0.012*like + 0.012*use + 0.012*kernel'),
(5,'0.023*pull + 0.019*torvalds + 0.017*people + 0.009*request +
0.009*actually'),
(6,'0.072*fix + 0.024*add + 0.013*error + 0.009*remove +
0.009*check'),
(7,'0.048*updates + 0.011*fix + 0.010*git + 0.009*fixes +
0.008*changes'),
(8,'0.023*code + 0.012*like + 0.011*use + 0.009*warning +
0.009*helper'),
(9,'0.017*device + 0.017*driver + 0.017*fix + 0.013*use +
0.012*module')
]
```

Fix stays an important word. *Updates* gets its own topic. Overall, we get slightly more variety, but some of the same concepts keep appearing over and over: *fix, memory, like, think, use*. Also, the contribution of each word to its topic is much smaller than when we have fewer topics.

Another thing to notice about the January-only data set compared to this one is the absence of *cpu* and *gpu*, words which were present in nearly every instantiation of the topic model we built earlier. This is because in a long-term software project such as the Linux kernel, different technical topics are important at different times. The *all* data set will show general issues that have always been important (*fix, memory*) but the single-month data set will reveal issues that were important for that particular moment in time (*gpu, cpu*).

What if we compared the January 2016 data set to an earlier single-month data set that was also about the same size? Would we be able to confirm the emergence of different technical topics over time?

To test this, let's construct a data set of e-mails from ten years earlier: January 2006. I have made this file available on the GitHub chapter page as well. When we run a four-topic, five-word, 100-pass analysis, we see the following result:

```
[
  (0, '0.010*git + 0.010*actually + 0.009*think + 0.009*kernel +
0.008*license'),
  (1,'0.016*license + 0.011*gplv2 + 0.011*linux + 0.010*thing +
0.010*kernel'),
  (2,'0.024*branch + 0.019*merge + 0.012*development + 0.011*actually +
0.010*tree'),
  (3, '0.018*code + 0.008*kernel + 0.007*user + 0.007*memory +
0.006*things')
]
```

This topic list shows that in January 2006, concerns included software licenses (*license, gplv2*), and growing discussions about Git as the new version control system (*git, branch, merge, tree*). By January 2006, Git would have been in use for about eight months on the LKML, and its presence in the topic list confirms Linus' participation in ongoing discussions about its use and how it works. An interesting point for further research would be to locate the point in time when Git disappeared as a topic of discussion for Linus, because by January 2016 it was certainly no longer appearing on the topic list. Other topics will certainly come and go over time. Topic modeling can be a great way to give an overall high-level view of what is happening in a group of texts over time.

Summary

We now have a basic understanding of how probabilistic topic modeling works and we have worked to implement one of the most popular tools for performing this analysis on text: the Gensim implementation of Latent Dirichlet Allocation, or LDA. We learned how to write a simple program to implement LDA modeling on a variety of text samples, some with greater success than others. We learned about how the model can be manipulated by changing the input variables, such as the number of topics and the number of passes over the data. We also discovered that topic lists can change over time, and while more data tends to produce a stronger model, it also tends to obscure niche topics that might have been very important for only a moment in time.

In this topic modeling chapter – perhaps even more than in some of the other chapters – our unsupervised learning approach meant that we experienced how our results are truly dependent on the volume, quality, and uniformity of the data we started with. Producing coherent topics from text is possible, but results will vary wildly depending on the initial documents in the collection. It is appropriate then that in the next chapter we will turn our attention towards using data mining techniques to address issues with data itself. We will use data mining techniques to identify data quality problems, including finding and fixing missing values and identifying anomalous data.

9
Mining for Data Anomalies

In the previous eight chapters, we have used data mining techniques to identify a wide variety of patterns in data. We have mined social networks, associations, matching pairs, and all sorts of interesting text patterns. Now we are going to turn the tables and use our skills to look for anomalies, or data items that do not match an expected pattern. Data anomalies happen for various reasons, but because they deviate from expectations or stand out in some important way, we can use our data mining knowledge to seek them out. In my toolbox of mining techniques, I like to think of data mining for anomalies as using the claw part of a hammer. Most of the time I am using a hammer to pound nails, but every once in a while, I need to turn the hammer over and use the claw to pull out a nail. Data mining is always about finding interesting patterns, but sometimes the pattern we are seeking is the one nail that is sticking out at a weird angle and needs to be pulled.

In this chapter, we will learn to answer the following questions:

- What are some of the different types of data anomalies, and why do they occur?

- How can we use visual mining, statistical methods, and machine learning to locate data anomalies?

- How can we implement these various anomaly detection methods using real-world data?

What are data anomalies?

An **anomaly** refers to something that is unexpected or a deviation from the norm. The classic example of an anomaly in data is an **outlier**, which is a data point that is distant in some way from the other data points in the collection. In addition to outliers, other types of anomalies could include data that is unexpectedly **missing**, or data that exhibits **errors**. In the grand scheme of the data mining process that we outlined in *Chapter 1, Expanding Your Data Mining Toolbox*, detecting data anomalies could be considered part of the data cleaning step, although in this chapter we will find that sometimes using data analysis techniques actually helps us with this cleaning task. In the next few pages, we will take a tour through these different types of anomalies, show what they might look like with real data examples, discuss why they happen, and outline a few simple ways to detect them.

Missing data

Even though missing data is not always the first thing people think of as a data anomaly, it can certainly be unexpected. In fact, how we handle missing data can definitely impact the rest of the analyses we perform on the data. So what do we mean by **missing data**? In a typical record-oriented data set, for example the kind of data a spreadsheet or relational database would contain, missing data will usually refer to **blank** or **null** data values. For example, if we have a record describing a person, and the birth date or first name for the person is missing, that could be an unexpected condition. On the other hand, the term missing data usually does not refer to rows or records that are absent entirely.

Now that we know what missing data is and is not, the question is how do we find these missing values and what do we do to fix them?

Locating missing data

A very common type of missing data is unexpected or undesired empty or blank values, zero values, and null values. In a data set expressed as a delimited file, such as a comma-delimited or tab-delimited file, an empty value may look like this:

```
Mary Smith,123 Main St.,,Anytown,CA,99123
```

In that example, the third data value is empty. Note the difference between the empty space in that record and the following, which is actually not empty at all. The record following has a space as the data value:

```
Mary Smith,123 Main St., ,Anytown,CA,99123
```

Whitespace in the form of a carriage return, new line, tab key, space key, and so on, is *not* the same as empty or null values.

In a relational database, columns may be set to be **nullable**, indicating that null values are allowed. In some **relational database management systems (RDBMS)**, a blank string can be passed as a valid data value into a non-nullable column. This action actually overrides the not-nullable setting. The difference between a null column and a blank value is a little tricky to see, but the following screenshot displays a snippet from PhpMyAdmin showing a small MySQL table called `apache_twitter`. In this table, there is one column that is nullable, called `details`, and the rest of the columns are set as not-nullable. The columns `svn_id` and `real_name` are not-nullable, but have no default value either:

Name	Type	Collation	Attributes	Null	Default
svn_id	varchar(30)	latin1_swedish_ci		No	
twitter_screen_name	varchar(20)	latin1_swedish_ci		No	*None*
real_name	varchar(50)	latin1_swedish_ci		No	
datasource_id	int(11)			No	*None*
project_name	varchar(30)	latin1_swedish_ci		No	*None*
details	varchar(100)	latin1_swedish_ci		Yes	*NULL*

Figure 1. Database table structure showing nullable and not-nullable columns in a table

The following screenshot shows what the table structure looks like when it is filled in with two of the sample rows. The first row is filled in with a blank `svn_id` and a blank `real_name`. These are not nullable, but they can be empty. The second row in the screenshot shows that the `details` column is set to *NULL*:

svn_id	twitter_screen_name	real_name ▲	datasource_id	project_name	details
	ApacheTomEE		370	Apache TomEE	https://svn.apache.org/re
	ApacheTomEE		372	Apache OpenEJB	*NULL*

Figure 2. Two sample records showing empty and null field values

The procedure for finding null or empty values will be different depending on what type of data storage system we are using. For an RDBMS such as MySQL, we can search for nulls with a SQL query like this:

```
SELECT *
FROM apache_twitter
WHERE details IS NULL;
```

Or, for columns where NULL values are *not* allowed but blank values *are* allowed, we could use:

```
SELECT *
FROM apach_twitter
WHERE real_name = '';
```

The quotation marks next to each other indicate that we are seeking an empty string.

Zero values

For numeric columns that are not-nullable, many times a default value will be set; usually a default of zero (0) is most common. However, this is quite problematic if zero is also an acceptable value for the column. For example, consider a column to hold quiz grades for students. A value of 0 should indicate that the student received no points on the quiz, either by getting every question wrong or by skipping the quiz entirely. If the student has an extension on taking the test, for instance he or she plans to take it another day but has not yet done so, perhaps a non-zero null value would be more appropriate and accurate. We need to be careful of setting zero as a default value when no data is entered into a numeric column.

Fixing missing data

Once the missing data values have been identified, we have to decide whether to fix them, and if so, how to do that. Over the next few pages, we will outline some of the choices for fixing this kind of missing data.

Ignore the problem rows

Our first choice could be to ignore the rows with the missing data. We could also ignore the columns that have a lot of missing values in them. Success with this strategy depends entirely on the application you are working with. If you have empty or null birth dates, that might not be a problem unless you are writing a program that depends on an accurate age calculation. A missing quiz grade may not be a problem until the end of the semester when it is time to submit the student's final course grade. Another option – and much more drastic than simply ignoring the problematic data – would be to delete the rows with missing data. Tread carefully, though, as this action is final and deletion may be too extreme for most cases. After all, by simply ignoring the problematic records, we give ourselves the option to locate the missing data later.

Fix the problem manually

If there are only one or two missing values in a data set, and if it seems likely that you could find the correct values by yourself, you could fill in the missing values manually. This approach obviously does not scale well to large data sets unless you have a very high tolerance for tedium. To determine whether a manual approach is even practical, we should first use a query to figure out how many rows are problematic.

We may get lucky and manage to find a way to update the rows automatically, for example by joining a complete data set to ours, or by updating groups of rows. For instance, if we have the postal code for every row, but many rows are missing a city column, we could use a JOIN in SQL or write a quick program to replace empty values from one data set with correct values from the other set. However, whether this option is available or practical is entirely dependent on what our data set looks like and what values are missing.

Sometimes we will have missing values that can be corrected after viewing the data presented as a sequence or a timeline. Consider an example like the one presented in the following screenshot:

219	3	2010-05-03	2010-05-04
229	3	2010-09-07	2010-09-08
238	3	2011-01-14	*NULL*
248	3	2011-03-03	2011-03-04
256	3	2011-04-04	*NULL*
266	3	2011-05-03	2011-05-04
279	3	2011-08-31	*NULL*
289	3	2011-11-01	2011-11-02
298	3	2012-01-17	*NULL*
307	3	2012-05-21	2012-05-22
317	3	2012-07-23	*NULL*
332	3	2012-08-09	*NULL*
336	3	2012-09-05	2012-09-06
344	3	2012-11-01	*NULL*
375	3	2013-03-20	2013-03-21

Figure 3. Data sorted by date, so that NULL values can be guessed based on previous patterns

This screenshot shows some log entries with *NULL* values for end_date. Can you guess what an appropriate end_date would be for these values, based on the other records? Based on the data we have, it looks like each end_date that is filled in is one day later than the start_date. These NULL values can therefore be replaced with a very good estimated end_date.

Use a fabricated value

Another option that some people use to handle missing values is to replace them with a fabricated phrase such as *N/A* (for not applicable), or the word *unknown*, or with a hyphen, or with a space. However, in most cases, I strongly caution against this approach for a few reasons:

- We gain little from it. It is usually very easy to find and avoid the blank or null columns by using a query, so what do we really gain from replacing these values with a new, fabricated value? That said, if there is a mix of null and blank values (or very problematic whitespace values) it might be helpful to standardize one representation of these, but there is little advantage to changing a null or blank value to a word like *unknown* or *N/A*.

- We have to manage the change. Since the new, fabricated value is constructed by a person, its meaning and existence in the system will need to be tracked and documented. As such, the meaning of this special value becomes one more piece of data knowledge that has to be retained and managed.

- We risk diluting the value of subsequent data mining activities. Suppose we are doing text mining and we have replaced a null or blank comments field with the words *not applicable* or *unknown*. In order to prevent our text mining program from targeting this phrase as important, we now need to program around it, perhaps by adding these fabricated words to our stopword list, or by ignoring all rows with the word *unknown* in a given column. This is a silly solution, first because we could have just ignored the column to begin with (see the *Ignorance is bliss* section). So we have simply made more work for ourselves. Second, now if the words *not applicable* or *unknown* truly are important to our program, we have jeopardized our ability to leverage this fact to learn something.

Use a central measure

If the blanks, nulls, and zeroes are causing a problem, one approach that works especially well with numeric values is to take impute a measure of centrality in the data, then replace the missing value with that. For instance, suppose we are calculating projected student final grades, but we have a few students who are missing a quiz here or there. If we absolutely had to **impute**, or substitute, a grade for these missing quizzes, we could take the class average for each particular quiz and replace the missing value with this new value. This solution may produce a more accurate projection of the grade than leaving an empty or zero value.

However, this replacement method is harder to use with some string data, after all, what is the central value of a first name? What is the central value of a favorite movie? Another risk of this solution is that it introduces data that is more than likely going to be incorrect. It is unlikely that our fictional student, once he or she takes the quiz, will actually achieve a score exactly equal to the mean score of the class as a whole.

Use Last Observation Carried Forward

In some data sets, we could choose to assume that if the data is missing, nothing has changed. For these cases, perhaps it would be easiest just to use the last known observation as the current value. This method, called **Last Observation Carried Forward** (LOCF), works well for data values that do not represent frequent changes, or where the changes are likely to happen gradually. For instance, many people use fitness trackers such as Fitbit or Jawbone to calculate calorie burn based on weight and amount of daily activity. The following shows an example of a Fitbit calorie and step tracking log:

Mar 19, 7:54AM	Run	7,971	4.27 miles	45:15	382 cals
Mar 17, 7:32AM	Run	7,526	4.04 miles	41:40	339 cals
Mar 16, 7:10AM	Run	3,436	1.84 miles	19:30	160 cals
Mar 15, 3:29PM	Run	7,739	4.15 miles	44:39	373 cals

Figure 4. Fitbit tracking log showing a calculated calorie burn based on last known weight value

The tracker software asks the user to enter a weight and stride length when they set up the device, and even if the user never updates the weight again, the last known weight will be assumed in order to track the daily calories expended. If the user updates the weight (or, less likely, the stride length), the new value will be saved and used for subsequent calculations. However, all the weight values are saved in order to draw a weight chart over time.

Use a similar value

Another approach to handling missing data would be to impute a value by choosing the replacement from a group of similar records. For example, suppose we are trying to fill in a missing value for how Sally Student would rate the movie *Fight Club*. We know Sally is female, born on January 15, 1996, goes to college in North Carolina, and plays volleyball. But for some reason we do not know what her score was for this movie. With **hot deck imputation**, we would find a list of students with similar attributes and randomly choose one of their scores to stand in for Sally's score. This method is based on an assumption that similarities between records on other attributes may have bearing on the missing attribute.

Use the most likely value

If we have data that supports it, another interesting idea would be to **impute the most likely value**. Suppose we have three or four columns that would allow us to predict the most likely value for some data we are currently missing. In our quiz example, if we have scores for the first four quizzes for a few hundred students, we may be able to use regression or another statistical technique to predict a few missing scores on the final quiz based on how other students with the same pattern of scores seemed to perform. As with the fabricated scores based on measures of centrality, the risk with this approach is that we could impute a value that ends up being totally incorrect. Probability tells us that the risk of being totally incorrect is low, but our tolerance for incorrect answers could change depending on the domain we are working with at the time.

Data errors

Data errors such as truncated fields, data type and character set errors, and logical errors such as nonsensical dates or garbage values, can also negatively affect our analysis if left untreated. **Data errors** such as these are somewhat more difficult to find than missing data, but for accurate data mining we must develop methods for locating them.

Truncated fields

A problem with data storage systems such as an RDBMS is that they have a fixed model designed in advance. This seems like a harmless idea until we realize that sometimes the data going into the system changes faster than the model, or sometimes the modeler cannot anticipate every possible type of data that the model must hold.

This happens to me a lot in my work when I am storing text data over a long time span – 10 or more years in some cases. I will design a model that I think will certainly have fields that are big enough to store every possible text artifact I could think of, but then someone sends an email message or an IRC chat line that is extremely long and I get a truncation error.

In one of my IRC chat databases from the community that is working to build the popular Puppet configuration management tool, I ran some tests and found that the longest chat messages were coming in at about 500 characters each. So when I decided to store this data for the long term, I created a table with a 2000-variable character line limit, thinking that surely 2000 characters would be large enough. Yet, after a few months, I noticed a few truncation errors, so I ran the following query to determine what was going on. The query shows each chat line and the length of the message, and puts them in order with the longest messages at the top:

```
SELECT line_number, LENGTH(line_message)
FROM puppet_irc
ORDER BY 2 DESC , 1 ASC;
```

The results were as follows:

line_number	LENGTH(line_message)
52	2000
420	2000
1601	2000
3138	2000
5589	2000
1346	526
1159	516
2601	503
1430	502
3266	502

Figure 5. Database table holding chat messages that were truncated at 2000 characters

When I query the text from line number 52, I see that this particular system message was the IRC channel itself issuing a listing of all the user nicknames on the channel; there were 973 nicknames in that list. Thus, the data was truncated upon being inserted into the table, cutting off the list of names at the letter D. Like with many data anomalies, there is no magical fix for this problem other than to expand the column length and re-enter the data. If we expand the column length, the future entries into this table will not be truncated, but all the previously truncated entries will need to either be ignored or re-entered.

Data type and character set errors

Data type errors manifest as mismatches between an expected data type and the actual values entered. Typically **type errors** happen because of a misunderstanding of the type of data that will be passed into the column or because the data changes after the table is designed. Examples of data type errors include:

- Storing a month-day-year style of date as a `date_time` column, which results in `00:00:00` being entered for the time portion.

- Storing decimals in an integer column, or using a column with too short a range or precision for a decimal number. The database will force the number to be truncated or rounded, sometimes silently, and sometimes in unexpected ways.

- Storing Unicode values in a Latin or ASCII character set column. Even though multi-byte character sets have been around for a while, the popularity of emojis and the integrated support for multi-byte characters in programming languages and browsers means that everyone working with data must consider Unicode for text nowadays. Many older tables were not designed to do this.

If you are looking at a data set in a relational database and want to know if it has multi-byte characters in it, we can compare the length of the text value to the number of characters in the text. For example, I have a table of Internet Relay Chat channel topics from Freenode. The MySQL query to find the multi-byte channel topics is as follows:

```
SELECT channel_name, topic
FROM fn_irc_channels
WHERE LENGTH(topic) != CHAR_LENGTH(topic);
```

This query can also be handy for finding relevant multi-byte data to use for tests.

As with truncation problems, the fix for data type and character set issues is to alter the table to fix the storage mismatch if it is a database issue, or update the code if the problem is in the processing of the data, and then re-enter the problematic data.

Logic or semantic errors

Just like when we are writing code, **logic errors**, or **semantic** errors, are often harder to find and fix than simple syntactic errors. A semantic data error might meet all the criteria for the database system, but simply does not make sense or does not mean what it was intended to mean. Semantic errors are often introduced to data sets unintentionally during the data collection phase, for example:

- Swapping the data that is supposed to go in a column with another column. First names and last names can be switched, phone numbers for work, home, and mobile could be confused, or there could just be simple off-by-one errors where several columns of data are entered incorrectly, one after the other.

- Entering dates in the wrong format. Different cultures express dates differently, some placing the month first and some placing the day first. This can cause data entry problems with day and month combinations where both day and month are numbered 12 or lower.

- Entering dates that are too early to be real, for example a system showing an email that was sent very far in the past or in the future, or where many dates are set to January 1, 1970.

The following are some examples of weird dates taken from a list of software package releases from the RubyGems web site. If we sort the gems by date, several gems show dates that precede the invention of gems or the Ruby language itself:

project_name	datasource_id	first_known_create
derpinderp	61240	1970-01-01
nakilon	61240	1970-01-01
blink_suv	61240	1991-04-16
suv	61240	1991-04-16

Figure 6. Nonsensical dates set too far in the past are syntactically correct for the database structure, but represent a logic error

A few more gems show creation dates that have not happened yet:

project_name	datasource_id	first_known_create
agi	61240	2915-09-06
gtl-sluggable	61240	2103-09-27
mk	61240	2020-12-18

Figure 7. Dates set too far in the future also represent a semantic data problem

It is clear that these dates are errors, even though they were formatted properly for the database.

At first it might seem like a good way to fix problems like these weird dates would be to add a logic check to our data collection program that disallows dates that fall outside some range. Another solution, if the RDBMS supports it, would be to add a **check constraint** to the database. This would generate an error when dates are entered that fall outside of the expected range. This is a straightforward solution, and much easier to implement than fixing the month/day switches or off-by-one column errors mentioned earlier.

Outliers

When we talk about data anomalies, we may also be looking for data points that represent very rare events. If 99 students scored 80% or above on a quiz, and one student scored 10%, this low score becomes very interesting. We call this rare event an **outlier** or a **novelty**. Depending on the type of data, outliers can be rare data points, or outliers could be represented as unexpected peaks or valleys in the data. The following graph shows a count of new projects being registered to the now-defunct Google Code project hosting site per month between 2011 and 2015:

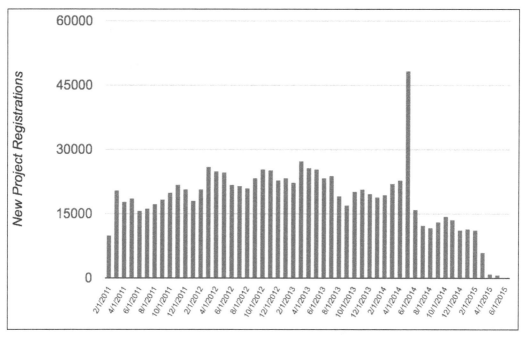

Figure 8. Graph of new project registrations to Google Code web site shows one outlier month

The large jump in projects registered in May of 2014 represents a huge increase; this is double the number of registrations of the months around it, and much higher than any other month in the data set.

If you are curious about why Google Code shows this huge spike in project registrations during May of 2014, I was too! From what I can tell from looking at the data, this large increase was caused by a huge influx of fake projects being added to the system all at once during the latter part of the month, with over 4,000 projects being created on May 25 and 26 alone. The vast majority of these projects have gibberish names like `01s4he49es8m` and `mnzghlhe` and they were created approximately once every minute for several days.

The following scatter plot shows a group of projects organized by their number of **source lines of code (SLOC)**, shown on the X-axis, and their number of Boolean expressions, shown on the Y-axis. While all the projects exhibit a positive correlation between the number of lines of code and the number of Boolean expressions in that code, a few projects really stand out for having very high numbers of both:

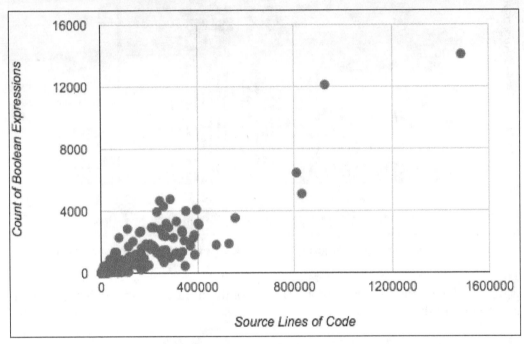

Figure 9. Scatter plot showing software projects organized by their source lines of code (SLOC) and number of Boolean expressions

In this section, we will learn about the different types of outliers and some ways to detect them using data mining techniques.

Visual mining for outliers

The human eye and brain comprise a powerful pattern recognition machine. It is no accident that our previous two examples used graphics to explain the concept of an outlier by encouraging our eyes to find discontinuity in a pattern. If we have the kind of data that will easily fit on a graph, **visual mining** for outliers is a viable option. Bar graphs, line graphs, and scatter plots are all great options for getting a quick sense of the shape of the data and for spotting wayward points or strange peaks and valleys. The following bar graph shows the impact of a sudden, prolonged service disruption on a software hosting site:

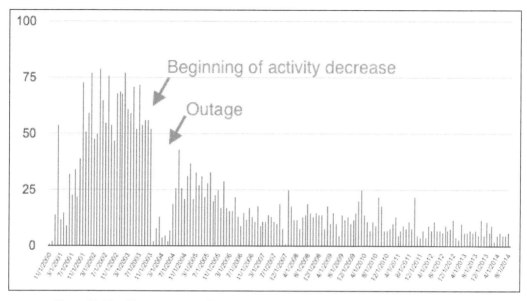

Figure 10. Monthly activity on software hosting site, showing the impact of a service outage

Even though the site was still technically available during the outage, the number of active connections during the low period was pronounced, and the site never really recovered to its pre-outage levels. Visual mining reveals that before the outage the site was experiencing a slight activity decrease, but that the outage may have exacerbated the problem and accelerated an already-downward trend.

Visual mining is best for univariate or bivariate data that can be viewed easily in two dimensions. The more complicated the data, the more unlikely it will be able to be mined effectively using visual mining.

Statistical detection of outliers

When we need a more robust solution, perhaps because we have too many variables or too much data to visually examine in a chart, we could try a statistical solution. What statistical method we use depends on how many variables we are measuring and how the data is distributed. Detecting outliers in **univariate** data sets, or those made up of a single variable, is simpler than detecting outliers in **multivariate** data sets. Detecting outliers in data that has a normal distribution is more straightforward than detecting outliers in data where we do not know the distribution, or where the distribution is skewed.

Detecting outliers with modified z-scores

If we have a normally distributed, univariate data set, the simplest method for detecting outliers will be first to estimate the center of the data set or the mean, then calculate the standard deviation of the data set. The standard deviation tells us how spread out the observations in the set are from one another. Outliers will be those that are farther from the center, measured in standard deviations from the mean. The number of standardized deviations from the mean where a data point is located is called its **z-score**. A simple outlier detection method is to find the data point with the biggest z-score, call that an outlier, mark it as such, remove it from the data set, and iterate through the test again. This procedure is called **Grubbs' Test** or the **maximum normalized residual test**. Grubbs' Test does not work well on data that has a lot of outliers, or on very small data sets.

The following is a Python program for detecting outliers based on a z-score for the SLOC count data set shown earlier. This univariate data set shows just the SLOC counts for 542 software projects. This program does not iterate through the data, but it does show the first outlier, and any points higher than this number are assumed to also be outliers. This code and the data file are both available on the Github site for this book, available at `https://github.com/megansquire/masteringDM/blob/master/ch9/zscore.py`.

The first thing we do in this code is that we import the Numpy library, which is installed with the default Anaconda Python distribution. Numpy is a frequently-used library that uses a powerful n-dimensional array as its primary data structure. After importing Numpy, we read in our data list and store it as a Numpy array:

```
import numpy as np
with open('sloc.txt', encoding='utf-8') as f:
    data = f.readlines()
data    = np.array(data,dtype=int)
```

Next we will use built-in Numpy functions to get the maximum, minimum, mean, and median of the data and print the results so we can learn a bit more about the distribution:

```
amax = np.amax(data, axis=0)
print("max:", amax)
amin = np.amin(data, axis=0)
print("amin:", amin)
mean = np.mean(data)
print("mean: ", mean)
median = np.median(data)
print("median:",median)
```

Next, we take the difference between each data point and the median value, and square those and sum them all together. The median of the square root of that value is called the `median absolute deviation`:

```
sumsqdiff = np.sum(pow((data - median),2))
print("sumsqdiff:", sumsqdiff)
sqrtdiff = np.sqrt(sumsqdiff)
print("sqrtdiff:",sqrtdiff)
mad      = np.median(sqrtdiff)
print("mad:",mad)
```

The program then creates a **modified z-score**, which is calculated from the median absolute deviation. The number 0.6745 represents about two-thirds of the standard deviation, representing a threshold at about half the distance between the first and third quartiles:

```
modzscore = (0.6745 * sumsqdiff) / mad
print ("Any value higher than",modzscore, "is an outlier.")
```

Any data point above this `modzscore` value can be considered an outlier. At this point, we can choose to prune these from the data set, or print them out, or take some corrective action.

Detecting outliers by combining statistics and visual mining

A traditional recommendation for finding outliers is to combine the concepts of the statistical test with visual mining to produce a **box-and-whisker plot**, or simply **boxplot**. A boxplot is a succinct way of showing a data distribution including the means, medians, quartiles, and outliers on a single chart.

The following is some simple Python code to generate a boxplot for the count of the SLOC for those same 542 different software projects. This code and the data file are both available on the GitHub site for this book, available at `https://github.com/megansquire/masteringDM/blob/master/ch9/boxplot.py`.

First we should import the `Matplotlib` library, which does come pre-installed with the Anaconda Python distribution. Next, we will open a file containing the data for this experiment:

```
import matplotlib.pyplot as plt
with open('sloc.txt', encoding='utf-8') as f:
    data = f.readlines()
```

We need to make sure that the data is stored as a list of integers and not as a list of strings, so we can use `map()` to convert them, and then store the result of `map()` as a Python list:

```
newdata = list(map(int, data))
```

Next we will set up a variable to hold the characteristics for our outliers, called **fliers** in boxplot parlance. This example shows the outliers as green o-shaped markers. More options for the flier markers are described in the Matplotlib documentation at `http://matplotlib.org/api/pyplot_api.html`:

```
flierprops = dict(marker='o',
                  markerfacecolor='green',
                  markersize=8,
                  linestyle='none')
```

Now we will use the `boxplot()` function of our Matplotlib object to process the data list, and the `show()` function to create the diagram:

```
plt.boxplot(newdata,
            showmeans=True,
            flierprops=flierprops)
plt.show()
```

In the generated diagram, the Y axis shows the number of lines of code, and each program is one observation in the sample:

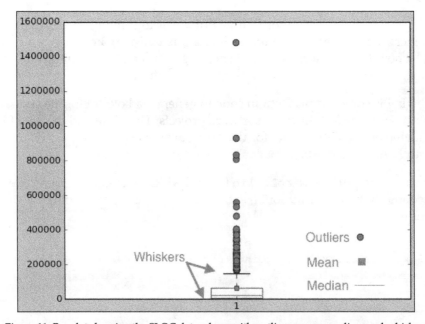

Figure 11. Boxplot showing the SLOC data, along with outliers, mean, median, and whiskers

I added a legend to indicate that green dots represent the outliers, the red line is the data median, the red square is the data mean, and the blue box shows the size of the first through third quartiles of the data. The black lines are the whiskers, or the maximum value of the 1.5 quartile.

In the boxplot example, outliers are shown visually, and are also defined quantitatively as any observation appearing above the highest whisker in this data.

Detecting outliers with machine learning

In this final section, we show how to use machine learning methods on data to find outliers. Looking once again at our SLOC data, suppose we want to compare SLOC count to the count of Boolean expressions in the code. As we saw earlier in the scatter plot, we should expect that as the lines of code increase, so would the number of Boolean expressions. However, we also know that there are outlier points in the data, indicating programs that have an exceptionally high number of Boolean expressions without a corresponding SLOC count, or vice versa. There are also data points that are high on both attributes, and which are therefore located farther from the rest of the data. An unsupervised machine learning approach could be directed to find clusters of data points that belong together, and call the rest of the data points outliers.

Before delving into how the clustering-based code works, let's quickly review the data on a scatterplot again:

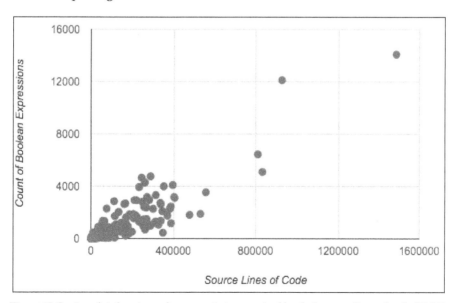

Figure 12. Scatter plot showing software projects organized by their source lines of code (SLOC) and number of Boolean expressions

We may be able to visually spot a few obvious outliers, but it gets trickier as we move closer to the main cluster at the lower-left of the diagram. Are *all* of those points considered one cluster? The rest of this section will be devoted to writing a program to help us automatically discern which of these points are outliers and which are part of the main cluster. The code for the clustering-based outlier detection, as well as the data file used in this example, are available on the GitHub site for this book at `https://github.com/megansquire/masteringDM/blob/master/ch9/clusters.py`.

> This code is loosely based on the example code that comes in the Scikit-Learn documentation, albeit much more simplified and streamlined. If you wish to view the original examples and additional documentation, the outlier detection examples are shown on their site at `http://scikit-learn.org/stable/modules/outlier_detection.html`.

Our first step is to import `Numpy` again and also a machine learning package called Scikit-Learn, abbreviated `sklearn`. From `sklearn`, we wish to use the `EllipticEnvelope` library, which will allow us to draw an elliptical curve around the points that are close enough together to be considered a cluster. We will also be plotting this data and the ellipse, so we need to use the `pyplot` portion of `Matplotlib` as well:

```
import numpy as np
from sklearn.covariance import EllipticEnvelope
import matplotlib.pyplot as plt
```

`Numpy` has a `loadtxt()` function, which comes in handy with multidimensional arrays:

```
X1 = np.loadtxt('slocbool.txt')
```

Next we set up an `EllipticEnvelope` object. The `contamination` argument is set to 0.02, which indicates that we want no more than 2% of our data to be considered outliers. The higher this number is, the smaller the ellipse will be, and the higher portion of the data will be considered outliers:

```
ee = EllipticEnvelope(support_fraction=1., contamination=0.02)
```

Next we set up the size of the grid, by plugging in the start and end points for the x-axis and y-axis, as well as the total number of observations for both X and Y:

```
xx, yy = np.meshgrid(np.linspace(0, 1500000, 542), np.linspace(0, 15000, 542))
```

We can fit the `EllipticEnvelope` object to our data, and tell its decision function to calculate a decision for each of the points in the observation set:

```
ee.fit(X1)
Z = ee.decision_function(np.c_[xx.ravel(), yy.ravel()])
Z = Z.reshape(xx.shape)
```

Now we are ready to draw the figure showing our scatter plot and the magenta-colored ellipse that has been learned for this data set. Remember that everything outside the ellipse can be considered to be an outlier. This code also shows how to add some simple labels to the chart axes and a title:

```
plt.figure(1)
plt.title("Outlier detection: SLOC vs BOOL")
plt.scatter(X1[:, 0], X1[:, 1], color='black')
plt.contour(xx, yy, Z, levels=[0], linewidths=2, colors='m')
plt.ylabel("count of boolean expressions")
plt.xlabel("count of source lines of code")
plt.show()
```

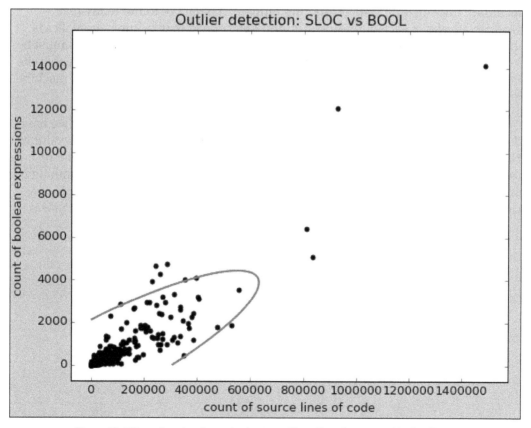

Figure 13. Ellipse showing the main cluster, with outliers shown outside the ellipse

After looking at the results, if you think the ellipse is too large or too small, it is easy to adjust the values for `contamination` and `support_fraction` when you create the `EllipticEnvelope` object.

We should remember that there are many more methods for outlier detection using clustering and machine learning. The **EllipticEnvelope** is just one technique. Scikit-Learn, and other machine learning toolkits, include many more options that could be better suited to different data distributions. This SLOC/BOOL data set is uniform and has just one main cluster in it. The attributes are for the most part positively correlated, and it is not a bimodal distribution. For these reasons, the Elliptic Envelope works well. However, if you are working with data that has a different shape, it will be necessary to find a technique that is better equipped to handle the particulars of that data set.

Summary

In this last chapter, we looked at a variety of different types of data anomalies, including missing data, data errors, and outliers in data. We found many real-world examples of each of these errors, and determined that locating anomalies is important, no matter how we choose to do that. Some of the data anomalies must be located and fixed by hand using queries and domain knowledge, while others invite more sophisticated data mining approaches such as statistical methods and machine learning techniques.

The interesting thing about detecting outliers with machine learning is that we have decided to use data mining techniques in order to do better data mining. The author Douglas Adams once said that a computer nerd is *someone who uses a computer in order to use a computer*. I draw the line at calling us *nerds* when we use data mining in order to improve our data mining, but perhaps – as befits the title of the book – we can say with pride that we are getting better at *Mastering Data Mining with Python*!

Index

C

CamelCase 164
centrality, of network
  betweenness centrality, 11, 12
  closeness centrality, 10
  degree centrality, 11
  measuring, 10
  other ways of measuring, 13
change detection problems 9
check constraint 228
classification problems 9
closed path 88
closeness centrality 89
clustering-based outlier
  reference link 236
clustering problems 9
coding 142
context-based similarity matching 58, 59
corpus 166
CRoss-Industry Standard Process for Data
    Mining (CRISP-DM process)
  about 6, 7
  business understanding 6
  data preparation 6
  data understanding 6
  deployment 7
  evaluation 7
  modeling 6

D

data
  datasets, merging horizontally 53, 54
  datasets, merging vertically 51, 52
  exploring 104
  merging 51
data anomalies
  about 218
  data errors 224
  missing data 218
  missing data, fixing 220
  outliers 228-230
data append 51
data errors
  about 224
  character set errors 226

data type errors 226
logic errors 227, 228
semantic errors 227, 228
truncated fields 225, 226
data, exploring
  datasources table 105
  rf_developer_projects table 106
data file
  URL 31
data, importing into graph structure
  about 96
  adjacency list format 97
  edge list format 97
  GEXF format 98
  graph data format (GDF) 99
  GraphML format 98
  JavaScript Serialized Object
      Notation (JSON) 100
  JSON link series 100, 101
  JSON node series 100, 101
  JSON trees 101, 102
  Pajek format 102, 103
  Python pickle 100
data mining
  about 2, 3
  big data 3
  CRISP-DM process 6, 7
  data science 3
  development environment,
      setting up 11-17
  Fayyad et al. KDD process 5
  Han et al. KDD process 5, 6
  machine learning 3
  methodology 8
  performing 4
  predictive analytics 3
  Six Steps process 7
  techniques 9-11
data quality 51
data science 2
data, social network
  centrality in subgraphs, analyzing 121-124
  change over time, finding 124-134
  cliques, analyzing 121-124
  network parameters 116-118
  simple network metrics, generating 113-116
  subgraphs, analyzing 118-120

datasources table
 comments 105
 datasource_id 105
 date_donated 105
data type errors
 example 226
degree centrality 90
density, graph 14
dependency modeling problems 9
deviation detection problems 9
directed network 82
disjoint sets
 about 58
 leveraging 58
distance 86
Django IRC chat
 about 175-178
 reference link 175
doc2bow() 206
document level analysis 139
doubletons 23

E

edge list
 about 95
 format 97
edges 82
ego network 51
entity 137
entity matching
 about 48-50
 attribute-based similarity matching 54
 attributes matching, methods 55
 context-based similarity matching 58, 59
 data, merging 51
 disjoint sets, leveraging 58
 effectiveness 61-63
 efficiency 60, 61
 evaluating 15
 machine learning based entity
  matching 59, 60
 techniques 54
 usefulness 63
entity matching project
 about 64
 code 70-75

dataset 69, 70
 difficulties, with matching
  software projects 65
 people names, matching 67
 project names, matching 67
 results 75
 topics and description keywords,
  matching 68
 URLs, matching 67
extractive method 186

F

Fayyad et al. KDD process
 data evaluation 5
 data interpretation 5
 data mining 5
 data pre-processing 5
 data selection 5
 data transformation 5
feature engineering 141
flaccid designator 165
fliers
 about 234
 reference link 234
FLOSSmole project
 about 69
 URL 69
frequent itemsets
 about 20
 diapers and beer urban
  legend example 20, 21
 mining 21-23

G

gazetteer 163
GDF format
 reference link 99
generalizable 63
general-purpose data collections
 Hu and Liu's sentiment
  analysis lexicon 142
 SentiWordNet 143
 Vader sentiment 143, 144

nodes 82
novelty 228
nullable 219
null data values 218
null words 197

O

objectivity score 143
opinion mining
  about 136
  reference link 137
opinion shifters 140
opinion words 140
out-degree 86
outlier
  about 218, 228
  statistical detection 231
  visual mining 230, 231
outlier, statistical detection
  outliers, detecting by combining
    statistics 233-235
  outliers, detecting by combining visual
    mining 233-235
  outliers, detecting with machine
    learning 235-238
  outliers, detecting with modified z
    -score 232, 233
overfitting 141

P

Pajek format 102, 103
partial matches
  about 168
  lenient scoring 169
  partial scoring 169
  reference link 167
  strict scoring 169
part of speech (POS)
  about 166
  named entities, classes 167
  tagging 166, 167
path 88
pendant nodes 116
Penn Treebank tagger 167

position of word 140
POS tagger 166
precision 61
profile 58
Python pickle 100

Q

Question Answering (QA) systems 162

R

real-world project, network
  about 103, 104
  data, exploring 104-111
  network data 112
  network files, generating 111, 112
recall 61
Reddit user page
  URL 185
regression problems 9
relational database management
    systems (RDBMS) 219
results, entity matching project
  about 76
  entity matches 76
  pairs, identifying 77-79
rf_developer_projects table
  datasource_id 106
  dev_loginname 106
  proj_unixname 106
rigid designator 165
Rmagick on RubyForge
  about 65
  references 65
Rmagick on RubyGems
  about 65
  references 65
RubyForge
  URL 67
Ruby on Rails
  URL 76

www.ingramcontent.com/pod-product-compliance
Lightning Source LLC
Chambersburg PA
CBHW060533060326
40690CB00017B/3477